AF173607

ANDY STARMORE
WE ARE LEEDS!

Dedication

to Nancy Starmore (Mum), Stevie B, John Mills,
Ron Dinmore and Marc 'Buzz' Burrows

About the Author

First and foremost, 46-year-old Andy Starmore is a massive Leeds United supporter and has been since he was a little boy. Over the past four years Andy has been a contributor to the official Leeds United magazine *Leeds, Leeds, Leeds.* Living on the south coast, he has been a freelance football writer since 1991, has covered some rugby union matches, mainly for the *Bournemouth Daily Echo,* and has submitted articles for the newspaper covering the World Superbikes at Brands Hatch and the Motor GP at Donnington Park. Andy has interviewed some high-profile footballers, including ex-Leeds players Gordon Strachan, Frank Gray, Joe Jordan, Ian Baird, Peter Lorimer, Jack Charlton and Mark Beeney. He has also produced articles for the football magazine *FourFourTwo* and written write-ups for national newspapers. During the 1991–92 season, as well as writing for the *Bournemouth Echo* Andy also did live reports for all the AFC Bournemouth home games for the local radio station 2CR, followed by post-match interviews with their then manager Tony Pulis (now manager of Premier League Stoke City). Andy's passion for Leeds led him to track down Leeds fans from all over the world, culminating in this publication of their stories.

ANDY STARMORE
WE ARE LEEDS!

DB PUBLISHING

First published in Great Britain in 2009 by The Breedon Books Publishing
Company Limited, Breedon House, 3 The Parker Centre, Derby, DE21 4SZ

This edition published in Great Britain in 2012 by The Derby Books
Publishing Company Limited, 3 The Parker Centre, Derby, DE21 4SZ.

© Andy Starmore, 2009

All rights reserved. No part of this publication may be reproduced, stored in
a retrieval system, or transmitted in any form, or by any means, electronic,
mechanical, photocopying, recording or otherwise without the prior
permission in writing of the copyright holders, nor be otherwise circulated in
any form or binding or cover other than which it is published and without a
similar condition being imposed on the subsequent publisher.

ISBN 978-1-78091-171-7

Printed and bound by Copytech (UK) Limited, Peterborough.

CONTENTS

ACKNOWLEDGEMENTS

Thanks to my eldest son Ben, my brother Baz and sister Alison, for sharing the ups and downs following Leeds. Thanks to my two little ones, seven-year-old Russell and five-year-old Harry, who already know that Leeds United are the only team to follow. How does it go boys? 'Leeds the best – Man U are rubbish.' Good lads! Thanks to my mum, who was born in Horsforth, leading me to worship the mighty Leeds. Thanks to my long-suffering partner Malena, who like many others is an understanding (I think) Leeds widow. Thanks also to Chris and Max Frampton, Clive (Clitty) 'you've got to laugh' Thompson, Chris Bradley, Scott Joyce, Robert Endeacott, Neil Jeffries, Gary Edwards, the Hampshire Whites, Matt Chiverton, Adie Farnell, Craig Reid, Les Rowley, Phil Caplan and Nick Spooner for their continued encouragement and support of me reaching my goal of actually finishing my first book. Thanks also to Richard Terry, Ricky Smithers, John Wood, Stuart Lewis, Jason Mesout, Jonny Burrell, Peter Poole and everyone who is featured in this book and agreed to tell their stories. Grateful thanks go to Breedon Books for allowing my words to be sat on the shelves.

Thanks to every Leeds fan in the world for being Leeds and for making our club one of the biggest and most supported clubs on the planet. Thanks to Paul Dews, for pointing me in the right direction. Thanks to the official Leeds United magazine *Leeds, Leeds, Leeds* for keeping us fans bang up-to-date with everything you need to know about the club. Thanks also to leedsunited.com for the same reason. Finally, in recent times, and I never thought I would say this, thanks to Ken Bates, for if it was not for him our club might be history.

Please note that since the book has been written some of the branches of LUSC (Leeds United Supporters' Club) have transferred over to become an LURMC (Leeds United Regional Members' Club). For information on how to become a Regional Members' Club, log on to leedsunited.com. Alternatively, telephone Lorna Tinker on 0113 3676242. A list of Regional Members' Clubs can be found at the back of the book.

FOREWORD

There are very few certainties in life, but one thing is for sure – and that is that the fans of Leeds United Football Club certainly do not get the recognition they so richly deserve. This book will undoubtedly put the record straight.

In the 2008–09 season, United's second season in the third tier of English football, Elland Road had the top three highest gates in the whole of the Football League, including much of the Premiership. As you will discover, the impressive army of Leeds fans stretches worldwide. These fans have had to endure more heartache than anyone could imagine, yet despite the hardships there is hardly a country, city or county anywhere that does not have the famous Leeds flag flying proudly.

Whenever a new player, or indeed a new manager, arrives at Elland Road, the first thing they comment on is the unbelievable support and passion shown by the hordes of Leeds fans week in week out, season in season out.

Players, staff and the directors will pass through this football club. The fans remain loyal to the club forever. Hands up and enjoy the ride.

We are Leeds – Marching on together.

Gary Edwards

INTRODUCTION

I know how *I* feel when it comes to waking up on a match day. It does not matter who the opposition are. It could be Liverpool at Anfield or Colchester United at Layer Road. It could be any match whatsoever at Elland Road or even a trip to Old Trafford, it really does not matter: I am off to watch Leeds United and that is all that counts. I am 46 years old but still get that unrivalled feeling of excitement the night before I set off to Elland Road or wherever Leeds are playing. It is like Christmas Eve as a child, except that you only get Christmas Eve once a year. The following morning is probably the only morning of the week that you cannot wait to fling off the duvet and prepare for the day ahead. When I have finished in the bathroom, having used my Leeds flannel for good measure, it is time to make the most important decision of the day. Which Leeds shirt shall I wear for this match? So many to choose from. Do I don the latest shirt to prove that I am right up there with modern times, or do I choose my oldest shirt, the 1972 FA Cup Final classic all-white no-sponsors'-name shirt, to prove that I have been a loyal Leeds supporter for a very long time? No, I've got it, I will wear the one with Bremner's name splashed all over the back. Can't go wrong with that. Am I sure? Yes, Yes...erm, YES! By now I am usually running a little late.

It is 16 April 2005, QPR away today and I cannot miss that train. No doubt there will be other Leeds United fans somewhere along the journey to reminisce with, dissect the current squad's capabilities and inadequacies with, swap opinions of how our manager is the right man for the job or should be shot at dawn, and generally 'talk Leeds'. All that excitement the night before is reaching new levels, now that I am on my way to follow my team and I know that the usual masses of white shirts and the usual chanting for Leeds is just around the corner. My Bremner shirt will be among them and I'm damn proud it will be. There's an added bit of excitement today. It is my son's 18th birthday, and having brought him up like every Leeds United father should, he was only ever going to support Leeds.

Needless to say, part of Ben's birthday present from the old man is a day out watching the team he and I have worshipped for what seems like an eternity. We step off the train and know that in just a few minutes time we will have the usual liquid refreshments for me, and the first legal ones for Ben. Familiar faces greet each other, all wearing something with reference to Leeds United. The noise is immense and even before the chanting begins, everyone is having to shout to the person just two feet away in order to be heard. The atmosphere is building, the chants begin and everyone knows Leeds are in town, and the day has only just begun. The time is fast approaching kick-off and we are still a fair distance from the ground, but help is on its way. A large 52-seater coach has just turned the corner and is about to stop right outside this particular public house and pick us all up to take us to Loftus Road.

When we arrive at the ground our tickets are for the upper tier, which is a great sign, given that at Loftus Road they usually only give the away supporters the lower tier. Not Leeds. We fill both – after all, we are Leeds! The game ends up as a 1–1 draw, with the highlight coming 24 minutes in when Seth Johnson cracks a dipping volley over the QPR 'keeper from the edge of the box. Two tiers at one end of the ground go completely loopy and even though it is a match that has no consequence whatsoever, with both outfits out of the running for a Play-off place and both sides totally safe from a relegation battle, it still gives you a tremendous buzz when Leeds find the back of the net. We hold onto our lead for much of the remainder of the match, until with just five minutes left Kevin Gallen levels for the hosts, which dampens the mood of the Leeds end.

The final whistle blows but the day is far from over. Now it is time to meet up with some West London Whites after the match for some opinions of the game and general 'Leeds talk' once again. Before you know it, you are looking at your watch and thinking 'Blimey, have you seen the time?' It's fast approaching the time to dart back to Waterloo to catch the last train back to my home in Bournemouth. Ben had already made his way back, with his girlfriend waiting patiently on the south coast – good to see he has got his priorities right though – Leeds first! It is a somewhat quieter journey home. After all that singing and shouting, not to mention the long day it has been since springing out of bed all those hours ago, a little shut eye comes into play – after a read of the matchday programme, of course. I finally turn the key of the front door and it is now well gone midnight, but it has been a great day out. I have been to watch Leeds United. And as I slip back under the duvet and lie there, slowly drifting off, a thought hits me. I live exactly 272 miles from Elland Road but have never lost the love I have for the club, and I wonder how many other supporters of Leeds, who live far away from LS11 0ES, share the same kind of love. A few questions then:

Ever wondered just how many Leeds United supporters there are around the world?

Ever thought of taking a trip to track some of them down and hear tales of their Leeds United experiences?

Ever wondered what the odds are of bumping into a fellow Leeds fan when standing on top of the Empire State Building?

Ever wondered, if you weren't there, what it must have been like in the San Siro with the bonding of fans and players after the AC Milan game?

Ever wondered how many Leeds fans there are in Scandinavia? Australia? Malta? Wherever?

Leeds United Football Club has been a massively supported club for a very long time and is one of the best-supported clubs in the world today, so to actually set off on a Michael Palin-style trip around the globe to meet many of these diehard Leeds United followers would be nice. But, let's face it, would the BBC pay for that? So, instead of investing an awful lot of cash, taking a year out and travelling the globe to find out a little bit more about what makes Leeds United fans tick, this book will aim to do that for you at a fraction of the cost. From Holbeck to the United States, from the scorching heat of the Saudi Arabian desert to the sub-zero temperatures of Russia, from the southern tip of Australia to Galway in the Republic of Ireland, the song is spot on: 'Leeds fans here, Leeds fans there, Leeds fans every…'– you know the rest! This book takes you on a fascinating journey and proves that these loyal-to-the-bitter-end supporters are a special breed. There are stories from all corners of the globe, including a kidnapping in Moscow, a celebrity Leeds fan Down Under and naked Finnish people running around the streets of Helsinki singing 'Stand up if you hate Man U'. There is also an account of a hair-raising boat trip across the Solent, all for the sake of Leeds United.

To give you some kind of idea of the size of following Leeds enjoy, Coca-Cola ran a competition where you could vote on the internet once a day, towards the end of the 2004–05 season, in order to have the opportunity to win a terrific prize for your club. The competition was open to all Coca-Cola League clubs in England and Scotland, with two prizes to be awarded to the randomly drawn winners prior to the Championship Play-Off Final at the Millennium Stadium on 30 May 2005. One prize was £10,000, to be awarded to a lucky individual who entered, while the other was a cheque for £250,000 to go to one club towards a new player. Every vote would go into the draw, but, obviously, the odds of winning would shorten if your club were to receive a large majority of the vote. Leeds United did not win in the end, but the amount of votes the club received showed what an enormous following they have. The team that won the big prize was Brighton & Hove Albion, who only received 26,020 votes. Queen's Park Rangers were in second place in the table on 69,431. QPR received a staggering 133,796 fewer votes than leaders Leeds!

This was the top 10:

1	**Leeds United**	**203,227**
2	Queen's Park Rangers	69,431
3	Sheffield Wednesday	43,310
4	Celtic	39,601
5	Luton Town	33,490
6	Aberdeen	33,304
7	Brighton & Hove Albion	26,020
8	Coventry City	25,793
9	Derby County	21,344
10	Nottingham Forest	19,151

Coca-Cola ran the competition again in 2005–06 and Leeds were runaway leaders once more. This was the top 10 for 2005–06:

1	**Leeds United**	**219,969**
2	Brentford	138,372
3	Sheffield Wednesday	137,075
4	Gillingham	103,860
5	Watford	78,899
6	Leyton Orient	72,512
7	Kilmarnock	71,229
8	Brighton & Hove Albion	68,730
9	Bristol Rovers	60,879
10	Stockport County	56,458

And guess what – we didn't win again!

We begin our journey in the heart of the city of Leeds itself, and from there we will be travelling across one side of the United Kingdom before an itinerary that passes through the Republic and Northern Ireland, the United States of America, Canada, the Caribbean, South America, Australia, New Zealand, up to Singapore and Thailand, over to Japan, fleeting visits to the South Pole, Saudi Arabia and Africa, onto Azabaijan, back to Europe and an extensive look at the Scandinavian Whites, more quick stopovers in Russia and the Ukraine, Greece, Malta, Holland and Belgium, before popping back to Blighty and finally arriving back in Leeds to complete the journey. In between, some of the chapters by number-one Leeds United fan Gary Edwards, who gives his views on many different issues concerning the club he and I, and indeed thousands of others, will forever worship.

Chapter 1

HOLBECK-KIPPAX

On the pitch – Leeds-born Whites:

Name	Joined	Left	Apps	Goals
David Batty	1987 & 1998	1993 & 2002	350/23	4
Len Browning	1946	1951	105	46
Walter Butler	1920	1921	3	3
Aidan Butterworth	1980	1984	64/10	17
Terry Connor	1979	1983	93/15	22
Brian Deane	1993 & 2004	1997 & 2005	179/22	45
Martin Dickinson	1979	1985	116/2	2
John Duthoit	1945	1945	2	0
Tom Elliott	2006	2007	1/3	0
Gareth Evans	2000	2000	0/2	0
Harrison Fearnley	1946	1948	29	0
Alan Fowler	1932	1933	15	8
Les Goldberg	1938	1946	33	0
Ernie Goldthorpe	1920	1922	6	2
David Harvey	1965 & 1983	1980 & 1983	445/30	0
Billy Heaton**	1937	1949	60	6
Jonny Howson	2006	CP*	71/26	12
Mark Jackson	1995	1999	15/8	0
Rod Johnson	1962	1968	25	6
Dennis Kirby	1947	1947	8	0
Aaron Lennon	2003	2004	21/22	1
Paul Madeley	1962	1980	712/13	34
Jack Marsden	1948	1959	75	0
James Milner	2002	2004	30/24	5

* CP stands for current player (apps and goals are up to and including the end of the 2008–09 season).

** Heaton was at Leeds for 12 years but only made 60 appearances. Someone called Adolf Hitler had something to do with this.

Where better to start this book than Holbeck and Kippax, in the heart of Leeds? One inhabitant is much-publicised super-fan Gary Edwards, who, in case you do not know, has only missed one Leeds United match, including all pre-season friendlies, anywhere in the world, since 1968. The reason he missed one game was because of an air traffic control strike in Spain, from where he was due to fly out to Canada to see Leeds in a pre-season friendly. He had a flight ticket and a match ticket, but if he had caught the next available flight, he would have missed the match by four hours. What sort of excuse is that? Come on Gary, shape up!

The dedication of this man is possibly – no, probably – unmatched by any other football fan in the world, but some of his Kippaxian compatriots do come close, making the Holbeck/Kippax Branch of the Leeds United Supporters' Club (LUSC) a super-branch for a super-fan. We will come to that later on, but for now, how did Gary Edwards begin his 'full-time' occupation as a follower of Leeds United Football Club? Gary is now a very well-known character among the Leeds faithful and his love for Leeds is and has been so immense that not even the chance to become a professional footballer himself, or the dream opportunity of a cartoonist's job with Thompsons of Dundee (who created *The Beano* and *Dandy*), could pry him away from following Leeds United, as he explains:

'My interest in Leeds United began during the 1963–64 season. Most of my mates' dads were big Leeds fans and used to travel in a minibus to all games and bring back programmes, which we'd all sit and read gathered on 'the Green', a big grass square at the bottom of our street where we would play football for hours on end. I remember the driver of the bus, Mr Tose. He was as blind as a bat. He wore really thick glasses and used to drive sat forward with his face inches from the windscreen. He used to think it was thick with fog every day when in fact it was bright and sunny. Amazingly they never had a crash – well, not a serious one anyway. I collected the match reports from newspapers and stuck them in my scrapbook, which I still have today. Leeds won promotion that season, I was eight. In 1966 I saw my first-ever Leeds game, which was Blackpool at Elland Road [26 March 1966 – Leeds lost 2–1 with Jack Charlton scoring Leeds's goal – two days later Leeds played the reverse League fixture at Blackpool's Bloomfield Road and lost again, 1–0].

'I went with my dad and his mate John Hamilton. It was John who had to act as 'first reserve' at games when Dad couldn't take me. The Blackpool match was unbelievable. I was actually at Elland Road, I'd heard all about it and now I was here. As the brilliant white shirts of Leeds emerged from the tunnel the noise was deafening. Gary Sprake spent nearly five minutes picking up toilet rolls and dozens of packets of chewing gum that had been thrown into his goalmouth by the crowd. I actually came out of the ground thinking we had won 1–0 when in fact we had lost 2–1. The ground had been that quiet when Blackpool had scored I hadn't even noticed. I was well and truly hooked from that moment on and have not missed a single Leeds game in Britain or Europe since the League Cup semi-final at Derby County in 1968 [Leeds won 3–2 with Rod Belfitt scoring twice and one from Eddie Gray].

'During the early stages of my Leeds-watching 'career' I neglected a couple of career opportunities of my own. I was the school goalkeeper and I had a trial at Huddersfield Town. I must have done something right because I was invited to a second trial on 30 September, the same day as Leeds were at West Ham. I missed the second trial. The following year Tottenham away got in the way of a trial at Doncaster Rovers. I also missed a couple of exams too, because of football, but I really worked hard on art. After weeks of a correspondence test I was offered a job as a cartoonist by Thompsons of Dundee. It meant leaving home and living in Scotland. No Dennis the Menace for me.'

Gary, whose unrivalled passion for Leeds has brought him many appearances on television and radio, including a slot on the *Trisha* show, where he agreed to propose to his long-time partner Lesley in a bid to show some loyalty to her as well as his beloved Leeds, is the Billy Bremner of the terraces. Bremner would break down brick walls with his bare hands for the sake of Leeds United and there is no doubt that this super-fan is of exactly the same ilk. The proposal 'to the lovely Lesley,' as Leeds manager at the time Kevin Blackwell described her on the telephone during the *Trisha* show, went ahead as planned in front of 29,607 people at Elland Road against Ipswich Town on 23 April 2005 – and Lesley said yes. Phew! The wedding itself took place just over a year later on 3 June 2006 – guess where? – Elland Road.

Gary originally formed the Kippax Branch of LUSC, along with Gordon 'Gord' Findlay and Malcolm 'Mally' King, way back on 31 May 1978. Kippax were somewhat unfairly forced to disband in 1995 after an incident when the branch had stopped off for a few beers in the quaintest of Cheshire villages, Alsager, on the way back from a match. The locals did not turn out to be that friendly and, as Edwards described 'A right old rumble took place and lasted fully half an hour. I had never witnessed anything like it before or since.' The branch were held responsible by some quarters, despite a lack of concrete evidence to prove the blame for the incident lay on their shoulders. There is no doubt that the branch was a popular one with other branches throughout the UK however, so when 60 of the Kippax members joined forces with Holbeck, in a mark of respect for Kippax they used to spell their branch name HolbecK. There is a brass band in Kippax and Gary possesses a T-shirt with the words Kippax and underneath '"Banned" Club'! Ray Fell, who is now the chairman of LUSC, was an original member of Holbeck, which is now run by Ralph Benson, the younger brother of Phil Benson. The elder of the twins is proud of his extra 20 minutes on this planet, but Ralph gleefully declares he is the taller of the two! Ralph has not missed many matches himself and is probably only about 20 games behind Gary Edwards and, with other members including Paul 'Robbo' Robinson (no, not the former Leeds 'keeper), Stuart Stephen, Barry Mortimer, Les Hince, Geoff Verrill and Danny Mills look-a-like Mick Halliday, these followers of Leeds United have clocked up around 17,500 matches between them. That is a lot of football! Before you get your calculators out, it's 1,575,000 minutes of footy, and that does not include injury-time and extra-time.

Gary Edwards alone has a record that is simply staggering. Up to the end of the 2008–09 season, he had watched 2,154 matches in a row (see the end of the book for an attendance record stat attack). That adds up to 193,860 minutes of football, or 3,231 hours, or 134.625 days, or just over four full months of solid football – and that does not include extra-time in Cup matches. It is also a statistic that does not include any of the countless friendlies and testimonials he has been to since 1968.

'Watering holes' are never far away when it comes to following Leeds, and one of the advantages Holbeck used to have was that member Les Hince ran his own public house in the heart of the city, the Viaduct, until the summer of 2006. Leeds supporters from all over the place were more than welcome to enter this establishment and when it came to the end of the season, whether the professionals out on the field of play had been outstanding or not, it was always party time at the Viaduct. And with the branch presenting a Player of the Year award after each campaign, there was always a star among the enthusiastic celebrations, too. In the past David Batty, Gary Kelly and the late great 'Gentle Giant' John Charles have all been guests, and in the summer of 2004 the Leeds United manager Kevin Blackwell turned up with the Whyte & MacKay Cup that Leeds had won after their 3–1 pre-season success at Hibernian. There was no Player of the Year award from the branch on that particular evening, though, given that it would have gone to a certain player who sat on the shoulders of Leeds supporters in glorious admiration in his final match for the club at Elland Road against Charlton Athletic, before he turned from hero to zero by heading off to Old Trafford.

Alan Smith was a great player for Leeds who gave everything for the club, there is no doubting that, but it is fair to say that what he did in joining 'that lot' from the other side of the Pennines hurt. And that is putting it ever so mildly. It was a mixture of bewilderment and anger. How could he have done such a thing? How could he have signed for them? It is also fair to say that, at least while Les Hince was in charge, Smith was no longer a welcome guest at the Viaduct. On one occasion a stranger entered the pub and asked to borrow a pen. Outside the Viaduct used to be a plaque dedicated to the loss of the two Leeds United supporters, Christopher Loftus and Kevin Speight, who were murdered in Istanbul prior to Leeds playing Galatasaray in a semi-final first leg of the UEFA Cup in 2000. When this individual, who had clearly not come in to buy a drink, asked for a pen, the bar manageress of the Viaduct and staunch Leeds fan Jo Barrett asked him why he wanted a pen. He replied, 'Alan Smith is outside looking at that plaque.' The young man was immediately escorted off the premises (without a pen) and had about as much chance of grabbing Smith's autograph as Sir Alex Ferguson had of being welcomed with open arms in the Viaduct. Barrett then turned her anger on the former Leeds striker and told him to leave in a somewhat direct fashion. Les Hince has since moved away from Leeds and now runs a pub in Rotherham. The Viaduct is now not quite the same…in more ways than one!

Chapter 2

NORTH-WEST WHITES, WEBBED FEET AND THE ISLE OF SAM

On the pitch - Northern-born Whites outside Yorkshire:

Name	Joined	Left	Apps	Goals	Born
Robert Abel	1931	1936	1	0	Manchester
George Ackerley	1910	1911	2	0	Liverpool
George Ainsley	1936	1947	97	33	South Sheilds
Thomas Alderson	1930	1930	4	2	Leasingthorne
John Allan	1912	1914	15	0	Newcastle
John Allen	1923	1923	2	0	Newburn
Tomi Ameobi	2007	2008	1/1	0	Newcastle
Anthony Arins	1981	1981	0/1	0	Chesterfield
Samuel Armes	1935	1938	82	9	Sunderland
James Ashall	1958	1960	91	0	Temple Normanton
Neil Aspin	1982	1989	240/4	6	Gateshead
Josh Atkinson	1924	1928	53	0	Blackpool
Simpson Bainbridge	1912	1919	69	15	Silksworth, Co. Durham
Edward Bannister	1946	1949	44	1	Leyland
Nick Barmby	2002	2003	21/10	5	Hull
Peter Barnes	1981	1983	62/2	6	Manchester
Norman Batey	1946	1946	8	0	Haltwhistle
Paul Beesley	1995	1997	33/6	0	Liverpool
Albert Bell	1923	1923	1	0	Sunderland
Thomas Bell	1922	1922	1	0	Usworth
Willie Bennett	1928	1933	11	4	Manchester
Jeremiah Best	1920	1920	11	1	Mickley
Robbie Blake	2005	2006	65/24	21	Middlesbrough
Billy Boardman	1920	1922	4	0	Manchester
Rob Bowman	1992	1996	5/4	0	Durham
Ted Buck	1928	1928	8	0	Dipton
Arthur Buckley	1936	1939	86	22	Oldham
Paul Butler	2004	2006	106	4	Manchester
Walter Butler	1920	1920	3	3	Skirlaugh

Name	Joined	Left	Apps	Goals	Born
Clarke Carlisle	2004	2004	32/6	4	Preston
James Carr	1935	1935	2	0	Ferryhill
Scott Carson	2003	2004	2/1	0	Whitehaven
Wilf Chadwick	1925	1926	16	3	Bury
Jack Charlton	1952	1972	773	96	Ashington
Trevor Cherry	1972	1982	477/8	32	Huddersfield
James Clark	1924	1924	3	0	Gateshead
Wallace Clark	1921	1922	13	0	Jarrow
James Clarke	1946	1946	14	1	Broomhall
Walter Coates	1921	1922	50	4	Kyo, Co. Durham
Thomas Cochrane	1928	1936	259	27	Newcastle
Thomas Coutts	1927	1927	1	0	Gateshead
Chris Crowe	1956	1959	100	27	Newcastle
Thomas Cunningham	1908	1909	1	0	Sunderland
John Daniels	1934	1934	1	0	Prestwich
Robert Danskin	1930	1931	6	1	Newcastle
Bobby Davison	1987	1991	92/18	36	South Shields
Robert Dawson	1953	1953	1	0	South Shields
Joseph Dougherty	1914	1919	1	0	Darlington
William Down	1920	1924	101	0	Ryhope
Thomas Duxbury	1924	1924	3	0	Accrington
Keith Edwards	1986	1986	34/17	9	Stockton-on-Tees
Walter Edwards	1948	1948	2	0	Mansfield
John Edmondson	1914	1919	11	6	Carleton, Lancs
Rob Elliott	2006	2006	6/2	0	Gosforth
Wayne Entwhistle	1979	1979	7/5	2	Bury
John Fell	1925	1926	13	1	Quebec, Co. Durham
George Fenwick	1913	1913	5	3	Durham
Frank Fidler	1951	1952	23	8	Middleton
Robbie Fowler	2001	2002	25/8	14	Liverpool
James Freeborough	1906	1908	24	0	Stockport
Des Frost	1949	1950	10	2	Congleton
William Furness	1929	1936	257	66	New Washington
Ken Gadsby	1936	1947	87	0	Chesterfield
Chris Galvin	1969	1972	11/5	2	Huddersfield
Thomas Gascoigne	1921	1923	20	0	Newcastle
Fred Goodwin	1959	1963	120	2	Heywood
Ernest Goodwin	1914	1919	20	3	Chester-le-Street
Danny Graham	2005	2005	1/2	0	Gateshead
Fred Graver	1924	1924	3	0	Craghead, Co. Durham

Name	Joined	Left	Apps	Goals	Born
Michael Gray	2005	2006	16	0	Sunderland
Harry Green	1930	1933	19	4	Sheffield
Brian Greenhoff	1979	1981	74/4	1	Barnsley
Jimmy Greenhoff	1962	1968	128/8	33	Barnsley
Sean Gregan	2004	2006	73/1	0	Guisborough
Anthony Hackworth	1999	2000	0/3	0	Durham
Peter Haddock	1986	1991	130/17	1	Newcastle
Tom Hampson	1934	1939	2	0	Salford
Peter Hampton	1971	1980	83	2	Oldham
Thomas Hampson	1938	1938	2	0	Salford
Peter Hampton	1972	1979	76/7	3	Oldham
Ray Hankin	1976	1979	102/1	36	Wallsend
Paul Hart	1978	1983	223	20	Golborne
Mark Hateley	1996	1996	5/1	0	Wallesey
James Henderson	1905	1907	80	0	Newcastle
Joseph Hilton	1949	1949	1	0	Bromborough, Wirral
Kevin Hird	1978	1983	181/19	21	Colne
John Hodgson	1945	1957	22	0	Dawdon, Co. Durham
Tony Hogg	1909	1915	101	0	Newcastle
Tom Holley	1936	1948	169	1	Sunderland
William Hopkins	1919	1919	7	0	Esh Winning, Durham
Tommy Howarth	1921	1922	46	19	Bury
Andy Hughes	2007	CP	56/19	1	Manchester
Charlie Hughes	1950	1951	23	2	Manchester
Phil Hughes	1983	1985	7	0	Manchester
Rob Hulse	2004	2005	51/8	20	Crewe
Alan Humphreys	1959	1961	44	0	Chester
Norman Hunter	1962	1976	724/2	21	Eighton Banks
Paul Huntington	2007	CP	26/5	2	Carlisle
Harold Jacklin	1921	1921	5	0	Chesterfield
Billy Jackson	1925	1926	39	2	Farnworth
Bob Jefferson	1906	1908	18	5	Sunderland
Adam Johnson	2006	2006	4/1	0	Sunderland
Sam Johnson	1911	1912	7	1	Colne, Lancs
Alf Jones	1960	1961	29	0	Liverpool
Harry Kay	1907	1908	32	0	Ainsworth, Lancs
Dom Kelly	1937	1937	4	0	Sandbach
Jack Kelly	1934	1937	64	18	Hetton-le-Hole
Mick Kelly	1934	1935	4	0	Sandbach
David Kennedy	1969	1969	3	1	Sunderland

Name	Joined	Left	Apps	Goals	Born
Billy Kirton	1919	1919	1	0	Newcastle
Tommy Lamph	1914	1919	11	1	Gateshead
Fred Lawson	1961	1964	51	21	Onslow
Andy Linighan	1984	1985	76	4	Hartlepool
Albert Lomas	1948	1949	1	0	Tyldesley
Dave Lucas	2007	2009	23/1	0	Preston
John Lukic	1978/82	1990/95	431	0	Chesterfield
George Lydon	1954	1954	4	1	Sunderland
John Lyon	1920	1920	33	3	Prescot
Billy McAdams	1961	1961	13	4	Manchester
Billy McLeod	1906	1919	301	177	Hebburn, nr Newcastle
Peter McConnell	1954	1962	53	5	Reddish
Albert McInroy	1935	1937	71	0	Walton-le-Dale
Frank McKenna	1956	1956	6	4	Blaydon
Duncan McKenzie	1974	1975	76/6	30	Grimsby
George McNestry	1928	1928	3	0	Chopwell
Jack McQuillan	1914	1915	20	0	Boldon, Durham
James Makinson	1935	1944	70	0	Aspull
Dave Mangnall	1927	1929	9	6	Wigan
Clifford Marsh	1948	1948	5	1	Atherton
John Martin	1924	1924	2	0	Bishop Aukland
Derek Mayers	1961	1962	24	5	Liverpool
Frank Mears	1924	1928	3	0	Openshaw
George Milburn	1928	1936	166	1	Ashington
Jack Milburn	1929	1938	408	30	Ashington
Jim Milburn	1939	1951	220	17	Ashington
Ron Mitchell	1958	1959	4	0	Morecambe
Tom Mitchell	1926	1930	152	21	Spennymoor
Ian Moore	2004	2006	25/42	5	Birkenhead
James Moore	1921	1921	28	4	Boldon
William Moore	1924	1924	6	0	Sunderland
Tom Morris	1909	1913	109	3	Grimsby
Jack Moss	1949	1950	23	2	Blackrod
Rob Musgrove	1920	1920	36	2	Ryehope
Tom Naisby	1907	1910	68	0	Sunderland
Tom Neal	1931	1935	23	0	New Washington
Kevin Noteman	1987	1989	1/1	1	Preston
Chris O'Donnell	1989	1990	0/1	0	Newcastle
Brett Ormerod	2004	2004	6	0	Blackburn
Neil Parker	1975	1981	0/1	0	Blackburn

Name	Joined	Left	Apps	Goals	Born
Keith Parkinson	1973	1981	33/6	0	Preston
Harry Peart	1913	1915	8	0	Newcastle
John Pemberton	1990	1994	56/12	0	Oldham
Terry Phelan	1983	1986	17/2	0	Manchester
Jimmy Potts	1925	1932	262	0	Morpeth
Joe Potts	1921	1922	10	0	Newcastle
Arthur Price	1945	1946	7	0	Rowlands Gill
David Prutton	2007	CP	56/13	4	Hull
Danny Pugh	2004	2005	40/17	6	Bacup
Dick Ray	1905	1907	44	0	Newcastle
Jo Richmond	1922	1924	60	19	Leasingthorne
Valentine Riley	1926	1926	1	0	Hebburn
Andy Ritchie	1983	1987	149/10	44	Manchester
Andy Robinson	2008	CP	27/14	6	Liverpool
Ronnie Robinson	1985	1986	27	0	Sunderland
Cuthbert Robson	1924	1924	17	4	High Wheatley
William Robson	1921	1922	11	0	Shildon
Ralph Rodgerson	1920	1921	28	0	Sunderland
Harry Roper	1929	1935	18	3	Romiley
John Rudd	1948	1949	18	1	Hull
Reg Savage	1934	1938	84	0	Eccles
John Scott	1950	1954	114	0	Crosby
Harry Searson	1948	1951	116	0	Mansfield
Alan Shackleton	1958	1959	31	17	Padiham
John Sheridan	1982	1989	261/6	52	Stretford
William Short	1919	1919	5	0	Gosforth
Bobby Sibbald	1966	1967	1/1	0	Hebburn
Harry Singleton	1905	1907	51	7	Prescot, Lancs
George Speak	1923	1925	32	0	Blackburn
John Stiles	1984	1988	61/20	3	Manchester
Steve Stone	2005	2006	7/8	1	Gateshead
Harry Stringfellow	1905	1906	16	1	Burscough, Lancs
Harry Sutherland	1938	1947	3	1	Salford
Jack Swan	1921	1924	116	50	Easington
Trevor Swinburne	1985	1985	2	0	East Rainton
Bob Taylor	1985	1988	43/11	13	Horden
William Thomas	1906	1908	10	2	Liverpool
Alan Thompson	2006	2007	19/6	5	Newcastle
Bob Thompson	1920	1920	25	12	Coundon Grange
Dick Thornton	1925	1925	1	0	Boldon

Name	Joined	Left	Apps	Goals	Born
Mark Tinkler	1991	1996	15/12	0	Bishop Aukland
John Trainor	1936	1936	4	0	Byker, Newcastle
Lee Trundle	2008	2009	7/3	1	Liverpool
Charlie Turner	1933	1935	13	0	Manchester
Arthur Tyrer	1950	1954	42	4	Manchester
Willis Walker	1914	1919	22	0	Gosforth
Jimmy Walton	1920	1922	71	4	Sacriston, Co. Durham
Tony Warner	2006	2006	14	0	Liverpool
Fred Whalley	1921	1924	91	0	Bolton
Norman Wharton	1939	1939	2	0	Askham-in-Furness
Thomas Wheatley	1953	1953	6	0	Hebburn
David White	1993	1995	37/15	10	Manchester
John White	1908	1910	64	0	Manchester
Mike Whitlow	1988	1991	75/20	4	Davenham
Charlie Wilkinson	1931	1931	3	0	Memdomsley
Brian Williamson	1962	1962	8	0	Blyth
George Willis	1953	1953	3	0	Shotton
David Wilson	1905	1906	21	13	Hebburn, nr Newcastle
Thomas Wilson	1906	1908	21	2	Preston
Roydon Wood	1953	1959	203	0	Wallasey
Bert Worsley	1932	1935	3	0	Stockport
Alan Wright	2006	2006	1	0	Ashton-under-Lyne

Blackpool

Across the Pennines, if you like your candy floss, enjoy wearing kiss-me-quick hats, are not afraid of heights and are partial to a bit of sticky rock, then it is fair to say that Blackpool would be a pretty good choice to either visit or indeed live. I can verify that, although I did not really have much choice in the matter. I spent the whole of my school life in the popular northern holiday resort. I must admit, though, that I cannot stand candy floss, kiss-me-quick hats are definitely a no-no and once I had broken a tooth after attempting to bite my way through the hardest stick of rock known to man, that particular avenue of culinary delights was off the menu for good. I did experience the views from the top of Blackpool Tower, though, and that was quite a spectacular sight. Although, being 12 years old at the time and not exactly the size of Giant Haystacks, my slight frame was being pushed backwards, forwards and sideways in the howling winds. We chose a good day to go up! When you looked at the clouds, they were moving so fast it gave you the impression that the tower was falling. And the iron railings that separated you from standing at the top of the tower or – erm – not, seemed as though they could snap at any moment. It is true to say that in all the time I lived in Blackpool, just the one trip up the tower was enough. I have always believed in keeping my feet firmly on the ground. Talking of heights, though, reminds me of when I went to see a friend in Boston in America for a three-week holiday. During that period, we had a day in New York and took a trip up the Empire State Building. Leeds had just played Stuttgart in the replayed European Cup tie in Barcelona – a tie they should have already been handed. Stuttgart had beaten Leeds 3–0 in the first leg of their first-round match in Germany. When the Germans came to Elland Road a fantastic performance from Leeds saw us win 4–1, not quite making it through because of their away goal. However, it was revealed that they had brought on an ineligible player from the subs bench late in the game. UEFA decided that the game should be replayed in a neutral country. We got the last laugh, however, with Carl Shutt scoring the winning goal in a 2–1 win in front of a strange-looking 7,400 people inside an eerie Nou Camp.

So anyway, I was standing at the top of the Empire State Building, proudly wearing a Leeds shirt, when this lad came up to me and asked in his broad Yorkshire accent 'ere mate 'ow did Leeds get on uther night?' I thought to myself 'hang on, I'm standing on the top of the Empire State Building in the middle of New York, and I still meet another Leeds fan'. This merely confirmed that the song is true, 'Leeds fans here, Leeds fans there, Leeds fans every…' and all that. I told him we had won 2–1, we talked Leeds for a bit and then both continued on our New York sight-seeing experience.

Going back to Blackpool, in my class at Worbreck High School, an all-boys school, there were at least 30 out of our 32-pupil class that were passionate about one football team or another. There were a few of us who supported Leeds and I was the one who brought a football to school every day. We would play at break time, at lunch and every single day after school. We would all have our favourite players and when I used to go for goal it had to be a Peter Lorimer shot. When I was on the wing I was Eddie Gray. To this day he is still my all-time hero. Sadly for me, though, my footballing 'playing' career took me to the heady heights of Sunday League football only; although I did manage to score eight goals in one match once and never missed a penalty (and yes, I did take them).

Prior to Sunday League football, my passion for Leeds was growing by the day during my time at Worbreck. My dad was into football but, sadly, he never took me to a match (I'm glad he didn't really, as he supports Tottenham!), so it was a case of saving my pocket money up and eventually, along with my mate Ian Costain, we planned my first trip to Elland Road. It was a day that will live with me forever. Saturday 3 February 1979 was the date and Coventry City were the visitors to Elland Road. Ian and I jumped onboard a train from Blackpool bound for Leeds via Manchester Victoria. The buzz and excitement I was feeling that day were simply incredible. Ian was and still is a big Blackpool fan, and having seen them in the first match I ever watched against Bobby Robson's Ipswich where Blackpool caused an upset and knocked them out of the League Cup 2–0, I always keep an eye out for Blackpool's results. On this occasion Ian was coming with me to Elland Road and in front of 22,928 people, with us sat in the South Stand, we watched Tony Currie score the only goal of the game to send us (or rather me) home delirious. I must have spent nearly an hour in the souvenir shop after the game, gobsmacked at all the items available to buy. It was heaven. It was better than I had ever expected, and I had expected a lot. I only had a couple of quid to spend and just could not decide what to take home to cherish. A period of 30 years has passed since that day, and the memory of what I actually bought has faded. Whatever it was, it was my prize possession until the next time. During the game the South Stand were singing songs to the Geldard End and Lowfields Road, and vice versa. The atmosphere was just the best feeling I had ever experienced in my life. The worst thing was to tear myself away at the end of the day. Satellite television was a long way off in those days, so when we saw that Yorkshire Television had brought their cameras to the match, on the Sunday I went round to Ian's house and, given we were back in Blackpool, we managed to get a weak signal from their television to watch the game again. It was like watching a snowstorm at night, but we could just about make out that it was a football match and we saw the goal again.

One day Ian was off to Sheffield to watch his beloved Blackpool play at Sheffield Wednesday and I was on my way to watch Leeds play Liverpool. We shared a train together to Manchester Victoria before he diverted to Sheffield and I headed for Leeds. It was a lousy day weather-wise, and while on the train to Leeds the snow got thicker and thicker. I got off the train at Leeds City Station wrapped in a thick winter coat, with my Leeds bobble hat and scarf keeping me warm, before making my way to Elland Road by foot. There was hardly anyone around, which was not a good sign. As I approached the ground, feet deep in snow, an old gentleman passed me and said a few words I would really rather not have heard: 'Match is off, young 'un,' he said. I could see the tallest floodlights in Europe in the distance and I thought, 'Well, I've got to see the ground if nothing else'. I dejectedly trundled to Elland Road, sat on a wall and had a good look at the stadium and spent half an hour in the souvenir shop, before trundling even more dejectedly back to Leeds City Station. Not surprisingly, the same thing had happened to Ian, with Sheffield Wednesday versus Blackpool also falling victim to the elements. But there *was* a surprise just around the corner. I was waiting on Leeds City Station for my train back to Manchester when who was to walk on the platform? Ian. He had taken a chance on meeting up with me (no mobiles in those days, of course) and the chance had paid off. By then we had decided that if we were not going to watch our respective teams we just wanted to watch a football match, so we looked at who else was playing in the area. Manchester City were at home to Aston Villa, so we thought we would go for that. We got there and it was off, too. That had to be that then, surely? No, there was one other that was not that far away. We arrived at Deepdale, Preston, for their match with West Ham United in the Second Division at five minutes to three. This time, the game was on, one of only six matches in the whole country. Although we were upset about not seeing our favourite teams, at least we were going to see a game of football. The misery was compounded, however, as we sat through a boring goalless draw!

Ian came to a few more Leeds matches with me and I returned the favour by going to a few Blackpool matches with him. It was quite expensive for someone still at school, so it was time to knock Blackpool on the head and become a junior member of LUSC Blackpool. Why hadn't I thought of that before? My first trip with them was terrific. Under the spectacular bright lights of my first night-time match, Leeds went behind three times against QPR before Trevor Cherry popped up with a late winner right in front of us in the South Stand. Cherry looked exhausted but ecstatic following this seven-goal thriller, a feeling mirrored on the terraces.

As a 15-year-old I became a member of LUSCB in their very first season as a branch. During the following campaign my Leeds-born mum and my Blackpool-born dad decided to move south to Bournemouth, where I have lived ever since. When I first moved down I got myself a job and made sure I was on the 7.41am train almost every other Saturday from Bournemouth to Leeds, via London, arriving in Leeds at around midday. I would then make the 45-minute walk I knew like the back of my hand from Leeds City Station to Elland Road. I would be back in Bournemouth for around 11pm. My first-ever wages were pitiful and apart from the odd single by The Police, Ultravox and Jasper Carrott's *Magic Roundabout*, all my money was spent on watching Leeds.

Back in Blackpool, LUSCB went from strength to strength and are still going strong now, although there are only two original members left: Gordon Stutley and secretary Steve Lean. Original members Dave Womack and Mark Jordan moved out of the area and Pete 'the good vicar' Bower did as I did and moved to Bournemouth. Malc Pearce is the current chairman of the branch, who has a strange ritual he enjoys inflicting on his fellow Leeds mates on long trips back to the seaside. Gordon Stutley describes Pearce's feet as 'webbed feet' and he is only too keen to show people his duck-like features, removing his shoes and socks for the entire journey back to Blackpool. 'It's not a pretty sight,' sighs Gordon.

Rochdale

Just down the road from Blackpool is the Lancashire town of Rochdale, where Leeds nut Stuart Robinson can be found. In the early 1970s, Stuart was just plain unlucky when it came to the FA Cup. Having collected enough tokens from the home programmes throughout the season in 1971–72, he was able to apply for tickets for the FA Cup Final showdown with Arsenal – which of course we won via Allan Clarke's delicious diving header. Sadly for Stuart, his application was unsuccessful. A year later was almost the same story. Enough tokens again. Able to apply again. Only this time he was successful and made his way to Wembley for the Final with Sunderland – and we all know what happened then (in case you don't, Leeds came second in the biggest shock an FA Cup Final had ever seen). At that time he vowed that he would definitely be there the next time we appeared in an FA Cup Final. Over three decades later we are all still waiting. In the spring of 1972, though, in the space of five glorious weeks, he was one of the lucky ones who witnessed some of the most outstanding football ever seen at Elland Road. Stuart, among thousands of jubilant Whites, watched the 5–1 thrashing of Man Utd, the famous 7–0 annihilation of poor Southampton, a 3–0 win over Arsenal and another romp, this time a 6–1 mauling of Nottingham Forest. We were simply 'Super Leeds'!

Carlisle

23 November 1985 was the last time Leeds United travelled up the M6 to Carlisle for a League match prior to the 2007–08 season, so imagine the small consolation of the fact that, despite Leeds dipping into the third tier of English football, for a bunch of Carlisle Whites it was a chance to see Leeds on their very

own doorstep for the first time in over 20 years. Leeds went to Brunton Park on Saturday 3 November 2007 on the back of 11 wins and two draws in what was a superb start to the 2007–08 season. And for 110 Leeds United Carlisle Regional Club members it was an occasion they were relishing. Sadly, it did not quite work out, with Leeds suffering their first League defeat of the season, going down 3–1. The bragging rights stayed with the locals for the time being, but that did not stop these loyal Carlisle Whites from enjoying not only an excellent start to the season, but also a 'Leeds on the Road' night, hosted by the head of the Regional Members' Club at the time, John Hemmingham.

The city of Carlisle is right on the border of England and Scotland and between the years of 1135 and 1154 actually belonged to the Scots. For the past 855 years, however, it has firmly been a proud English city. When Hemmingham compèred the 'Leeds on the Road' night, though, there was a very special welcome for a Scot we all have massive respect for. Peter 'Lash' Lorimer was on the panel to answer questions and tell some stories of his time wearing the glorious white of Leeds United. Alongside him was another ex-United favourite, Brendan Ormsby, and Rugby League legend Karl Harrison, who used to turn out for Halifax and Great Britain and is a huge Leeds United fan. Branch secretary Steve Brierley, Roy Clapperton, Gary Ward and the Underwood brothers, Mark and Paul, fired questions at the trio during an excellent evening, one of many 'Leeds on the Road' nights that have been a huge success since Ken Bates initiated the idea. Lorimer played in the first match member Norman Dalton attended way back on 23 November 1974, in a 2–1 success at Carlisle United, with Joe Jordan and the never-knew-what-he-would-do-next Duncan McKenzie scoring for Leeds. Dalton also explained how one member of the Carlisle posse rarely sees Leeds these days yet travels to almost every game. 'One of the Carlisle Whites, who shall remain nameless, very rarely watches the full game but regularly leaves his seat and frequents one of the Elland Road bars. His record used to be six minutes watching the game, but he has since surpassed that by not even going to his seat and just staying in the bar!'

Isle of Man (or Sam!)

Just before we move off down south to meet some southern-based Whites, we'll take a quick trip across the Irish Sea to the Isle of Man. An island famous for its tailless Manx cat, gambling casinos, the annual TT (Tourist Trophy) motorcycle races and for being a tax haven, the island spans 220 square miles, and although it is a dependency of the British crown, it is not a part of the UK. In a book that will be covering thousands of miles all over the planet, this is the first 'virtual' overseas trip.

It is a four-hour ferry to the mainland for the Isle of Man Leeds United Regional Members' Club (IoMLURMC) when they make the trip to see Leeds around eight times a season. Leeds are one of the best-supported English clubs on the island and Steve Cain, who is the secretary of the IoMLURMC, is keen to attract more members. At the time this book went to print they had 15 members, including Lee Hardman, a mascot for the Leeds versus Walsall match in 2007–08, but Steve Cain was hoping that figure would rise to around 60 very soon. The club hold their meetings at the Heron pub in the capital, Douglas, which is run by landlords Paul and Sandra Morley, who are also staunch Leeds supporters. Paul Morley was actually on Leeds United's books at one stage, but never quite made it as a professional footballer.

In 1999 Ray McKeenan decided to start up an Isle of Man Leeds United Supporters' Club and Joe Jordan (no, not the toothless fearsome Scot that once donned the Leeds United number-nine shirt – and then joined a silly club) was elected as chairman. Their first visit to Elland Road as a supporters' club was against Southampton on 28 November 2008, when Michael Bridges scored the only goal of the game to sink the Saints in injury time. 'It was great to take so many IOM supporters to their first game,' Cain says. 'Many supporters probably still would not have been to Elland Road had it not been for the formation of the club. The club changed over to be a recognised members' club in February 2008. Andy Quayle is now the treasurer, Floyd Wilson the chairman and David Craine the vice-chairman. Many of our supporters over here make their own travel arrangements for various games as it is far cheaper to book flights [35 minutes to Liverpool's John Lennon Airport, then an hour and 15 minutes in a minibus to ER] well in advance of games and in small groups. However, we do try to attend as a club as often as we can. We normally go over on the ferry, which is always dodgy given that the bar opens at 7am! The members' club is full of characters, with our chairman Floyd Wilson being one of them. During the World Cup in 2006 he painted a St George's flag on the side of his house. Then there's John Faragher, who despite always taking the mickey out of foreigners on European tours, was born in Germany and now has a Polish fiancé. He is now regarded as the Polish Ambassador on the Isle of Man. One of our members, who will remain anonymous, had a match ticket and a camera to look after in Barcelona in our Champions League run, and he lost them both and spent the game outside the ground in tears. Not funny at the time, but looking back, it is now!'

Here is a question for you: What have London's West End theatre-goers got in common with Leeds United? Answer: Samantha Barks. It is fair to say that the massive majority of Leeds United supporters know how to belt out a tune or 12, but it is also fair to say that *Marching on Together* and *Glory, Glory, Leeds United* may not be quite appropriate for a bit part in the musical *Oliver!* Sam Barks was a contestant on the BBC's *I'd Do Anything* reality show to find the next Nancy for the West End stage version of the film. The talented youngster comes from the Isle of Man and Steve Cain said, 'We all went to Elland Road for the Walsall game in League One on 22 March 2008, not only to support Leeds, but Sam Barks as well. We all took posters of her which said "Vote for Sam". We were all fully behind her. We have even renamed the Isle of Man the Isle of Sam!' Sam's *Oliver* dreams were sadly not to be realised.

The Isle of Man Whites have not been ignored by Leeds United Football Club in the past either, with players such as Peter Lorimer, Norman Hunter, Eddie Gray, Mick Jones, Allan Clarke and Lucas Radebe all making the effort to visit as guest speakers for very special evenings. Cain adds, 'We even had Peter Ridsdale over for one evening telling us how to live our dream, which was really enjoyable at the time. He told us that £8 million had been made available to David O'Leary to buy Frank Lampard, but Peter insisted that David did not think Lampard was worth that money. A few months later you wondered whether the £8 million really was available to David O'Leary. We are planning on other 'Leeds on the Road' nights in the future.'

As this book just about bids a fond farewell to these loyal Isle of Man Whites, prior to boarding the ferry back to mainland Britain they leave us with their collective choice of their all-time favourite player, who is Gordon Strachan, and their all-time Leeds XI, including subs, manager and assistant manager, which is as follows:

Nigel Martyn, Gary Kelly, Tony Dorigo, Billy Bremner, Lucas Radebe, David Batty, Gordon Strachan, Peter Lorimer, Allan Clarke, Tony Yeboah, Eddie Gray. Subs: Gary Speed, Gary McAllister, Carl Shutt. Manager: Howard Wilkinson. Assistant manager: David O'Leary.

Cain: 'I think you can tell that we're quite a young members' club!'

Chapter 3

LIVING NEXT DOOR TO CARDIFF

On the pitch – Welsh-born Whites:

Name	Joined	Left	Apps	Goals
Mark Aizlewood	1987	1989	76/5	4
Steve Balcombe	1978	1982	2	1
Nathan Blake	2004	2004	2	0
Terry Casey	1961	1961	4	0
John Charles	1949 & 1962	1957 & 1962	327	157
Alan Curtis	1979	1980	35	6
Byron Davies	1953	1953	1	0
Malcolm Edwards	1971	1971	0/1	0
Neil Edwards	1989	1989	1	0
Brian Flynn	1977	1982	174/4	11
Cliff Francis	1937	1937	1	0
Thomas Hallett	1962	1962	1	0
Carl Harris	1973	1982	136/40	29
Dennis Hawkins	1966	1967	4	0
Billy Hudson	1951	1951	4	0
Matthew Jones	1997	2000	16/17	0
Eric Kerfoot	1949	1958	349	10
Glan Letheran	1974	1974	1/1	0
Awbrey Powell	1935	1948	119	25
Billy Poyntz	1921	1922	29	7
Ian Rush	1996	1996	38/4	3
Robert Simmonds	1984	1986	7/4	3
Gary Speed	1988	1995	291/20	57
Gary Sprake	1962	1973	505/2	0
Byron Stevenson	1973	1982	102/8	5
Gwyn Thomas	1975	1984	92/11	3
Michael Thomas	1989	1989	3	0
Harold Williams	1949	1955	228	35
Terry Yorath	1967	1976	165/32	12

Leeds fans here, Leeds fans there…where shall we go next then? It is fair to say that CF11 8SX is a postcode for a place that is not somewhere Leeds fans enjoy visiting, and it is not a place where you would normally expect to find too many Whites roaming around.

When United do visit Cardiff, it is more a case of get there, play the match, hope to get a win (which is sadly rare) and get out – as quickly as possible. In January 2002, appalling scenes of violence from the home supporters of Cardiff City were fully in evidence, before, during and after the FA Cup third-round tie at Ninian Park. Nigel Martyn played in goal that day and actually feared for his life, as bottles, coins and anything the Cardiff fans could lay their hands on were thrown at the Leeds players. The Leeds supporters were also subjected to some intense intimidation from a set of football fans who should have been punished way above the meaningless fine of just £20,000 they actually did receive. Not surprisingly, despite taking the lead through Mark Viduka, Leeds, who at the time were top of the Premiership, came off second best and were dumped out of the FA Cup 2–1. Bottles of urine were showered into the Leeds end by an element in football that surely belongs in the Dark Ages. It was, indeed, a day to forget for every Leeds fan present. And one which may well have put some children that attended off the beautiful game forever. Thanks Cardiff. Your hospitality will always be remembered. One Leeds United fan, David Holden, mentions on the brilliant website www.leedsfans.org.uk, 'For the first time I wished I had not got my Leeds coat on, in fact I was in a minority of one wearing a Leeds kit!' It is true that you do not see too many Leeds shirts in Cardiff, so spare a thought for people like Alan Collett, Howell Roberts, Colin Joliffe, Jim Taylor and Andrew Lloyd, who live on the doorstep of arguably the most-supported club in Wales.

Together Messrs Collett, Roberts, Joliffe, Taylor and Lloyd, with much enthusiasm and a great passion for Leeds United Football Club, formed the South Wales Branch of LUSC in 1993. Branch secretary Stuart Salvage joined the ranks shortly after they formed. And along with other members of LUSCSW, Salvage remembers that awful day in January 2002 only too well.

'In all fairness it was a cracking atmosphere they [Cardiff supporters] generated but what happened that day was despicable really,' said Salvage. 'Some people were saying that the Cardiff fans were on the pitch celebrating and everything but that's just rubbish as far as I'm concerned. They were there trying to provoke everyone. They fully deserved their win on the day and you've got to hold your hands up, but the atmosphere was volatile to say the least and standing on that terrace made you think, and I think it got to the Leeds players.

'With regards to the bottles and coins and everything being thrown on the pitch at the players it was disgraceful, and certainly more action should have been taken against Cardiff City Football Club. Both sides, even Leeds, got warned about their future conduct, which was a joke. Everyone got provoked by the Cardiff fans and all they got was a minimal fine. I still maintain to this day that if that had been Leeds United fans on the pitch we would have been thrown out of the FA Cup, no question about it. It may have been the fact that they are a Welsh team that they didn't take any action against them.'

'And we've had our ups and downs' go the lyrics in *Marching on Together*, and that day has to be one of the biggest *downs*, so what about a big *up* for LUSCSW? 12 September 1995 was one such day LUSCSW and, indeed, any Leeds United supporter will remember with great pride. And Salvage and Co. were some of the 14,000 people lucky enough to witness the proceedings first hand. Howard Wilkinson was in charge at Elland Road for his last full season at the helm, and when the UEFA Cup got underway in that campaign, and Leeds were drawn against Monaco, a trip to the south of France was just too good an opportunity to miss for LUSCSW. Minibus fuelled up, they headed to Leeds where they parked up in Beeston before flying from Leeds-Bradford airport to the Principality. A special evening ensued as Tony Yeboah scored a brilliant hat-trick to send Leeds fans into delirium.

Despite losing the second leg at Elland Road 1–0, United safely booked their passage to round two without too much difficulty. On the way back LUSCSW were among the jubilant supporters boarding a plane bound for Leeds-Bradford airport. What was I saying about 'ups and downs' though? When they arrived back in Beeston, ready for the final journey back to South Wales, the minibus was there alright but, sadly, missing its wheels. Did it spoil what had been an amazing trip? Not a bit. That's the spirit lads!

Howell Roberts is a founder member of the branch, who had been going to matches prior to the birth of LUSCSW for 12 years, and he recalls his first away match following Leeds, one which anyone present could never forget. Tuesday 22 May 1982 was a night that was so full of mixed emotions that your body was exhausted with feelings of pride and sadness by the end of it. The venue was the Hawthorns, home of West Bromwich Albion. The occasion was the last match in the top flight for eight years. Leeds had to draw that evening in order to escape the dreaded relegation. Even after a 2–0 defeat, avoiding the drop could still have been achieved, had West Brom done Leeds a favour by beating Stoke City a couple of days later. Given the fact that the Hawthorns was a complete wreck after they had beaten Leeds, however, it was hardly likely they were going to play their hearts out to save Leeds United. Stoke City were a poor side at best but they managed to beat West Brom 3–0 and Leeds were doomed.

'All my mates were going and I was the only one that had a car that was roadworthy, so I got conned into driving and it ended up being one of those matches that will always stick in the back of your mind,' said Howell. 'We stopped off at a Travellers Lodge on the way back and we could hear these inspectors of the West Midlands police calling Leeds fans animals and thugs and all sorts.

'Not even the day we won the Championship, at Sheffield United in 1992, have I ever seen a vocal support like the one at West Brom in 1982, and I've never seen anything like it since. You didn't have the cherry pickers at that match. You were talking hardcore fans.' It was indeed a vocal support that was simply awesome. If you were there, you do not need reminding that from the half-time whistle, right the way through to the final whistle of our season and what was to be the final whistle in the top flight for far too long, it was non-stop singing. West Brom fans were not just spectators at a football match, they were witnessing an incredible show of support for a football team from the opposition. With five minutes remaining and the score still 1–0 to West Brom, every Leeds fan inside the Hawthorns was praying for an equaliser, one which would have changed the course of Leeds United's history. Instead, Cyril Regis made it 2–0 to the Baggies, which did not go down too well. Well, alright, that is a bit of an understatement. The correct description of what happened immediately after Regis broke all our hearts, was 'all hell was let loose'. What had been simply an unbelievable support by the Leeds faithful turned into sheer anger and violence. In those days, the 12-foot iron girders to prevent supporters getting on the pitch were fully erect, but it was amazing how they still stood there after thousands of Leeds supporters attempted to bring them down. Outside the Hawthorns, concrete walls came down in a sea of raging frustration and the immense pride of the support that evening had suddenly, in a Cyril Regis split-second, turned to anger, which was soon followed by sadness. It seemed inevitable that Stoke City would beat West Brom days later, and it was.

Getting back to South Wales, there are plenty of other Leeds fans in the region and, as Stuart Salvage explains, they help each other out whenever they can: 'Whether we take a minibus, a couple of cars or link up with other supporters, it's Leeds United as far as I'm concerned and there's always a hard core of us go to practically every game. That's the beauty of it really, we've got the contacts of other supporters and we help each other out. Whether it's the guys from the South West or West Midlands or the Shropshire mob it doesn't matter. It's a good base down here, there are a lot of people who are interested in Leeds United Football Club.'

Stuart mentions the South-West Whites, with whom member Dave Jones has been following Leeds for over three decades and recalls his first match, which was at White Hart Lane on 1 September 1973. 'As a mere 10-year-old my dad took me in the hope of me becoming a Tottenham fan, but he failed,' laughs Dave. 'I remember standing on a wooden stool my dad had made for me. We won 3–0 and the Revie team, Bremner, Giles, Clarke and Co., were playing. I was hooked and the rest is history. I was a bit too young to take in just how good that team was but Leeds were *the* team then.' Dave may not have realised it at the time, but he was witnessing the best period in the club's history, with Billy Bremner's brace and Allan Clarke's goal completing Leeds's third win at the start of the 1973–74 season. Leeds would go on to win their opening seven matches, only equalled in the club's history at the start of the 2007–08 season in the third tier of English football. Leeds remained undefeated in the opening 29 games of that fabulous title-winning campaign and eventually lost just one game at Elland Road all season (surprisingly 1–4 against Burnley) and four in all.

Dave Jones has since been back to White Hart Lane on many occasions to see Leeds in action, and he recalls an incident in 1998 that triggered his dislike of our former chairman Peter Ridsdale. 'George Graham, our manager at the time, was about to leave Leeds to take over at Spurs,' Jones says. 'Ridsdale came to the Leeds fans at half-time to let us know what was going on. I left my seat to go down to pitchside and felt an excruciating pain in my knee. It turned out I had dislocated it and I was stretchered out of the ground. At Edmonton General Hospital it took two attempts to put the knee back and they couldn't knock me out because I had had one or two beers before the game. That was the first time I blamed Ridsdale for everything! When I left the ground we were leading 2–1. It ended 3–3.'

The South-West Whites travel to every game throughout the season, and they always include three other loyal United fans, as Jones explains, 'There is Acker Hurd, who lives in Glastonbury, who has no transport but does not miss a game, home or away. He lives for Leeds, raises money by selling a scratchcard in the pubs of Glastonbury throughout the season and you couldn't meet a nicer bloke. He turns up week after week despite some of the worst hangovers ever seen. There's Neil 'Sumo' O'Dare, who is responsible for sampling all the food on our trips. He really has eaten all the pies. We just wish he wouldn't insist on listening to *Late Night Love* on the radio when coming back from midweek trips. Geoff Hann, who is our minibus driver for some trips, knows the location of every

KFC in the country and will never go without a portion as his post-match meal. I just hope they are a future shirt sponsor for Geoff's sake!'

Les Evans is the chairman of the South-West Whites and is another lifelong Leeds fan from this part of the world, who recalls a slightly longer trip to Italy on 20 October 1998 than they originally had planned. It was his first European trip for a UEFA Cup second-round first-leg tie against Roma, which United lost 1–0 despite putting on a plucky performance for the travelling Leeds following. 'It was due to be a day trip, quick tour of the sights, game in the evening and then back to Blighty,' says Les. 'So all goes well until we get back on the plane with the lads having played well and only lost 1–0 with good old Alfie Haaland playing a blinder. We got to the plane, settled into our seats, checked out the stewardesses' legs and looked forward to a pleasant kip before landing back in Luton. Then nothing happened. A widgit on the plane had broken and a replacement one had to be shipped out from the UK before we could take off. We all trooped off the aircraft and were transferred to a hotel for the night with the airline promising us the new doodah would be in place first thing in the morning. Unfortunately, come the morning, and after being bussed back to the airport, the news came that the plane with the replacement piece had also broken down so we were stuck in Rome. Or, more accurately, in an extremely decrepit airport near Rome. Facilities were pretty basic to say the least, food basically being cheese and ham sandwiches, and tempers were beginning to fray when we spotted a way to wreak our revenge. For reasons best known to themselves, the airport authorities had selected that day to film a commercial for Italian TV to encourage people to use their distinctly dodgy facilities. So, cameras and lights appeared, actors and actresses took their places and the action began – with about 50 bored, hungry and pretty miffed Leeds fans looking on. All went well, with the assembled cast giving the impression of going about their business in a sophisticated European airport, until choruses of *We Are Leeds*, *MOT* and ribald comments to the actresses interrupted proceedings. After about 17 takes they admitted defeat and gave up. Vengeance was ours!'

The South Wales LUSC have since become a Leeds United Regional Members' Club.

Chapter 4

WE'RE IRISH AND WE'RE PROUD OF LEEDS

On the pitch – Irish-born Whites:

Name	Joined	Left	Apps	Goals	Eire or NI
Rob Bayly	2004	2008	1/1	0	Eire
Jim Beglin	1989	1989	20/1	0	Eire
Wesley Boyle	1996	2001	0/1	0	Northern Ireland
Robert Browne	1935	1946	114	0	Northern Ireland
Thomas Casey	1949	1949	4	0	Northern Ireland
David Cochrane	1937	1950	185	32	Northern Ireland
Wilbur Cush	1957	1960	90	9	Northern Ireland
Ken De Mange	1987	1987	19/1	1	Eire
Jonathan Douglas	2005	2009	151/15	11	Eire
Harry Duggan	1925	1936	196	49	Eire
Peter Fitzgerald	1960	1960	8	0	Eire
Robert Fullam	1923	1923	7	2	Eire
Johnny Giles	1963	1975	523/4	115	Eire
Ian Harte	1995	2003	270/16	39	Eire
David Healy	2004	2006	88/32	31	Northern Ireland
Billy Humphries	1958	1959	26	2	Northern Ireland
Denis Irwin	1982	1986	82	1	Eire
Gary Kelly	1991	2006	516/15	4	Eire
Robbie Keane	2000	2001	38/18	19	Eire
Andy Keogh	2003	2003	0/1	0	Eire
Jim McCabe	1948	1954	161	0	Northern Ireland
John McClelland	1989	1992	26/3	0	Northern Ireland
Eddie McMorran	1948	1949	40	6	Northern Ireland
Stephen McPhail	1996	2004	72/34	3	Eire
Simon Madden	2007	2007	1	0	Eire
Cornelius Martin	1946	1948	49	1	Eire
Alan Maybury	1995	2001	14/4	0	Eire
Liam Miller	2005	2006	31/2	1	Eire

Name	Joined	Left	Apps	Goals	Eire or NI
Eugene O'Doherty	1920	1920	2	4	Eire
Jimmy O'Neill	1973	1973	0/3	0	Northern Ireland
Noel Peyton	1958	1963	117	20	Eire
Alan Sheehan	2008	CP	21/2	1	Eire
Frank Taylor	1949	1949	3	0	Northern Ireland
Jim Twomey	1937	1949	111	0	Northern Ireland
Nigel Worthington	1994	1996	43/12	1	Northern Ireland

Republic of Ireland

Back to our virtual trip then and, ah, Fishguard. Just up the road from Cardiff and a two-hour ferry away is what is simply a beautiful country, the Republic of Ireland. There's no doubting that. It offers stunning scenery with a deep, rich history and a hospitality second to none.

According to the Irish poet W.B. Yeats, Galway is 'the Venice of the West'. Once again, there is some stunning scenery to behold in this beautiful part of the world. One such place is Aughnanure Castle, built in the 16th century. It takes your breath away. However, for a few of the locals of Galway, it is not their favourite piece of architecture. Not by a long way. That honour goes to a building far, far away from the west coast of the Republic of Ireland – you might know it – Elland Road.

They love the place so much that it was too hard to resist setting up a Branch of LUSC. So that is exactly what Gerry McDermott, Liam Keogh and James McManus did in 1984, making it the oldest LUSC Branch in Southern Ireland. Along with Paul Madden and Joe Connell, they fly over to Elland Road around 15 times a season. Some of their members hail from another Republic, the former Czechoslovakia. Karel Kalivoda and his wife Alena Kalivoda, along with their grandson Petr, continue to enjoy their ties with the Galway Whites and meet up at Elland Road as much as they can.

Over in Wexford, on the other side of Ireland, back in 2003 the Wexford Whites can boast that they beat Manchester United. All keen golfers in this part of the world, they organised a 'United Challenge Trophy' against the enemy at the Mitchelstown Golf Club in County Cork. The 11-a-side matchday singles contest was organised by Batt Power. Simple rules – first to six wins. The Wexford Whites got off to a good start with David O'Sullivan taking the first leg. Leeds then lost the next two to go one leg behind, before Pat O'Farrell, landlord of the popular O'Farrell's Bar, Gerry O'Riordan and Joe O'Brien rattled off three victories to give Leeds a two-leg lead at 4–2, which then became 4–3. Batt Power then restored their two-leg advantage, leaving the Wexford Whites just one leg from victory. Just like our teams over the years, though, Leeds do not *do* simple, and all of a sudden the match was tied at 5–5, with one leg to go. Up stepped Michael McElroy, who had ultimate responsibility for winning the match for Leeds. Eighteen holes later, there was nothing in it. Sudden death then. Over to the par 4, 20th hole. McElroy's opponent was in trouble. McElroy was now 25ft from the pin. Get it down in two and victory was with Leeds. He rolled the first putt close. And the second? Sank! Victory to Leeds – against Man Utd! We do not hear that anywhere near enough. It was time to celebrate at O'Farrell's Bar, where Leeds were presented with the victory shield.

We now move up the coast to the Republic's capital Dublin and on to Michael Verdon who, despite living across the water, has held a season ticket at Elland Road for the past 16 years. He even gets to around seven or eight away games a season. 'It's very frustrating living this far from Leeds and it's cost me a fortune,' he admits. 'I would possibly be a rich man were it not for my love of Leeds, but I would not change a thing. I find it hard to understand some locals in Leeds moaning about prices of match tickets. I reckon I've been to about 750 matches. I've commuted from Dublin for about 600 of them and then the rest was when I moved over to Leeds between 1971 and 1974. I followed the lads everywhere in that time in what was probably the best period in the club's history.'

Michael fell in love with Leeds after watching them play in a friendly in Dublin, with the likes of Bremner, Giles, Lorimer, Eddie Gray *et al* strutting their stuff. 'Watching that Super-Leeds side in all-white under the floodlights was awesome. I had no chance. Hooked! So I made plans to go and watch them in a proper match, which was at Old Trafford against Manchester United. We won 1–0 with a goal from Mick Jones. Best, Law, Charlton and all that lot were totally outplayed. I had only just discovered the joys of sex but now I had found the one thing that was even better. Any Leeds win is simply brilliant but beating Man Utd and on their own patch? It does not get better than that. I am very lucky to be able to tell this story, though. I was probably the only Leeds fan in Dublin or possibly the whole of Ireland at the time, so I had the cheek to travel with the Man Utd Dublin Supporters' Club for reasons of costs. I was able to travel incognito until the game. When Jones scored, my cover was well and truly blown. Suffice to say I had to make my own way back to Dublin! Sore losers!'

Nowadays the support for Leeds in Dublin has risen dramatically and Michael believes that behind 'that lot', Liverpool and Celtic, Leeds are the fourth-best-supported club in the Irish capital, with fans meeting up for live games at the Sean O'Casey pub just off O'Connell Street. Has he managed to include the rest of his family among the Dublin Whites though? 'It was no problem luring my wife to becoming Leeds. It was in the marriage contract. But I have failed as a father to two of my four kids. I got it right with two of them but the other two grew up in the 1980s during the Liverpool dominance. They reckoned there was something seriously wrong with me trekking off to Elland Road every second week and rarely returning home with a win. What they don't realise, though, is that Leeds fans are simply the best football fans in the world.'

Just before we head off north of the Irish border then, Michael gives us his all-time Leeds side:

Nigel Martyn, Paul Madeley, Terry Cooper, Billy Bremner, Jack Charlton, Norman Hunter, Peter Lorimer, Allan Clarke, John Charles, Johnny Giles, Eddie Gray. Subs: David Harvey, Paul Reaney, Mick Jones.

Northern Ireland

The number of Leeds United supporters north of the Irish border in Belfast is so vast that Alfie Bell, a lifelong fan, says 'It's impossible to put a figure on it!' Among them are many characters, including Marty Steele, who, it appears, has a twin brother. Bell, who has travelled to around 150 Leeds matches said, 'It's actually a bit of a laugh as Marty has a bit of a split personality. Good guy Marty and not so nice Marty. My wife and I produced a Marty "twin" picture on the computer. It came out really well and he now has a framed copy in his living room.'

Another staunch Belfast White is rather more laid-back Nick Patterson. On a trip to PSV Eindhoven in 2002 (UEFA Cup fourth round, first leg – drew 0–0) the casual approach was not ideal, as the trip turned into an embarrassing experience, as Alfie Bell explains. 'Nick is from County Fermanagh and likes to take things slowly and in his stride, as most county lads do. Anyway, Nick was walking around Amsterdam with the group when they approached a cordoned-off section of the footpath in which workmen had dug a hole, and this was clearly marked out with red tape. Nick being Nick was just walking around without a care in the world, admiring the high buildings when the group shouted a warning about the hole. Nick reacted just a little too late, and on trying to prevent himself from falling into the hole grabbed onto a postcard rack that was close by. Unfortunately, the postcard rack was not chained to the ground and poor Nick and postcards fell into the hole, much to the amusement of the rest of the group and the local Dutch people sitting in a restaurant across the street.'

Patterson also provides the entertainment for the Belfast troops on trips to watch Leeds by singing cartoon theme tunes, including his two favourites, *Banana Splits* and *Hong Kong Fuey*! However, on one particularly long trip to Elland Road, various renditions of the aforementioned would have perhaps worn a little thin after a lengthy hold-up north of the border. Bell explains 'We were travelling to Leeds in a coach that broke down in Scotland and we waited for four hours for a replacement. The funny thing was that the lads were all looking for something to eat and drink and there was a bar just around the corner and no one had bothered to take a short walk to check out our surroundings. We were all totally gazumped when we passed it in our replacement coach.'

The Irish, known for their hospitality, certainly know how to enjoy themselves. At the end of each season, no matter how our team has fared, after the final game at Elland Road it has become a tradition for them to enter every public house from the ground back to the centre of Leeds. And we are not talking about a few orange juices! They also play a football match for Jordan's Dreams at the end of every campaign against Leeds fans from Beeston, which is followed by a hearty barbecue and a couple of ales. Alfie Bell explains that one particular end-of-season will not be forgotten in a hurry – the 1991–92 title-winning year. 'There's been some terrific games I've been to but against Norwich City after we'd just won the title in 1992 it was fantastic. I was offered £700 for my ticket but there was no way I was parting with that. The ground was full at 2pm and the atmosphere was unbelievable. Wallace scored a wonder goal to celebrate in style, even though it was obvious the players had been celebrating all week!'

Chapter 5

ACROSS THE POND AND BEYOND

On the pitch – American-born Whites:

Name	Joined	Left	Apps	Goals
Mike Grella	2009	CP	0/12	0
Jemal Johnson	2006	2006	3/2	0
Eddie Lewis	2005	2007	92/3	9

America

All aboard our first long-haul flight then, it is time to cross the pond to basketball-loving, American football-loving, baseball-loving US of A. When I visited Boston just two years prior to America staging the 1994 World Cup Finals, they still did not have a clue about the wonderful world of football. I even visited a local radio station in Boston and spoke with the sports editor. He too knew nothing of the world's biggest sport. Trying to explain to him that Foxboro Stadium in the heart of the city was to be a venue for the football World Cup was like trying to explain the offside rule to a cross-eyed monkey on dope. But hey, let's not have a dig at the Yanks too much. After all, Eddie Lewis was more than alright by us. Whatever you think of America, the country has become a better place since the birth of a certain organisation in the heart of the jazz-land city of Chicago in 1992.

In the space of just three years, what was originally the Chicago branch of LUSC grew from a mere acorn to a sturdy oak tree and eventually became what it is today, the Leeds United Supporters' Club of North America (LUSCNA). Geographically, it is the largest LUSC branch in the world, with members stretching from the Californian coastline right across to the bright lights of New York and Boston. From the sun-drenched beaches of Florida back up to the Rocky Mountains of Denver, Colorado and then even up into Canada, LUSCNA are flying the white flag of Leeds United. And, it is fair to say, the *Yorkshire Evening Post* had a large part to play in the birth of LUSCNA, albeit unwittingly. Mike Bellwood, who now lives in Boston and is the secretary of the branch, originally settled in Chicago. He then found out that there was a pub called the Abbey that regularly showed English football. When Leeds played against Rangers in our ill-fated European Cup second-round second-leg tie in 1992 (lost 2–1 on the night and 4–2 on aggregate), Mike Bellwood could not resist the temptation to wander down to the Abbey to take in the action. He took along cuttings from the *Yorkshire Evening Post*. It was not long before others in the establishment noticed and before long there were around a dozen Whites cheering our boys on. Obviously, because of the outcome of the game it was not the best of occasions, but on the plus side the Chicago branch was born.

New York had already set up their branch and a year later the two branches merged to become the USA branch. It was not long before word began to spread all over the US, and with email contact new members were springing up all over the place. This also included members from Canada, so in 1995 the branch once again changed its name to the North America branch.

Mike Bellwood recalls a memorable UEFA Cup night in Boston in 2000. 'The home game against Roma was outstanding. It was 0–0 after the first leg, so the Boston Whites met up at the Irish Embassy for the return at Elland Road. It was a great performance and Alfie Haaland in particular was magnificent. With about 20 minutes to go Harry Kewell popped up with the winner. Alan Smith then came on for the last 10 minutes, wound two of the Roma players up, who both lost their cool and got sent off and the 'time to go' chant resounded around the pub! The following season [the Champions League campaign] we went to watch all the games at Café Paradiso in the North End, the Italian section of Boston. Cappucini, panini and beer, coupled with the games versus Milan and Lazio, made for some great afternoons. "White flu" [i.e. leaving the office with some feeble excuse to go and watch Leeds] was very prevalent during the UEFA Cup and Champions League days when the matches kicked off over here at 2.45pm.'

Right over the other side of the US, by the golden sands of Palm Beach, the wealthy suburbs of Hollywood and the bright lights of Los Angeles, lives Californian White Andy Smith. Through the wonderful world of the internet, he now listens to matches live on the radio via his computer, but when Leeds are live on the television across the pond it is not so convenient. 'When Leeds kick-off at noon in the UK, it's 4am over here,' he explains. 'The pubs throw you out at 2am and then reopen at 4am. I've kipped in my truck [registration number 4 LUFC – he has a motorbike as well with registration number LUFC] in the parking lot a few times during the gap before. When I listen to Leeds on the radio through the internet I can generally do the *We are the Champions, Champions of Europe* song topless and bottomless – but I guess that's a bit too much information!' Yes Andy, it is.

Andy was born in Cheltenham but moved to Scarborough with his Scottish parents at a young age and grew up partly in the Yorkshire holiday resort and partly in Hong Kong. Living in California for some 15 years, the 41-year-old had quite an amazing day out at the American Formula One Grand Prix back in June 2004. Not only did he manage to take his Leeds United flag onto the grid of the F1 meeting, but he also managed to track down the *American Speed* TV commentator Bob Varsha before the race. At a scorching Indianapolis speedway circuit Andy used his persuasive powers to get Varsha to mention the mighty Leeds in his commentary. The deal was that Andy's company would make a donation to a charity of Varsha's choice, a deal which Varsha was only too happy to strike. So how on earth was he going to manage to sneak in Leeds United while commentating on motor racing? To the confused American listener, the exact words were, 'McLaren will rise like a Phoenix from the ashes, just like the mighty Leeds United will march back into the Premiership next season.' Nice one Bob. And Andy of course!

Andy can thank his mum and her twin sister, Aunt Anna, for his never-ending love for the club, as they took him to countless games as a youngster. And for his mum's 80th birthday celebrations, she enjoyed a guided tour of Elland Road by the 1992 Championship-winning defender John McClelland. Andy's mum and dad were able to have their photo taken holding one of Billy Bremner's Scotland caps, which was a huge thrill, particularly for his mum. She was, however, a little upset at not meeting her Elland Road hero, Eddie Gray. After worshiping the man for years, she was hoping he would be there, but, on her return to their home in Cheltenham, she got a terrific surprise. She pressed the answerphone button, and a certain Eddie Gray had recorded this message: 'Hello Margaret, Eddie Gray, the manager of Leeds United here. Sorry I couldn't be there for your special day but I had to train the players. Hope you've had a great birthday.' Now let's be honest, how many managers in the country would bother to do that?

Adrian Dingle is another passionate adopted American White, living in Atlanta. And he is convinced that the support for Leeds in his neck of the woods is among the best of all the English clubs. He says, 'Outside the part-timers for Man Utd, Arsenal, Liverpool and lately Chelsea, we rank very highly. In Atlanta there are seven or eight of us that meet on a regular basis. My guess is that if you took a survey of the few hundred people who consider themselves real English football fans, we would be right up there among the genuine hardcore as the largest group.'

Robert Alderman, who now lives in Fort Lauderdale, began life with Crystal Palace on his doorstep but, as he puts it, 'there was no peer pressure to support the local team and my mum came from Keighley', so he just had to start following the Whites. Palace against Leeds was always on the cards as being his terrace 'debut', and so it proved. 'It was in 1969, during the 1969–70 season,' he says. 'And Gary Sprake made one of his infamous gaffs to gift Palace an equaliser after Lorimer had put us one up. I remember my first trip to Elland Road as well, which was also against Crystal Palace. I went up to Leeds on a Crystal Palace coach with some school friends. I was terrified that I would be identified as a Leeds fan. Third Division Palace pulled off a shock 1–0 win in the fourth round of the FA Cup, so on the way back I couldn't have given a toss! In the early 1990s I took my American girlfriend with me to watch us play Aston Villa. It turned out to be a boring 0–0 draw, so she never came again! It was much better when I drove up to the Stuttgart game in the European Cup in 1992, though. It was an incredible come-from-behind performance [3–0 down from the first leg – won second leg 4–1 – Leeds going through 2–1 in a replay after Stuttgart fielded an ineligible player in second leg] and a great atmosphere on the Kop. I drove up from London and had some good banter with some Stuttgart supporters who were staying at the same B&B.'

Go on then Robert, what is your all-time Leeds XI?

Nigel Martyn, Paul Reaney, Terry Cooper, Billy Bremner, Rio Ferdinand, Norman Hunter, Peter Lorimer, Allan Clarke, John Charles, Johnny Giles, Eddie Gray.

Did you know there is another 'Leeds United' in this world? Well, if you didn't, you're about to find out – it's in the US. 'Leeds United of Pennsylvania' is an Under-16 outfit coached by one Gary Ross, who, funnily enough, happens to be an ardent Leeds fan. Born in Grimsby, he harboured hopes himself of one day pulling on the Leeds shirt at Elland Road. The now 42-year-old was a promising prospect on the field and began with the Nottingham Forest youth set-up. He also played for England Schoolboys in 1986. He then moved across to America on a soccer scholarship, leading him to play professionally in the US for a number of years. And as for his up-and-coming teenagers, what more inspiration does a youngster need than to put on the white strip of Leeds United every time they step onto a football field? Gary buys all the kit, trackies and whatever else is needed directly from Elland Road, and he insists that no red is to be worn at any time, not even in training! The ex-pat has a website, which tells you all about his soccer academy in the US, and the address is: www.soccerschool.com. For the record, his US professional career saw him start with Harrisburg Heat for the 1992–93 season before moving on to Delaware Wizards between 1994 and 1996. A brief spell at Baltimore Spirit was then followed by a two-year stint at Philadelphia Kixx.

Brian Schoenfelder has, funnily enough, done the opposite of those escaping the British Isles to settle in the US. Originally from Columbus, Ohio, he now resides in London and has since made up for lost time in following Leeds. Almost 300 games crammed into the nine years he has been in Britain is not bad going, considering it is still 195 miles to travel to a 'home' match. A true loyal Leeds fan, there is no doubt of that, he explains why he thinks the Leeds following is such a vociferous one. 'I think that part of it is that Leeds is a one-team city, which is very passionate about its football. Leeds is the third-largest city in the country behind London [nine teams within 20 miles in the top two divisions] and Birmingham [five teams in the top two divisions within 20 miles]. The other reason Leeds have got such a great support is that things are just much better in Yorkshire! I have got a mate who is also mad on Leeds, Paul Cadd, and we shared a room on a pre-season tour of Sweden once. While he was asleep in the middle of the night he just started talking loudly. The only thing was that every other word was some sort of profanity. It was both funny and scary at the same time!'

Brian Schoenfelder's dream Leeds United side, in a 3–5–2 formation, looks like this:

Nigel Martyn, Lucas Radebe, David Wetherall, Norman Hunter, Gordon Strachan, David Batty, Billy Bremner, Gary McAllister, Eddie Gray, Tony Yeboah, Jimmy Floyd Hasselbaink.

Altogether there are members of LUSCNA in 27 states across America, plus members in Canada and even Argentina. In California they have 21 members, in New York there are 19 and in seven other states there are at least 10 members. Ian Slade looks after the membership in Canada and Gary Wilson and Simon Toplis run their excellent website, http://www.luscna.com/.

Canada (and talking of Ian Slade…)

On the pitch – Canadian-born Whites:

Name	Joined	Left	Apps	Goals
Kevin Sharp	1992	1995	11/7	0

Just before we head off to warmer waters, we'll take a quick diversion up to Toronto in Canada, where Ian Slade plays a big part in the running of LUSCNA. There are around 20 Leeds supporters in the Greater Toronto Area (GTA), who meet up whenever Leeds are on the box. Ian himself left the British Isles back in 1996 but his love affair with Leeds United remains as passionate as ever. His Leeds watching 'career' began way back in 1970 as an eight-year-old, when Peter Lorimer's goal at Crystal Palace was wiped out by one of Gary Sprake's howlers, throwing it into his own net with five minutes left to play. Even though he hails from Surrey, Ian was captivated by Don Revie's heroes of the 1970s and it was in 1970 that he decided that Leeds were the team for him. 'When I first became interested in football, they were the best,' says Ian. 'Despite being from Surrey, where there was a lot of support for Chelsea and other London clubs, I somehow took a liking to Leeds and that support never changed. For this reason, I've never been one to criticise out-of-town support and can see why children in the 1980s would support Liverpool, in the 1990s would support Man Utd and today, Chelsea. As a non-Yorkshireman supporting Leeds, I have never been made to feel any different from the home-grown support, i.e. we're all "Marching on Together"!'

It was eight years after he was bitten by the Leeds bug before Ian made his first visit to Elland Road, but he made up for lost time by holding a season ticket from 1990 until 1996. 26 August 1978 will always be etched onto the brain of this adopted Canadian. Leeds made the day of his first visit complete by comfortably beating Wolves 3–0, courtesy of goals from Ray Hankin, Frank Gray and Tony Currie. 'I don't remember much about the game,' Ian says. 'But I remember the whole day was a fantastic experience. The train journey to and from Leeds, the walk to Elland Road, standing on the Kop. And for my first game away at Palace, I was just shocked at how disliked Leeds were by the home support – which of course was where we were sitting! I would say that since then, one of the best games I've been to was the FA Cup tie against QPR in 1987. A sell-out crowd [unheard-of in those days] and the crowd willing the underdogs – Leeds – to victory from a goal down, achieved five minutes from time by a diving header from Brendan Ormsby in front of the Kop. Unbelievable reaction from the crowd as that winning goal went in. Probably the 6–1 victory at Sheffield Wednesday in the Championship-winning season [1991–92] was the best match I've been to away in terms of everything. The atmosphere, the performance. It was a televised Sunday game, and although Sheffield Wednesday were poor, an imperious performance by the whole Leeds team ensued, highlighted by a Lee Chapman hat-trick. We had great seats high up in the

Leppings Lane stand, from where you could see the movement and passing style open up the Sheffield Wednesday defence time after time, added to which the support for Leeds seemed non-stop all afternoon.'

Having attended roughly 300 Leeds matches in his time, how does he feel now being so far away from Elland Road? 'I left the UK in 1996 and through the early O'Leary years when we had a young, vibrant, attractive team to support, it was very frustrating. I missed out on being able to watch them regularly and being able to join in the great European adventures. However, the way that things have worked out in the second half of my absence, it has probably been a lot easier to take, being so far away from the action.' Prior to emigrating across the Atlantic, along with fellow members Mark Belshaw and Ian Cokeyne, Ian joined the Wellingborough branch of LUSC. As mentioned at the front of the book, since chairman Ken Bates came on board, he has now implemented the LURMC. A lot of fans have mixed feelings about making the swap from LUSC to LURMC, so how does Ian feel about it? 'I've been a member of the supporters' club for a number of years now. Firstly with Wellingborough and now with LUSCNA, and I have always enjoyed the camaraderie of meeting and travelling with fellow supporters. The question of the allocation of scarce match tickets is always a difficult one, but, as far as I was concerned, I always found it to be fairly handled within the branch as a whole. I never liked Ken Bates from his Chelsea days, he was too outspoken and radical, and wouldn't have ever considered him as the saviour of Leeds United, but that's what he's done. I don't agree with some of his actions (ticket prices, alienation of the supporters' club *et cetera*), but he knows the business of football and therefore I trust and hope that he is making these decisions with the best interest of Leeds United Football Club. Put it this way, who would you prefer to be running Leeds, Bates or [Peter] Ridsdale? In my opinion, it's no contest.'

One of Ian's hairier moments watching Leeds came in 1992, when we played away in a European Cup match with Glasgow Rangers. No tickets were allocated to Leeds, so Ian had to find another way of obtaining a ticket. He was successful in his quest but was relieved when he arrived home safe and sound. 'It was quite strange really because I had a young lady friend visiting me from Ireland for the week in question but she was prepared to cut short her visit when I explained that I had to travel up to Glasgow for the game,' says Ian. 'And before anyone asks, yes I did see her again after that week, which was even more of a surprise! I had acquired a ticket through some contacts my boss (a Scotsman) had with the SFA I believe, which involved getting the train to Glasgow from Northampton via Edinburgh to pick up the ticket. I had arrangements to stay with some distant relatives in Glasgow and although I had, beforehand, felt confident about travelling to the game alone, I must admit to feeling relieved when they picked me up from the station, took me to their home for something to eat and drink and then insisted on driving me to and from Ibrox. Being on my own, I reasoned that it would be quite easy to avoid detection as I wouldn't have to speak to anyone. So imagine my horror when, having taken my seat, the Rangers fan next to me turned round and said "You're from Northampton aren't you?" Of course, he had got his tickets via the same source and had been told that he would be sitting next to an English Leeds fan.'

So, how did it feel when Gary McAllister silenced the whole of Ibrox with a goal for Leeds in the opening two minutes? 'I had no problems sitting on my hands and not leaping from my seat, especially when I saw the reaction that some Leeds fans got when they weren't able to do likewise. I have to say that sitting with the home support isn't always the easiest thing to do. All things considered, though, everything worked out as well as could be expected and having the guy next to me knowing my circumstances certainly made watching the game easier than might otherwise have been the case.' Leeds went down 2–1 at Ibrox and we were knocked out of the competition following the second leg at Elland Road, which was another 2–1 defeat and led to Leeds going down 4–2 on aggregate.

So then Ian, do you have an all-time Leeds XI plus a few subs? In a 4–4–2 formation, this is it:

Nigel Martyn, Paul Reaney, Tony Dorigo, Billy Bremner, Lucas Radebe, Norman Hunter, Gordon Strachan, Allan Clarke, John Charles, Johnny Giles, Eddie Gray. Subs: David Harvey, Paul Madeley, Tony Currie, Gary McAllister, Tony Yeboah.

'I'm too young to have seen John Charles play but if the reports are to be believed, there's no way that he could be left out of any all-time Leeds team. If the team has to only include those players that I've seen, then I'd replace Charles with Yeboah and bring Hasselbaink in as one of the substitutes.'

Cayman Islands

Heading south now, and if you are going to become an ex-pat and get together with fellow Leeds supporters as often as you possibly can, then you could do far worse than the luxurious surroundings of the Cayman Islands in the

Caribbean. Grand Cayman to be precise, situated to the west of Cuba and Jamaica. That's exactly what Dave Newlove did. A former season ticket holder at Elland Road, he had found out that even fans as far away as Singapore had set up a branch of LUSC, so he decided he would attempt to do the same on this British-owned island.

Born and bred in Leeds, Dave began his working life as an employee at the Yorkshire Bank in Headingley. Subsequent promotions took him first to Dublin, from 1998 to 2002, before he moved to Grand Cayman in February 2002. Newlove says, 'I had read about the formation of the Singapore Whites in *LLL* [the Leeds United magazine] and once I had settled the family into Cayman Islands life, decided to form an LUSC club on Grand Cayman if there was sufficient support. I advertised in the national newspaper here, the *Caymanian Compass*, asking any Leeds fans to email me, and I initially had five responses. So, with my eldest son Thomas, aged 10 at the time, we had six members. This has grown to 18, which isn't bad with a population on Grand Cayman of only 40,000. We watch the games at Fidel Murphy's, a popular Irish bar on Seven Mile Beach. Sky Sports coverage is beamed in and Fox Sports World [the US sports channel] show regular League games too. Fidel Murphy's has great staff – Mark, Derek, Manuela, Petra and Stella, and they really look after us. Then there's Noel, the Arsenal-supporting landlord who says that there are much better supported clubs on the island, but at least we have managed to mobilise ourselves, unlike the Arsenal and Man U supporters. The Guinness in Fidel's is not half bad either. Our membership consists of about eight from Leeds plus Jonesy from Harrogate, our secretary Pete Tristram from Stoke, our treasurer Colin Reid from Stafford, the island's FIFA representative from Gillingham Paul Macey, Steve Whitley from Jersey, Mad Stevie Roughead from Berwick on Tweed, Ian Bell from Beverley and Andy Brown from London.'

Trinidad & Tobago

Moving further south still, approaching South America this time, we stop where Hurricane Ivan, back in 2004, suddenly took a change of direction and hit Grenada instead of the island of Trinidad & Tobago, much to the relief of another staunch Leeds ex-pat Simon Giffin. He moved with his family to the laid-back tropical island in 2001, and he blames himself that on the same day Kevin Blackwell failed to capture the signature of Stern John, as he explains, 'I would like to apologise to Blackwell, as I could have made all the difference to that deal. When it was announced that a deal had almost been agreed with both Leeds and Coventry, Stern John was in Trinidad for the World Cup qualifier against Mexico. This was the same day that Hurricane Ivan was about to hit and everyone was told to stay at home. No one in Trinidad took this seriously, preferring to believe "God is Trini and will look after us", but having seen the photos of Grenada, where the hurricane hit after it took a last-minute change of direction, we were very lucky. All of this meant that I was encouraged to go to the Trinidad Hilton to see whether I could meet with Mr John to persuade him. Unfortunately, despite seeing a few of the players, he evaded my clutches and the rest is history. I could have made all the difference.'

Simon left for hotter waters just 48 hours after the first leg of our Champions League semi-final with Valencia in 2001, and also blames himself for the spectacular demise of the the club over the next few seasons. 'The blame has been laid at many doors,' he says. 'But I can exclusively reveal that my absence may be one of the key factors – as my occasional returns to the UK always seem to coincide with an up-turn in fortunes (I managed a run of nine unbeaten games on trips back on one occasion). Yet whenever I tune in from abroad the news is more gloomy.' So there you have it. Hurry back Simon, the club needs you occupying your season ticket seat.

Chapter 6

THE EDWARDS VIEW PART I

There are many stars on the terraces of Elland Road week-in week-out, but, it is fair to say, there is one who stands out in the crowd. Having written two books on his life following Leeds already, and about to publish a third page-turner, Gary Edwards has dedicated his life and soul to Leeds United Football Club. He has missed one game, including all friendlies, testimonials and the rest, since 1968 and even ended up getting married to Lesley at Elland Road in 2006. So when I asked Gary if he would be willing to contribute to this publication, he was only too happy. He only had one very important stipulation. And that was that wherever there is a mention of 'that lot' from Old Trafford, the 'M' and the 'U' in Manchester United, within any quotes from Gary himself, as in his own books, remain in lower case, to render them insignificant. Only too happy to oblige! So then Gary, how many trophies do you honestly believe Leeds should have won, on top of the silverware we did actually capture?

'It could be argued with some justification that we could have won the FA Cup in 1967. And we most definitely should have won the 1973 European Cup-Winners' Cup, the 1975 European Cup, the 1971 League title and the 1972 League title (making it a League/FA Cup double). Among trophies that we could have won but didn't on our own account are two FA Cups when we lost in consecutive quarter-finals at home against Portsmouth in 1997 and Wolves in 1998. The League Cup in 1996 against Aston Villa [lost 3–0 at Wembley] – good old Wilko played for a draw at Wembley! And, of course, the famous "Treble" attempt in 1970 where Leeds were so, so unlucky it's not true. Also, on Leeds' return to the old First Division back in 1964–65, they lost the FA Cup in extra-time 2–1 against Liverpool and the title to manchester united on goal average.'

So a mixture of some quite bizarre refereeing decisions, some occasional below-par performances and some, well, plain bad luck, has resulted in Leeds not quite claiming possession of as many trophies and winners' medals as perhaps we really should have done…actually there is no perhaps about it.

Gary's life-long love of the Whites stretches back further than when he started out on his mammoth consecutive match record back in 1968 and, in terms of referees, it's from that pre-1968 period that he picks out one particular official that he *did* like.

'Roger Kirkpatrick was by far the best referee I saw in the 1960s – and to date, actually. He was brilliant. The sign of a good referee is the one who gets through a game unnoticed, and by and large this is true. But Kirkpatrick was flamboyant and often played up to the crowd. I haven't spoken to a single supporter from any club who didn't like Kirkpatrick. He physically demonstrated his decisions so that the crowd knew exactly why a certain free-kick had been awarded. I remember an Everton fan once running on to the pitch at Elland Road and as two policemen moved in, Kirkpatrick intervened. The police backed off and the fan stood there as the referee wagged his finger at him and gave him such a dressing down before putting his arm round him and leading him back to his place on the terrace. Everyone in the ground, including Everton fans and the two policemen, laughed at him as he sheepishly slid over the wall and disappeared. Other well-respected referees of that era were Jack Taylor and Jim Finney. Less respected, in Leeds fans' eyes, were Clive Thomas and, of course, Ray Tinkler and Ken Burns. Much has been said already about Tinkler and Burns, but Thomas is also high up there with them. Clive Thomas once famously booked the entire Leeds defensive wall as they shuffled backwards for a free-kick at Arsenal and then only minutes later, in the exact reverse situation, ordered Leeds to stop arguing and take the free-kick. The Arsenal wall was barely yards back and the ensuing free-kick was easily cleared. Leeds had many run-ins with the Welsh official and a few years back, several years after his retirement, in his biography, he made no secret of the fact that he disliked Leeds immensely.

'I know it's easy to pick out isolated incidents, but you instinctively know when a referee is against you. In the late 1980s George Courtney was in charge of the Barnsley/Leeds FA Cup clash. Leeds were winning 1–0 with minutes to go when a Barnsley forward had a desperate, long-range shot at goal. The ball was so off target and so high that in a bid to save time another Barnsley forward, in the line of fire, leapt up and stopped the ball with his hands. The forward who had originally shot at goal charged forward and hit the falling ball with a cracking volley into the roof of the Leeds net. Even Barnsley fans didn't cheer initially, but they did seconds later when Courtney, who was standing a couple of yards away, gave a goal. Leeds won the replay 4–0. Roger Dilkes was brilliant one week and awful the week after, regardless of the result. Dilkes was an astonishing Bill Oddie look-a-like. Roger Milford, with grey, permed, flowing locks was possibly the best referee around at the time. Into the 90s and Uriah

Rennie was a difficult referee. He made some horrific decisions but always refused to relent even after seeing TV replays proving his actions wrong. I know it's easy to criticise with hindsight and TV cameras, but players are punished on replays so why not referees? Rennie was actually demoted a few years ago for below-par performances. Widely acknowledged as the worlds best referee is bald Italian, Pierluigi Collina [now retired]. You'll hear no argument from me.'

The 'Glory Years' at Elland Road were of course the Revie years, and who can forget the fantastic array of talent on display each time the 'Mighty Whites', as they most certainly were, stepped out onto a football pitch in those days? Revie is described by Gary as a manager who 'had he been at any other club in the country, his huge achievements would have been appreciated for what they were – outstanding. But he was manager of Leeds, enough said. His total devotion to Leeds should have been rewarded with even more silverware than the club attained.'

Revie, of course, left Leeds for the England job in 1974 and Gary is not quite so complimentary about his replacement at the club – one Brian Clough – who lasted an infamous 44 days in the job. In 2009 Clough was the main subject of the critically acclaimed film *The Damned United*, a film which the Clough family were not happy about, but, as Gary rightly points out, it is not the Clough family who should be upset, it is the Revie family. 'After Don's departure, in my opinion Clough should never have been appointed as Leeds manager. The board of directors, not noted for their tactful qualities, employed a man who had systematically targeted Leeds for extreme verbal abuse over the previous three seasons or so. He constantly criticised Revie and once publicly told Eddie Gray that if he had been a racehorse, he would have shot him. There weren't many Leeds players who escaped his wrath and it was quite understandable that once at the club he was clearly loathed, and certain players resented his presence. That said, once the club had hired him they should never have fired him, but as I said, the directors weren't exactly switched on.'

And after Clough? 'Jimmy Armfield replaced him and was one of my favourites. Gentleman Jim, as he was often referred to, was a laid-back pipe smoker, and in his first season he guided Leeds to their first-ever European Cup Final. The events that night are known to everyone in football, but the fact remains that Armfield had revamped an ailing side and steered them away from the foot of the table and to that Final. After reaching the FA Cup semi-final in 1977 and the League Cup semi-final in 1978 Armfield had quietly replaced Revie's ageing stars and had built the foundations for a side that promised much. However, the board wasn't particularly satisfied and dismissed Armfield.

'Jock Stein then came and went, ironically in 44 days. I feel, as many did at the time, that Stein had eyes only for the Scotland job. He came to Leeds but never signed a contract and weeks later he had replaced Ally McLeod as manager of Scotland. Enter Jimmy Adamson. I must admit I was an "Adamson Out" campaigner from the start. I didn't like him. He was never "Leeds" from the start. Once again, the directors had issued us with a total mismatch. Demonstrations occurred at regular intervals after games, demanding Adamson's removal. I have many newspaper cuttings of me and some of the lads outside Elland Road with my "Adamson Out" flag. During his reign, me and some of the lads were sat in the Nags Head before a match, when a detective and some police officers came in. They were carrying a large tape recording machine. They placed it on the bar and played this voice, a Geordie voice, and asked if it was familiar. The whole pub shouted, "Jimmy Adamson!" The police smiled but left without asking any further questions. The voice was the Yorkshire Ripper [although subsequently this was discovered to be the infamous hoax Yorkshire Ripper]. During the pre-season game at Grasshoppers Zurich the Leeds team walked out on to the pitch to have a look at the ground. About 400 Leeds fans were in the stadium and chanted the team's name. Just then Adamson walked out and was greeted by the chant "Adamson Out! Adamson Out!" Jimmy Adamson resigned in October 1980. The decay was so deep-rooted that old favourite Allan Clarke was unable to arrest Leeds' slide into the Second Division. Initially, Clarkey had stabilised the side and began bolstering the defence. Leeds finished ninth in the table and were looking forward to better things. An ambitious buy, Peter Barnes for almost £1 million, proved to be his undoing. To this day Allan Clarke remains one of Leeds United's greatest fans. He was replaced by Eddie Gray in the summer of 1982. I've met Eddie many times and he is a courteous and friendly fella. But when he became manager he also proved he has a ruthless streak when needed. He was the man who gave David Seaman a free transfer and sold fans' favourite Terry Connor. Eddie began to build a side of immense skill, but they weren't nearly physical enough. This proved to be the downfall of Eddie, as teams with half the talent roughed Leeds up week after week. The directors sacked him in October 1985. Obviously, Eddie Gray returned to the club he loves in different capacities and is as popular as ever.

'Billy Bremner once said, "Now that I've played for Leeds United, the next step is to manage them." He did just that when he replaced Eddie Gray. It was a slow start for Bremner, but in 1987 he took us to the brink of a double victory. We were beaten in the promotion Play-off Final against Charlton 2–1 and Billy's team lost 3–2 in the FA Cup semi-final with Coventry. The following season, as

Leeds faltered, the directors sacked him. I always felt a bit sorry for Billy. If we had won promotion that season the directors maybe would have given him some money to spend, something they hadn't done previously. He was sacked in September 1988. Sadly, Billy died of a heart attack in 1997. But as the song goes, "For the sake of Leeds United, he would break himself in two". Of that there is no doubt whatsoever.

'Howard Wilkinson replaced Billy. "Sergeant Wilko" set about his task admirably. Although he wasn't exactly Mr Charisma, he did have a very dry sense of humour as he demonstrated on the occasions he visited supporters' club meetings. Of course, Wilko went on to be the most successful manager since Revie, winning promotion in 1990 and then the Championship in 1992. Everything was going great, when Wilko had what can only be described as a relapse. He tore the title-winning team apart, decimating what was widely acknowledged as the best midfield in Britain if not Europe, and the following season we narrowly avoided relegation. He began making strange decisions and making silly quotes, like "the first half we were shovelling custard but in the second half we began pushing marmalade upstairs". Well, that's clear enough. He sold leading scorer Lee Chapman in February for a mere £250,000, when even by then he had scored 19 goals. That left us without a striker and months later Wilko had to bring Chapman back on loan. The Sergeant sold favourite David Batty and replaced him with Carlton Palmer. Wilko gave Eric Cantona to our fierce enemy manchester united. It was a move which transformed them and won them their first title for 26 years. Shortly afterwards they came to Elland Road fully armed with Cantona and beat us 4–0. Wilko was finally overpowered, sedated and sacked.

'George Graham was next in the hot seat. There is absolutely no doubt in my mind that Graham used Leeds only as a stepping stone to get back into football. He had been kicked out of football following the well-publicised bung scandal. During his exile and near to the end of his suspension Tottenham chairman Alan Sugar said, "Graham should not be touched with a barge pole." Leeds were the only club who offered him a return to football. At the start Graham stabilised the Leeds defence, but he had no intention of taking the club any further. He had public fallouts with top players, including the top scorer at the time, Tony Yeboah. He simply refused to play him. Yeboah was desperate to play but there seemed no way through Graham. For a League game at Sunderland, because of injuries, Graham was forced to put Yeboah on the subs bench. A further injury on the field meant that Graham reluctantly had to send Yeboah on. Within minutes Yeboah picked the ball up on the halfway line, turned and unleashed an amazing shot at goal. The startled Sunderland 'keeper watched helplessly as the ball crashed off the crossbar and, luckily for him, to safety. After the game Graham was asked to describe Yeboah's effort. Graham replied that he didn't see the incident as he was fastening his shoelaces at the time. Not long afterwards, Alan Sugar came and offered Graham the Tottenham manager's job. Despite claiming he wasn't interested, Graham was soon at White Hart Lane.

'Much has been said about David O'Leary, Graham's assistant and then replacement, but my version is that he was brilliant from the outset. He groomed the youngsters from the excellent youth policy, instigated by Howard Wilkinson, and built a side that reached two European semi-finals. Unfortunately for him, he lost the plot and the Bowyer/Woodgate trial, his book, loss of respect from players and several other factors were the reasons why he was sacked in the end.

'Terry Venables was never going to be a success at Leeds United. It simply wasn't going to work. And after being lied to and misled by the Leeds directors it was obvious that he simply had no intention of taking Leeds United anywhere, except the drop.'

That is exactly where El Tel was leading us until he was given the boot and a tidy little cheque. Peter Reid was then given the unenviable task of turning around the club's fortunes. Ironically, he began with a whopping 6–1 win over Charlton at the Valley (Viduka 3, Kewell 2, Harte), managed to save the club from relegation during the 2002–03 season, was taken on permanently and then ended his seven-month reign as gaffer with a 6–1 reverse at Portsmouth. So how did Gary take the news that Reidy was coming on board?

'I was working on a job one morning when I got a phone call from a mate of mine telling me Leeds had just appointed Peter Reid as manager. The club had just relieved Terry Venables of his duties and this new appointment came out of the blue. At the time, Leeds were spiralling down the table at an alarming rate and I didn't have much confidence in Reid's appointment. With one, no, both hands tied behind his back because of the previous regime, Reid rallied what troops he had at his disposal and Leeds gained a brief stay of execution. I felt sorry for Peter Reid. With no money, he had to put together a string of loan players who couldn't even speak the same language. His commitment was never in doubt and when the inevitable happened, Reid was shown the door. He'll never be regarded as the best manager in the world, but his honesty and determination are second to none. He loved the Leeds fans and on many an occasion said that they were the "most passionate fans I have ever seen". Coming from a one-time manager of Sunderland, that statement carries some weight. I liked Reidy.'

And then we move on to the club's next boss – Kevin Blackwell.

'Kevin Blackwell dropped into the hot seat with only one player at his disposal. Blackwell had an impressive array of coaching badges to his name and he had to push every single one of his players to the boundaries if he was to succeed at Leeds United. Gone were the days when he could claim to have rescued Leeds from oblivion with so few players around him, even though it was a phenomenal achievement. Steadily he built a side capable of making the return to the Premiership, but sadly it didn't happen. I am only a supporter on the terraces and Blackwell has qualifications coming out of his ears, so you have to respect him as a manager. However, I cannot help thinking that he sometimes got his tactics wrong. I stood by Blackwell throughout his time at Elland Road, but I blame him for the poor performance in the Play-off Final at the Millennium Stadium in Cardiff. Over 40,000 Leeds United fans groaned in unison when their team was announced. Unbelievably, in the club's most important game in years, Leeds were to play only one man up front. Of course, the inevitable happened. Watford added another man to their attack and Leeds were on the back foot throughout the game. They never stood a chance, losing 3–0. Could it be possible that Blackwell is overqualified and that sometimes he looks too deep at a situation instead of using simple logic? I firmly believe that the squad of players he put together was 100 per cent better than their performance showed. I had a little chat with Blackwell on a pre-season tour in Norway in the summer of 2006. I have met him on numerous occasions and he's a smashing fella. I asked him why he had played 4–5–1 at Cardiff. He replied that he hadn't. He insisted that he had played 4–3–3. Worryingly, I think he believed it.'

Following the departure of 'Blackie', the Leeds faithful eagerly tuned into Yorkshire Radio, LUTV and any kind of media possible to find out who was to become his replacement, and the answer was to raise more than a few eyebrows. Gary Edwards couldn't agree more. 'From the outset, I have to say that it was completely unnatural to have Dennis Wise as manager of Leeds United Football Club. It was even more unnatural to have to like him. It just didn't seem right to see him organise the famous "huddle" before and after games. Admittedly he was manager of the club when we dramatically wiped out the totally unfair 15-point deduction by the Football League, but it soon appeared as though it was his right-hand man, Gus Poyet, who was the main man. This was proved right when Poyet left Leeds to take up a similar position at Tottenham. On his own, Wise was left to look like a fish out of water, and Leeds lost a lot of ground in their fight for promotion. He continually overlooked the promising youngsters at the club and did not alter the side, or perhaps didn't know how to alter the side, when it was obvious that things weren't happening with the present system. I remember Ken Bates saying that he'd never have Wise as his manager "because he's family, and I wouldn't want to have to sack him." Well, Mr Bates did bring Wise in as his manager, but he didn't have to sack him. No, after calling for loyalty from the Leeds fans, Wise learned of a vacancy at Newcastle United. It was for a director of football and the successful applicant would be based in London. Of course, our man Wise was off faster than a rat up a drainpipe. Wise famously said of the 15-point deduction, "Not only have they cut my arms and legs off, they've cut off my balls as well!" Well that's precisely how Leeds fans felt when Bates installed Wise as manager. Like I said at the beginning, it was all too unnatural.'

Next in the Elland Road hot seat was a manager following in the footsteps of Don Revie, Allan Clarke, Eddie Gray, Billy Bremner and David O'Leary. All these famous names were players for Leeds who went on to become managers of the club as well. Back in 1992 Leeds had a wonderful midfield that carved open defensive doors with a special blend of speed (literally – Gary Speed), hard tackling (David Batty), precision passing and movement (Gordon Strachan) and finesse (Gary McAllister). And it's the latter that returned to Elland Road in the capacity of first-team gaffer. He was a hugely popular choice, which ultimately and very unfortunately did not quite work out for Macca. He will always be a welcome guest at Elland Road, though, and will always have the affection of the fans. So go on then Gary, what is your opinion of Gary Mac?

'You could not wish to meet a nicer bloke than Gary McAllister. Whether or not that was the reason for his departure from Elland Road, we may never know. One thing is for sure, however, that the Leeds players appeared to stop playing for Macca. By and large these were the same players that were playing well and playing some beautiful football during the first 12 months or so, but then unfortunately other teams seemed to get to grips with our "flowing, passing movement" and "lovely one-touch stuff". When this happened, Leeds didn't seem to know what to do next. Certain players showed a definite lack of enthusiasm and this was followed by confusion and frustration among the Leeds faithful. Although I still feel some sympathy with Macca, I do agree that a change was necessary. Having said that, Steve Staunton was brought in as a defensive coach, and quite frankly, he simply did not deliver the goods. Who knows, if Macca had been given a better assistant, he may have fulfilled his obvious commitment to Leeds United Football Club. It has also got to be remembered that Gary McAllister was devoted to this club and was the man who gave Fabian Delph his big chance, and what a find Robert Snodgrass proved to be. I, for one, will always be grateful for Macca's attempt to guide this club of ours back to where it truly does belong. I wish him all the good luck in the world, if ever anyone deserved it, then for me it's this fella.'

The departure of Gary Mac meant that the next manager to take charge of Leeds United would be the 25th boss of the club in addition to the three managers who were in charge of Leeds City. On the face of it, 25 managers is not bad when you consider Leeds United are 90 years old, but the worrying trend of recent times meant that McAllister's replacement would be the club's eighth manager (if you include Eddie Gray as caretaker in 2003–04) in the last seven years. Chairman Ken Bates looked to the North West for an up-and-coming Yorkshire-born boss with drive and ambition that goes with the territory of any Leeds United supporter. To many it was a somewhat surprising appointment, but one that could prove to be a stroke of genius from Bates. For Gary Edwards, the capture of former Blackpool boss Simon Grayson was almost like seeing an old friend coming home.

Gary remarks, 'I was brought up on a coal board estate in Kippax, seven miles east of Leeds. We lived on a road called The Drive, which runs through the whole estate. Not many years ago, Simon Grayson married a girl who lived on The Crescent, just around the corner from our family home. The first team I ever saw Leeds play was Blackpool back in 1966. From then on I've always had a soft spot for them, even though they beat us in my first-ever game! When Leeds played at Blackpool in 1971 it was the last meeting of our teams, as Blackpool began a sad decline down through the divisions. Unfortunately, in 2004 we began the first leg of a similar journey. I've always had an eye on Blackpool's position in the League with the hope of our teams meeting again, and when we descended even further, into the Third Division in 2007, I thought, "At least we can play Blackpool again." I've never been a lover of "Him Upstairs" but I couldn't believe it when He allowed Blackpool to switch divisions with us when they won a Play-off Final at Wembley and then leapt into our place in the Championship. Of course, Simon Grayson was the manager of victorious Blackpool and had raised a few eyebrows among those clubs looking for a new boss.

'Although only playing a handful of games for Leeds back in the 1980s, Grayson has now returned to the team he supported as a boy. It's still early in Grayson's managerial reign at Elland Road, but already he's shown signs of becoming a very competent manager indeed. His tactical awareness, man-management and drive are clearly evident. Besides, my mate Kev cuts his dad's hair in Kippax, so everything's looking rosy.'

Chapter 7

BETTER TO WIN BEHIND A PYLON THAN LOSE IN FRONT OF ONE!

Brazil

On the pitch – Brazilian-born Whites:

Name	Joined	Left	Apps	Goals
Jose Vitor Roque Jnr	2003	2004	7	2

Moving further south, we now head off to a nation that boasts an amazing record in world football. A nation that produces football genius after football genius. A nation that conjures up memories of World Cups past in glorious party gold. Names that roll off the tip of the tongue with effortless ease are names that anyone with an ounce of love for the game will have heard of. Names which conjour up memories of magical moments. Names such as Bebeto, Cafu, Carlos Alberto, Denilson, Dida, Edinho, Garrincha, Jairzinho, Kaka, Rivelino, Rivaldo, Ronaldo, Ronaldinho, Romario, Socrates, Zico and one Edson Arantes do Nascimento, better known as Pelé, give you that purring feeling of watching a wonderfully pristine conditioned engine capable of the best attacking football ever seen. The Brazilians have never known how to defend; it is simply not in their makeup. They have always, throughout history, seemed to play with 10 attackers and a goalkeeper – who usually has very little to do. Five times they have become World Champions and they are the only nation to have played in all 18 World Cup Final tournaments. They are also the only South American country to have won the World Cup in Europe and, if you are watching them against any other side than your own national team, the irresistible manner in which they play their football almost guarantees that they are the majority of people's second-favourite team. Brilliant consistency over many years and the knack of producing world stars of the beautiful game has not made anyone jealous of them – unless you're Argentinian perhaps, meaning most fans can just sit back and admire a country that encapsulates all the finest qualities of the game.

Having said all that, as Leeds United we were perhaps dealt a raw deal back in the 2003–04 season when Jose Vitor Roque Junior signed for the club, playing seven times and scoring two goals. In those seven games he played in his usual central-defensive role, but the pace of the English game was far too quick for this Brazilian World Cup-winner and Leeds failed to triumph in any of the five League games he featured in. His record for Leeds was simply awful. In his seven matches, Leeds lost six. Peter Reid's side at the time scored just six goals and conceded a hefty 26. The only victory was a second-round League Cup win after a penalty shoot-out over Swindon at Elland Road following a 2–2 draw. His two goals were against Manchester United in our 2–3 after extra-time League Cup third-round tie at Old Trafford, but he was also sent off in one of his appearances and substituted twice, and his last appearance was in the diabolical 6–1 trouncing we received at Portsmouth in what turned out to be Reid's final match as manager of Leeds. Roque Junior then went off for a Brazilian friendly, and, to the relief of the majority of Leeds fans, returned with an injury – which meant that he would not wear the white of Leeds United again. Without being disrespectful to an obviously otherwise super-talented player, he just could not quite get to grips with the English game. He joined Leeds in September 2003 for what was supposed to have been at least one whole season, but he returned to AC Milan, where he had collected a Champions League-winners' medal prior to joining Leeds, only four months later.

So, despite Roque Junior's obvious qualities, having picked up the two biggest prizes in world football prior to arriving at Elland Road, we never got to see why he was so highly rated. It was an interesting period for one Leeds supporter, who was keeping a beady eye out for the defender all the way back in Roque Junior's homeland Brazil. Ian Bloom, who was born in Hull but says his 'heart and soul have always been in Leeds,' moved out to São Roque in the state of São Paulo at the age of 25 back in 1986. Now some 5,967 miles (give or take a mile or two!) from Elland Road, he is doing his best to spread the love of Leeds United to this football-loving country. And he is in a perfect position to be able to do so as well. Teaching English in São Paulo City, he has a bunch of photos from Elland Road in his classroom, which the students are forever enquiring about. 'I spread the word of Leeds United to all my students and all over town,' beams Ian. 'I have a lot of students nowadays who ask me where they can get a Leeds United shirt and I feel proud that I'm doing a good job of "spreading the Leeds United word". As you probably can imagine, Brazilians are very passionate about their football. In fact, three of Brazil's biggest teams are São Paulo, Palmeiras and Corinthians, who are all based 60km from where I live. These clubs have a fanatical following. My team in Brazil is São Paulo FC, so needless to say I cannot stand either of the other two teams I've just mentioned. I proudly wear my Leeds shirts as often as I can over here, though, or should I say as often or as quickly as my wife can get them washed! Everyone asks me about my Leeds shirts. Of course, many people over here have heard of Leeds and used to watch them on Sky TV when we were in the Premier League. But when someone who does not know about Leeds asks me what shirt I'm wearing, I answer, "It's a Leeds United shirt, the best team in Europe" – and that seems to satisfy!'

Ian and his Leeds-loving wife Regina Bloom christened their daughter Laura at an English church in São Paulo City, and Ian is proud to admit that he 'put a Leeds United badge inside her pocket just for that extra special blessing.' Bloom junior is yet to see her first Leeds match in the flesh but Ian remembers *his* introduction to Leeds United like it was yesterday; although as he recalls he did not actually see much of the action. 'It was against Huddersfield Town on 5 April 1972 and we won 3–1 with goals from Mick Jones, Peter Lorimer and Eddie Gray in front of 46,148 fans. One thing I remember very well, though, was the fact that I watched the game from behind a pylon, which was strangely placed inside the stadium, impeding the view of everyone who was behind it. It didn't spoil my enjoyment at all, however, as the saying must have been at the time "It's better to win from behind a pylon than to lose in front of one"! But I'm not sure this saying ever existed! This is probably the best and most exciting match I've ever seen as I was only 11 years old and it was my first trip to Elland Road.'

All those thousands of miles away from Elland Road Ian was just as upset as anyone closer to home when news came through that Leeds were relegated from the Premiership, but like so many of us he is convinced we will be back in the promised land before long. 'The day Leeds got relegated into the Championship I was listening to the game on the internet and I just broke down in tears! I just couldn't believe it. But when we got relegated into League One, although I felt very sad, I felt the writing was on the wall because of the tremendous debt a certain chairman had got us into before they just walked away. So I think today we are at the turning point in Leeds United's history and I'm very optimistic. I think that the 15-point deduction made a lot of people angry and determined, after all, we Yorkshire folk are very strong and determined people, and wrapped up in Leeds colours we become even more so. We all have a lot of pride and love in the club and its history.'

When Leeds were in the Premiership, Ian, Regina, a solicitor friend/Leeds fan called Charles and a student of Ian's called Lila would head off down to a pub named O'Malley's in São Paulo at 7am to watch Leeds live on Sky, accompanied by bacon and eggs washed down with a couple of early morning pints of Guinness! The Guinness has been put on hold for the moment, but it is surely just taking its time to ferment into a wonderful rich taste of success once the club is back on its feet and back where it firmly belongs – in the Premier League.

When asked to name his all-time favourite player and Leeds XI plus manager, Ian quickly retorted, 'I can't choose one player because there's been too many, so I would have to say Don Revie's 1972 FA Cup-winning lads – all of them.' For the record, here is the line up for that wonderful Wembley afternoon:

David Harvey, Paul Reaney, Paul Madeley, Billy Bremner (captain), Jack Charlton, Norman Hunter, Peter Lorimer, Allan Clarke, Mick Jones, Johnny Giles, Eddie Gray. Sub: Mick Bates. Manager: Don Revie.

Argentina

On the pitch – Argentinian-born Whites:

Name	Joined	Left	Apps	Goals
Luciano Becchio	2008	CP	47/9	19
Alex Sabella	1980	1984	26/1	2

Brazil and Argentina have never exactly been the best of buddies when it comes to football. It is a bit like England v Scotland, Rangers v Celtic, Barcelona v Real Madrid, Leeds United v 'that lot' or Inter Milan v AC Milan, only you have to multiply that feeling of antagonism. There is no love lost between any of these bitter aforementioned rivals, but the big guns in South America take some beating when it comes to tribal warfare on the terraces. For Ian Bloom, though, he has a link from his adopted Brazilian home to that of a good friend over the border in Argentina, Peter Hudson. Peter and Ian have a common bond that makes them quite unique in South America. One living in Brazil, the other in Argentina, but best of buddies. And why? Leeds United, of course. Peter, a journalist for some 19 years now, caught the Leeds bug via his father when he was just three years old. Born in Christchurch, New Zealand, he moved with his parents to England in 1966 and lived in Leeds until he was six. 'Leeds was thus the first place I remember and has a lot of emotional ties for me,' says Peter. 'I still think of it as one of my main emotional homes and was sorry to leave. My parents had split up and my mother and I moved to Cambridge while my father stayed in Leeds. So I used to get taken to one or two matches near Cambridge, Ipswich or Norwich and maybe the odd match in London, and then a match or two when I went to visit my father; although I was usually there for longest in summer, when there were no matches on. That means many of my memories are of seeing us on TV. I was at the famous Colchester FA Cup match of the 1970s, but let's skip over that.

'Football was a big part of my relationship with my father and Leeds United has a special emotional charge for me. I go to matches whenever I am back in England nowadays; although that's increasingly less these days. On average over the last two decades it's been around every three years. The last match I saw us against was Preston in 2004, when I was back for my father's funeral. Here's the email I wrote at the time to the Leeds United email list:

'I attended my first match for four years on Saturday and probably the last for the next few, as I was back in England for the funeral of my father, Michael Hudson. My father had attended home matches regularly since the 1960s and it seemed an appropriate tribute to use his season ticket one last time. We were not very close, but the one thing that brought us together was Leeds. He took me to my first match (I think against Crystal Palace) sometime around 1970 and in the 1980s we used to see each other basically every two weeks to go to the home games after a few pints. It was a bit emotional when I got up to the West Stand and saw his name written on the back of the seat. I guess my experience of the match will have been different from most others, but since this is the only chance I'll have to do a match report for a while, these were my impressions:

First, the football. How the mighty have fallen, eh? This is a different planet to the Premier. In fact, I think it was probably worse than the old Second Division days, which is the last time I was going home and away. At least those sides had a few half-way decent players, like John Sheridan, Andy Ritchie, Ian Baird and Ian Snodin. The problem with the current lot is that the majority of them are just not very good. There's hardly anyone with the imagination or flair to break down a defence. No wonder we haven't scored for ages. On the other hand, I don't see us going down, for which full marks to Kevin Blackwell given the players he's having to work with. Having said that, it looked worse the further forward you go. I had not seen any of the current players before (no Second Division

English highlights in Argentina, unfortunately) and it took me a while to work out who everyone was. That said, I thought all our defenders looked good, even if there were a couple of moments of panic that would have been punished by a better side. Kelly in particular I thought was excellent, given his limitations. He ran around a lot, got in some excellent tackles and even managed to get at least some of his passes to a player in a white shirt, which is as much as you can probably ask of him. I thought Kilgallon looked alright too, especially going forward.

The midfield was poor to average, but I thought Richardson was better than some reports I'd read. He misplaced a lot of passes, but was one of the few who at least looked like he might show some imagination, even if a lot of it didn't come off. Gregan never broke out of a jog, but I thought he looked like he could be a tidy player. If the problem is fitness then I wouldn't be surprised if he does well. But if he still can't move any faster than that in a month or so, I'd say we've wasted £500,000. Lennon can certainly run very fast, but I wanted to see a bit more than that before putting him in on a regular basis.

The attack, though, was just poor. On this showing, Ricketts would enter my all-time worst Leeds strikers. The only plausible reason for putting him on the pitch is the comedy value of the crowd cheering on the rare occasions he won a header. Oh, that and the fact that the alternative was bloody Deano.

Last but not least, the crowd. Bloody hell, I hear people complaining on here about our fair-weather supporters, but for 30,000 people out to pay out a fair sum of money for that excuse for entertainment I think shows what wonderful fans we've got. The singing was excellent, too (not in the West Stand, obviously; although even there a number of us applauded energetically on several occasions). Several renditions of old favourites as well as a decent rendition of *WATC-COE* literally brought a tear to my eye. The bloke sitting next to me probably wondered why I kept blowing my nose and rubbing my eyes, but was too polite to ask.

All in all, a great day out. The football was mainly crap, but I love Elland Road and since it was central to my relationship with my father, I spent an emotional 90 minutes, reliving everything it means for me on and off the pitch. And to top it off, we won. (1–0 – Danny Pugh.)'

This adopted Latin American White fled the British Isles in his mid-20s, starting out by working on a building brigade in support of the Sandinistas (political party) in Nicaragua, Central America. He then travelled around for a while before taking up a trainee journalist post on a small financial newsletter in Santiago, Chile, before moving to Lima in Peru in 1994. Three years later he upped sticks to travel east across the border to settle in Buenos Aires, where he has lived ever since. 'For several years I was working as a correspondent for the *Economist* and *Newsweek*, although I parted company with them three or four years ago and have since worked freelance on a variety of publications,' adds Peter. 'I also took a year off to manage a local rock band. This was very enjoyable but I made no money at all and ended up back in journalism.'

Peter Hudson could have possibly passed on some of his economic expertise to a former chairman of ours with the same first name not so long ago, something Leeds were not worried about in the glorious days of the early 1970s. Peter recalls his feelings at the time and remembers a coin collection where Leeds really did stand out. 'I guess the best match I remember then was the 1972 FA Cup Final (I was nine), which I saw on TV round at a friend's house in Cambridge. I remember us playing well (although it may be my memory is playing tricks on me, I really can't remember much about the match itself), but more importantly we got the right result and it was all the sweeter because I was the only Leeds fan in my school. I also have fond memories of the coin collection that was issued by Esso (I think) with all the winners of the FA Cups over its 100-year history. It was completed by a larger gold-coloured medallion to commemorate our victory. I had the complete set and it was a treasured possession, although I've lost it since.'

Peter Hudson spent the majority of his Leeds-watching 'career' in the dark days of the 1980s and recalls an ironic moment at Boundary Park, Oldham, for the second leg of Leeds' Play-off semi-final. 'I was living in Manchester at the time and had got a ticket in the seats with the Oldham fans. As the match wore on it became apparent that there were quite a few of us and by the end the locals had worked out who we were, so when they got their second goal at the end of the match, apparently sealing victory, one man leaned over and said something patronising like "Never mind son, there's always next year." Of course, I was very happy to repeat the comment back to him when Keith Edwards scored straight from the kick-off to take us through on away goals. He found it difficult to see the irony. There were not that many great matches in those days, though, my memories are more of some of the poor players we had: Brendan Ormsby, David Rennie, John Stiles, Mark Aizlewood, George McCluskey, John Pearson, etc. We had real weakness in depth in those days. Since I've been here in South America I've been a member of LUSC North America for several years, and have found it a lifeline. They have supplied me with videos and helped get tickets when I have been back in England. I have persuaded a few of my Argentine friends to take an interest in Leeds and even bought a shirt for one of my friend's boys, but none of them are fanatics. Not a very promising prospect for starting up a local supporters' club branch, really.'

Peter decided to make an extended trip across the Atlantic in 2000 to his former stomping ground, but what in prospect looked to be an exciting holiday actually turned out to be a disastrous one in more ways the one. 'Overall, my experience of following Leeds on my trips back home has been fairly depressing,' sighs Peter. 'I remember particularly the trip in 2000, planned around the most attractive Leeds fixtures. I arrived in the UK full of optimism on the day of the away leg of the match against Galatasaray, which I saw us lose from a barstool in a London pub; although the fact that two of our fans were stabbed to death made the football seem unimportant. I then saw three matches live: a 1–0 away defeat against Aston Villa, a 4–0 home defeat against Arsenal (voted the worst match of the season by the fans, it was also the first and last Leeds match my Argentine girlfriend agreed to accompany me to) and the return leg against Galatasaray, a 2–2 draw that saw us knocked out of the UEFA Cup. Actually, I only saw the second half of the Galatasaray match, because it was Easter and all the trains were booked solid so I had to hire a car, but got stuck in a three-hour traffic jam coming out of London. Oh, and every match I went to was preceded by a minute's silence for our murdered fans, which meant I was already depressed even before I had to watch the football.'

And just how does English football compare to that of the Argies? 'Argentine football is a bit like what I remember of English football in the 1980s, only more so. That is, there is still real passion there that hasn't been squeezed out by commercialization, gentrification and all-seater stadia (although people are trying). The buzz you get when the teams come out in a big game has to be experienced to be believed. The fans chant throughout the match and there is a real enthusiasm for the game at all levels. In fact, I stopped playing five-a-side here, because many Argentines seem unable to just have a casual kick-about and since I'm not very good I used to get heavily criticised. The downside is that football here is run by a bunch of crooks who make Ronnie and Reggie Kray look like models of virtue, the stadia are mainly decrepit, hooligan thugs are nurtured as a weapon for controlling clubs or for doing dirty deeds for local politicians and people are killed on a fairly regular basis. Also, most good

Argentine players get flogged off quick to Europe, so the only really good players left are those youngsters who are just about to get sold or the aging players (eg Veron) who have come back to play out the final year or two prior to retiring. Having said all that, I still go to a few matches every season and heartily enjoy it.'

It is fair to say that you won't see too many Leeds shirts in and around Buenos Aires but there is one roaming about that Peter wouldn't mind bumping into again, after a trip to a launderette a few years ago. 'I used to get my clothes washed in a little launderette in an upmarket part of Buenos Aires and it was there that someone stole my Leeds shirt, one of the old polo neck models, with "Yeboah" on the back. As far as I know, it was the only item of clothing that they ever had stolen, so it obviously attracted someone's attention. They paid me the value of the shirt in free laundry services, but it didn't make up for the loss.'

This book has more than once touched on the injustices that have befallen Leeds United over the years, and the 'ups and downs' that the club have enjoyed and endured, but Peter Hudson believes that in some ways we are a club that gets a kick out of either. He says 'Leeds have always thrived on misfortune and injustice, real or otherwise. In fact, I sometimes think we enjoy it more than success. The old Second Division days in the 1980s were pretty terrible from a footballing point of view, but I know several people who rate them as the best time to have been a Leeds fan in terms of atmosphere and passion. In fact, another one of the matches I enjoyed most was the drubbing we received at Stoke (actually I seem to remember we got hammered twice at Stoke and I believe I was at both of them, so maybe I am mixing the two games together). Anyway, the Leeds fans were tremendous, singing all the way through the match, and I remember laughing at the chant of "next goal wins" when we were something like 7–0 down. Given the rubbish we generally had to put up with on the pitch, it was this sort of passion that made the games worth going to, and the "them-and-us" siege mentality was part of that. I can well imagine that spirit back at Elland Road given recent events.' For the record, the 7–0 match finished 7–2 to Stoke with Ian Baird and John Sheridan on target for Leeds. The other game Peter is referring to is the 6–2 drubbing we received from Stoke a season earlier (1985–86 – Neil Aspin and Ian Snodin on target for Leeds). Ironically Leeds beat the Potters in each of the two home fixtures in those seasons. In 1985–86 it was 4–0 to Leeds (John Stiles, Ian Baird and two goals from Peter Swan), and a year later it was 2–1 to Leeds (John Sheridan and Baird again on target).

Back in South America, Peter can now keep in touch with events at Elland Road far better than in years gone by with new technology, but prior to the computer age it was frustrating trying to find out how Leeds had fared; although he did have one plus point. 'The first few years I used to catch up with results on the World Service on a short-wave radio, and if for any reason I couldn't tune in or there was no reception when the football results were on, I had to wait around two weeks for the papers to arrive at the Anglo-Chilean Cultural Institute to find out the results. I did meet my first Chilean girlfriend there when I was checking the papers, though, so there was an upside. I remember when we won promotion to the old First Division in 1990 I was in a car with some Chilean friends travelling from Santiago to Valparaiso on the coast and I made my friends stop so that I could tune into the World Service stood beside the road to find out we were up. My friends helped me celebrate, but it was all a bit muted by the fact that they had no real idea what I was so excited about. Talking of Chile, I introduced a subsequent girlfriend of mine to English football and explained the finer points to her, on which basis she decided to become a Man Utd fan just to wind me up (she always was excessively argumentative), a decision she maintained for the duration of our relationship. Fortunately, we pipped Man Utd to the title the next year, so I was able to rub her nose in it and we split up before they started winning for fun.'

Peter's dad originates from Australia, his mum from Germany, and when Peter turned 12 he was about to meet his gran on his father's side for the very first time, but things did not quite go to plan. 'The day she arrived at Heathrow, Leeds were playing QPR in London and I was offered the choice of either going to meet my gran at the airport or going to the match. I figured that she was going to be exhausted after a 24-hour flight, so it would be better to let her get settled in first. She was going to come down to Cambridge to visit me and my mother, so we were going to have plenty of time to get to know each other then. So, she arrived and travelled up to Leeds with my father, while my mother and I went to see Leeds at Loftus Road. But the strain was evidently too much for her, because a few days later my gran dropped dead of a heart attack and I never met her because I had chosen to go to see Leeds play instead. I was racked with guilt about this for some time, although I now guess it's just one of those very unfortunate things that seem to be part and parcel of my life as a Leeds fan.'

Before we set off on the next journey in this extraordinary itinerary of Leeds supporters across the globe, Peter leaves us with his all-time favourite player and his all-time favourite XI. Given he was born in 1963, it is no surprise to learn that Tony Currie takes the accolade as the number-one player for Peter Hudson. 'I think it must be my age. I am a bit too young to really have appreciated the classic Leeds side and Currie is the first player I really remember standing out.

Duncan McKenzie was good, but a bit too nonchalant. Currie just oozed class. Scored some great goals, too. My favourite player of all time is Johan Cruyff. Again, I think it's an age thing, one of the first footballing memories I have is the 1974 World Cup.'

And the all time Leeds XI?

'I find it hard to do this. I guess it would have to be the classic Harvey-Bates-Reaney-Madeley-Charlton-Bremner-Giles-E,Gray-Hunter-Clarke-Jones, with a few extras thrown in from other periods, like John Charles and Tony Currie. Truth is though, I didn't ever see Charles play and I don't remember the classic side well enough to really say. If I had to assemble a first 11 out of players I really remember, it would be:

Martyn, Sterland, Radebe, Matteo, Dorigo, Batty, Strachan, Currie, Dacourt, Yeboah, Hasselbaink. Subs: Woodgate, Sheridan, Chapman.

The only top-class manager we have ever had (for all his failings) was The Don. Honourable mention to Eddie Gray, who I don't think got a fair crack of the whip, so he would be my assistant.'

Chapter 8

THE AUSSIE CONNECTION

On the pitch – Australian-born Whites:

Name	Joined	Left	Apps	Goals
Jacob Burns	2000	2003	6/2	0
Tony Dorigo	1991	1997	205/4	6
Hayden Foxe	2006	2006	15/6	1
Joel Griffiths	2005	2005	0/2	0
Harry Kewell	1995	2003	227/15	63
Neil Kilkenny	2008	CP	19	1
Jamie McMaster	1999	2004	1/12	0
Paul Okon	2002	2003	21	0
Mark Viduka	2000	2004	162/4	72

Australia

From South America we venture further to a country on the other side of the planet and a city that used to host the Australian Formula 1 Grand Prix every year and boasts a fanatical Branch of LUSC. The Adelaide Branch of the Leeds United Supporters' Club is the branch furthest from Elland Road, so living some 12,191 miles from their sacred place of worship may prompt you to think that such a distance would eventually eradicate thoughts of the Whites. Nothing could be further from the truth – and try telling that to a bunch of supporters who follow Leeds with as much passion as the Holbeck-Kippax crowd. Remember the old saying 'absence makes the heart grow fonder'?

LUSC Adelaide was born out of pure luck and opportunism. John Thompson-Mills (JTM) works as a sports broadcaster for Australia's ABC, which is the equivalent of Britain's BBC, and it was during a radio station competition that the seed of LUSC Adelaide was sown. Pete Lupton, who is now the secretary of the branch, entered the competition and, while he was on air, could not resist the temptation to let everyone listening in Adelaide know that he held a real passion for a football team named Leeds United. JTM's ears suddenly pricked up and, armed with this important information, he arranged to meet up with Lupton, who was keen to set up a branch in the southern hemisphere.

Lupton received a phone call from a friend in Leeds, who suggested he should start a branch in Adelaide. He thought it was an excellent idea but did not really know how to go about it until the chance meeting with JTM. JTM then used his position within the radio station to good advantage and announced on air that there was to be a meeting at the Woodside Hotel in Adelaide Hills on 20 May 2001, and that anyone was welcome if they supported the Whites. It may not sound like it was a great response as only eight people turned up, but after two months of spreading the word the branch held its inaugural AGM at Frostbites, and by the time that meeting had finished there were an impressive 59 members on board. Subsequent meetings, which took place at the British Hotel in North Adelaide, saw the branch organise the LUSC Adelaide banner, polo and t-shirts, and arrange to have a special patron, United's former midfield ace David Batty. The first match that they all sat down together for was on 13 October 2001, a 1–1 draw with Liverpool at Anfield with Harry Kewell scoring for Leeds. This was watched at the Earl of Aberdeen, before they moved on to the Arkaba, which is now their spiritual Leeds United home.

Membership since the first AGM has fluctuated up and down, and at the time of going to print the membership was spot on 60. On 27 October 2001 more than that figure of members plus guests packed into the Arkaba for their first match at the hotel to watch Leeds play out a 1–1 draw with the enemy from Old Trafford. Australia's very own Mark 'The Duke' Viduka gave Leeds the lead and it was almost a dream day out for the branch until, with just a few minutes left on the clock, Ole Gunnar Solskjaer silenced the Arkaba with an equaliser.

Lupton says, 'I realised that day that we had arrived. We moved our committee meetings to the Arkaba after that and it became our "home ground".' Wherever they have gone together to watch Leeds on the box, however, it has been far from a ray of Adelaide sunshine in terms of their record in matches. The opening five games saw no victories, two draws and three defeats, so Lupton came up with the idea that the branch puts up 10 Australian dollars for each match until they achieve their first win. 'Once that happens we can then use however much is in the kitty to crack open the champagne,' explained Lupton at that time. It was to be just short of a year after the draw with Man Utd when they finally did open the bubbly. And it was well worth the wait, given it was again against 'that lot', with a Harry Kewell goal on 14 September 2002 settling the match at Elland Road. Smiles that day were clearly stretching from Elland Road all the way round the globe to South Australia.

Of course, there is nothing quite like actually being at the game itself, but when you are thousands of miles away and a trip to Elland Road would take more than a day to make, not to mention the enormous cost, it is not surprising to hear that few members get to see their beloved Leeds in the flesh very often. JTM did make the long haul to the northern hemisphere in 1998, however, and spent six months travelling around Europe with his wife Kathy, which included almost two months in Yorkshire. Taking in a few Leeds matches was high on the priority list and he enjoyed 10 games in some style.

JTM explains, 'The trip was not work related, but as I had spoken to Martin Tyler [a Sky Sports TV commentator] in the course of the 1990, 1994 and 1998 World Cups we had arranged to meet up when I got to the UK. So I met him for the Sheffield Wednesday game, which was on a Sunday afternoon. I sat on the TV gantry with him and Andy Gray and had my photo taken with them. We won 2–1 [Hasselbaink and Woodgate scoring] that day after they had scored an early goal, so that was a good day.

'Martin then arranged tickets for the press box at Anfield and at Old Trafford, so wearing no colours I made my own way there and sat with the journos for those two games. The Anfield game was special. It was a 3–1 win after Robbie Fowler's penalty had put Liverpool in front with only about 15 minutes to go. Alan Smith made his first-team debut for us and scored with his first touch, then two goals from Jimmy Floyd Hasselbaink secured a rare win [only the second win at Anfield since 1 January 1972, when goals from Allan Clarke and Mick Jones secured a 2–0 victory – the first win since then came in 1995 when Brian Dean scored the only goal of the game].

'As I was leaving the press box I bumped into Peter Ridsdale and told him how far I had travelled just to see the match. Alright, it was a slight exaggeration but it was such a brilliant day. The hardest thing for me, though, was trying not to be too excited sitting in the press box each time Leeds scored! Martin also arranged tickets for me to see a match in London when we were there over Christmas and New Year, but it wasn't a Leeds game. Again I sat with him and Andy on the gantry for the Chelsea versus Man Utd match.

'Actually, he didn't organise tickets for the gantry but tickets for the press box, which back then were at pitch level. I didn't like the view so I blagged my way up to the gantry for a much better view of what turned out to be a dull

0–0 affair. So Martin Tyler was fantastic because I tried through the club to get tickets to the other away games, and ones at home for that matter, but they wouldn't oblige! I suppose it was a bit selfish to insist to my wife on seeing so many games, but we were going so well then. David O'Leary had just taken over and Leeds were everyone's second-favourite team. I was born in Bradford, so we were always going to spend some time in Yorkshire and seeing Leeds as much as possible was a priority for me.'

JTM's 10 games he watched while in the UK included one defeat (sadly 3–2 at Old Trafford), three draws and six wins. It started on 25 October with a goalless draw at home to Chelsea, which was O'Leary's third match in charge after the departure of George Graham. He then returned to Elland Road for the 1–0 third-round Worthington Cup win over Bradford City, where Harry Kewell grabbed the goal. A trip to Derby County was next on the agenda, with the match finishing 2–2. Robert Molenaar and another goal from Kewell secured a point for Leeds. It was then back to Cup action and a 0–0 draw with Roma at Elland Road, which was sadly not good enough to go through, as the Italians had already taken a 1–0 lead from the first leg of this UEFA Cup second-round tie. JTM then enjoyed three victories on the bounce, starting with the 2–1 win at home to Sheffield Wednesday, followed by the 3–1 success at Liverpool and then a 4–1 win against Charlton Athletic back at Elland Road. Lee Bowyer, Kewell, Hasselbaink and Smith all got on the scoresheet against the Londoners. This was followed by the disappointing 3–2 loss at Old Trafford before two goals from Bowyer and one each from Hasselbaink and Molenaar saw them thump West Ham United at Elland Road 4–0. The final match on JTM's mini-Leeds tour saw an emotional David Batty make his comeback for Leeds after his transfer from Newcastle United, in the 2–0 win against Coventry City at Elland Road. David Hopkin and Bowyer were on target for Leeds.

Clearly it is not a trip that is made very often, mainly because of the cost, but also because of the time needed to make a trip like that worthwhile. So when Leeds United FC decided to visit Australia in 2002 it was a dream come true for the Adelaide Whites. Terry Venables led the team on a Far East tour, which saw them reaching the city of Melbourne for a game against Colo Colo at the Colonial Stadium. Leeds did not disappoint as Harry Kewell's goal proved to be the only goal of the match, but it was not just the result that mattered, in fact that was secondary really. The priority was that it was a chance for the Adelaide Whites to all get together for the very first time as a group and show their love for the club at an actual match. Around 50 members made the trip by one form of transport or another. Some flew, some went by car and half of them travelled on a 12-hour train journey.

JTM chose the train option and enjoyed a fantastic trip with LUSC Adelaide. He says, 'On the afternoon of the match, about 300 Leeds supporters met up in a pub in the centre of Melbourne for a few pints and it was awesome. We had two nights in Melbourne and realised that something like this might never happen again. On the train you can imagine what 25 of us got up to. I remember we drank the train dry. Suffice to say that when we got to Melbourne a couple of the members could hardly walk. In fact, after that, we hardly saw them for the rest of the weekend because they were so sick! I'm not suggesting there was any trouble on the way there or on the way back, it was just a bit boisterous to say the least.'

Ian 'Swags' Cotterill, who runs the branch's excellent website (www.geocities.com/leedsunitedadelaide) recalls, 'JTM is probably our most celebrated Leeds fan, working for ABC, and he gets to meet all sorts of celebrities. So while we were on the train to Melbourne he kept popping the odd "name" here and the odd "name" there into the conversation. Andy "Nudge" Briggs kept bending down to pick something up. Each time a "name" was dropped, down Andy would go with "whoops there goes another one" routine until the penny dropped. But John kept on name-dropping and Andy kept picking them up.'

Now that they do not get to watch their heroes on television given that Leeds are no longer in the Premier League, the branch do still get together for other organised events. Every Christmas, as Yorkshire invariably watches the snow falling out of the sky, these United fans don their Leeds shirts, shorts and sandals as they head for the beach and set up their annual barbecue. One of the members takes the turn of being Father Christmas and hands out presents to the junior members, while the more mature (in terms of age only!) members of the branch consume what seems like half the ale in Adelaide!

Six months after one such festive occasion, in June 2004, when some members had just about recovered, the branch organised a football match with the Adelaide Hills Hawks, and every single one of them wore a Leeds shirt – naturally. Want to know the score? Of course you do. In brief, the first half saw the Hawks take the lead with a highly dubious goal that looked as offside as Colin Suggett did for West Brom when 'that goal' effectively cost Leeds United the First Division Championship in 1971 – what was it, 15 yards offside?! Half-time then: Adelaide Whites 0 Adelaide Hills Hawks 1.

Worse was to come as the Whites went further behind before the fightback began. Paul 'Bebbo' Bebbington pulled a goal back and then Nudge grabbed the equaliser, but a late Hawks goal with just a couple of minutes remaining won the game and the Whites to their first-ever defeat, in their only match to date!

Full-time score: Adelaide Whites 2 Adelaide Hills Hawks 3.

The Adelaide Whites Team:

Goalkeeper:

Emmanuel Lelas

Defence:

Terry Bradford, 'Nudge', Steve Draper, Mark Downey

Midfield:

Mike Parry, Big Les, Lyndon Parry, Rob Tiley

Attack:

'Bebbo', Rob Barone

Subs:

Matt Francis, Darren Aesche, Pete Lupton, 'Swags', JTM

Player-coach:

Les Wake (Big Les)

Director of football:

Fred Goldstone

On 21 May 2006, Watford halted Leeds's return to the Premier League with a painful 3–0 win at the Millennium Stadium. 'Swags' took the chance that we would be in that Final a couple of months prior to the match and booked his flights and hotels for a six-week trip. 'I was one of the thousands who queued for tickets on that sunny spring day under the freezing shadow of the Revie stand. Five and a half hours I endured, but I was one of the lucky ones. Some had been there for hours only to find themselves in the wrong queue. The funny part was when the management at one o'clock decided to put the "members only" banner up, which was greeted with ironic cheering from the crowds. The only problem I had during the six weeks was getting away tickets, as season ticket holders were given priority over members' clubs and the allocation was quickly sold. But I had a cunning plan for the Sheffield away game. I stayed with my Uncle Clifford in Sheffield for the first week, which included Easter and the game at Bramall Lane. Cliff, being a season ticket holder at the Lane, managed to get me and a mate Trevor tickets. The only problem was they were in the Blades end! I think Cliff must have had a bit of sympathy for us, because when Bakke's own-goal went in we were the only ones still seated. And when Healy's cracker hit the back of the net, Trev and I could only nudge each other. Clifford had gone for an early pint…what a pity! The whole trip cost about £3,000, but that included looking up old friends and relatives, so a few trips to the pub and restaurants. Also a week in Cardiff at the Ibis Hotel, which I was lucky to get with the Heineken Cup Final being played on the Saturday. All in all it was a bit of a gamble not knowing whether Leeds would make the Play-offs, but as it worked out the only disappointment was the shambles in Cardiff.'

Chapter 9

112 HOURS IN THE AIR AND STILL NO GOALS

On the pitch – New Zealand-born Whites:

Name	Joined	Left	Apps	Goals
Tom Alderson	1930	1933	4	2
Danny Hay	1999	2002	3/3	0

New Zealand

John Mallinson is one of a few New Zealand Whites who have the longest journey to Elland Road of anywhere in the world. Just the flying time, including stops, is a whopping 28 hours, but the 51-year-old retired accountant and author of a book entitled *Top New Zealand Shares* doesn't mind one jot, and manages the trip once a season. 'The most direct route to Leeds is to fly Singapore or Emirates Airlines to Manchester, which is around 28 hours,' John says with a shrug of the shoulders. 'Most people would say that was hell but in fact it's very easy. The music, video games and film entertainment on the planes these days are superb and if you take a sleeping pill the time passes very quickly.' His last couple of visits have not been the happiest given he witnessed the 1–0 FA Cup defeat at home to Hereford on 20 November 2007, preceded by the 1–0 Championship defeat against Wolves at Elland Road on 10 September 2006. If 112 hours (round trip times two) of jumping on and off planes to watch two defeats and no Leeds goals, yet still maintaining an undying love of the club, is not dedication, what is? John did not used to live so far from Elland Road. In fact, he was born in Horsforth into a family who all supported Leeds. Both his parents were born and raised in Pudsey and claim to have attended the very first match played under floodlights at Elland Road, a 4–1 friendly win over Hibernian on 9 November 1953. In front of a crowd of 31,500, John Charles scored twice and Raich Carter also netted a brace. The floodlights cost £7,000, which were the most expensive in the country at the time, and they proved so popular that every Monday night after that, for some time, Leeds would play a friendly against a Scottish side under the lights. The 260ft diamond-shaped floodlights, the tallest in Europe, were erected in 1974, well, on three sides of the ground anyway. The fourth pylon was put up in 1978. Each pylon contained 55 lamps.

So the older generation of Mallinsons saw history in the making at Elland Road some 56 years ago, and the baton was passed to the next generation on 4 November 1967. Leeds were at home against Arsenal. United won 3–1 with Mick Jones scoring his very first goal for the club. The first of Jones's 111 goals for Leeds United was sandwiched between a Peter Lorimer penalty and an Eddie Gray goal. At the age of 10 it was John's first Leeds match. His dad Stuart took him along, along with his granddad, Lawrence, who as it turned out was attending his last Leeds game. John's brother David Mallinson, at the age of eight, was also getting behind the lads. John Mallinson would have to wait a little bit longer to see one of United's all-time greats, Billy Bremner, as he was suspended for the Arsenal game, but it was still a fantastic day he says he will never forget. 'We had great seats, front row by the tunnel, which in those days was on the halfway line,' he reflects. 'Elland Road was very different then, only the West Stand survives today. My grandma said she used to pay sixpence to get in the Scratching Shed. David and I were very excited and in awe of the size of the crowd and the noise. We were hooked!'

The Mallinsons may have missed out on seeing our fiery red-headed Scottish midfield genius on that occasion, but there were to be many other matches following this victory over Arsenal where it was a privilege to witness not just Bremner, but the whole Don Revie side. And John picks out one such occasion which will always live in his memory. 'The best atmosphere at Elland Road for me was the European Cup semi-final home leg against Barcelona in 1975, where we won 2–1 in a very tough game. Johan Cruyff and Johan Neeskens were both playing for Barcelona. Billy Bremner burst the back of the net for our first and then they equalised from a free-kick. Allan Clarke scored the winner in the second half. We were crammed like sardines in the lower South Stand, so had a perfect view. The quarter-final against Anderlecht was interesting from a weather point of view. It was so foggy at one end of the ground, you couldn't see it from the other. We took the referee's word for it that we'd won 3–0! Watching the lads beat Manchester United has always been a highlight. The first time I saw that was when my brother and I went to Old Trafford in the 1973–74 Championship year to see us beat them 2–0 (Mick

Jones and Joe Jordan scoring). We nearly did not get in the ground as it was full with over 60,000 [60,025 to be precise], a big crowd for Old Trafford in those days. Then we came back from New Zealand for Christmas 1995 and watched us beat them 3–1. Even Thomas Brolin played well! And Tony Yeboah scored a tearaway goal [a Gary McAllister penalty and a Brian Dean goal completed the scoring for Leeds].'

Along with his Hull-born wife Jane Mallinson, who also supports Leeds, John has two boys who were born in Auckland, Ben, now 23 and Alex, 21, and yet, even though they could not possibly have been born further away from Elland Road, they listened to their parents and keep Leeds firmly in the family. Prior to Ben and Alex coming on the scene John worked at Price Waterhouse in Leeds after graduating from Leeds University. He and Jane, shortly after getting hitched, moved to Wortley, so it was easy to walk to Elland Road. They then upped sticks to the other side of the planet in 1982. On the way to their new life down under they stopped briefly in Los Angeles, just when the 1982 World Cup was on. Looking for somewhere to watch England's ill-fated goalless draw with Spain, which ultimately knocked Ron Greenwood's team out, John said, 'Football was big in New Zealand at that time because they had qualified for the tournament, but football was not big in the States then. The only coverage we could find was on a Spanish language TV channel. Kevin Keegan missed a sitter and England were out of the Cup.'

Travelling back to Blighty for Christmas 2001, John, Jane, Ben and Alex went to see three Leeds games. And they saw their fair share of goals to boot, 16 in all, although Leeds only got half of them. All at Elland Road, they started with a 2–2 draw against Leicester (Harry Kewell and Mark Viduka), then followed that up with a 3–2 win over Everton (Viduka and two from Robbie Fowler). Their final match before their 28-hour journey back to the southern hemisphere was a disappointing but exciting 4–3 reverse against Newcastle United (Lee Bowyer, Viduka again and Ian Harte on target).

Back down under, the New Zealand-based Mallinsons are constantly reminded of that horrible May afternoon in 1973 when Leeds lost to Sunderland in the FA Cup Final, as their Auckland home is on a road called 'Sunderlands Road'. 'Perhaps I should ask the council to rename it,' quipped John. Apart from the Mallinsons, though, are there other Leeds supporters in their neck of the woods, and just how big is football in Kiwi land? John says, 'There are a few Leeds fans over here and it's not unusual to see someone wearing a Leeds top or T-shirt. Football in general though is very big in New Zealand. While rugby union and rugby league are the big spectator sports, more people play football than any other football code over here. Kiwis are sport mad and are extremely competitive at everything. Auckland is 37 degrees south of the equator and in the middle of the Pacific Ocean so has a very mild climate. It has great facilities for sport so anyone can play football at any level. At the grand old age of 51 I'm still playing football and my team consists of supporters of Leicester, Birmingham, Arsenal, West Ham, Oldham, Derby and Wigan, but no other Leeds fans. My football club has 16 senior men and women's teams, which play full winter seasons in organised leagues, and over 1,000 juniors, who start playing at the age of five. We also play in summer leagues.'

In the 2000–01 season Leeds United embarked on a European adventure, finally going out to Valencia in the semi-finals of a Champions' League run that nobody outside Leeds saw coming. John recalls watching the games down under. 'It was all very exciting,' he says. 'All the games were shown on the box over here, from the early away defeat to Barcelona right the way through to the Valencia game. New Zealander Danny Hay played in the Barcelona game. Time is 12 hours ahead in New Zealand, give or take an hour for daylight saving, so the games were shown at 7 and 8am. It was late to work on those days! The TV coverage here is very good, although it has not yet extended to League One. Nearly all the Premier League games are shown live, as are Champions League games, Spanish and Italian League games.' John also sums up his thoughts on the massive Leeds following. 'It's a one-team city with a large fan base so it is a matter of time before the right combination of business management and football management is found to return the club to the top. Leeds fans support the club when they can see a genuine attempt is being made for success by the management and players. Certainly the 15-point deduction was an outrageous penalty and fired up the players and the fans early in the 2007–08 season.'

Given the fact that John Mallinson has followed the Whites for over 40 years, when asked to pick his all time Leeds XI with three subs, a manager and an assistant, he comes up with an interesting line up. Only six of Revie's side make it to the starting XI, and look who he chooses for assistant manager:

Nigel Martyn, Gary Kelly, Terry Cooper, Jonathan Woodgate, Rio Ferdinand, Peter Lorimer, Billy Bremner, Johnny Giles, Eddie Gray, Mark Viduka, Allan Clarke. Subs: Gordon Strachan, Robbie Keane, Paul Madeley. Manager: Don Revie. Assistant manager: Gus Poyet.

'Billy Bremner and Gordon Strachan were very similar,' enthuses John. 'Both were fiery Scotsman, hugely skilled, strong leaders and goalscoring midfielders. We've had many great strikers over the years. In recent years my pick would be Mark Viduka. For a big man he was very skilful and a great finisher. It's also always entertaining to watch Robbie Keane at Tottenham, as well as the other former Leeds players there.'

Chapter 10

EASTERN PROMISES AND A LITTLE HELP FROM THE CLUB

On the pitch - Asian-born Whites:

Name	Joined	Left	Apps	Goals	Born
John Armand	1922	1929	79	24	India

Singapore

Heading back from the southern hemisphere, we are now going to be landing at Changi International Airport, Singapore. When you arrive at Changi and enter the arrivals lounge and the main body of the airport, it is simply a perfect example of what lies ahead. The airport is stunning. Super clean and reputedly the best-kept airport in the world. When you see it, you find that notion difficult to argue with. It is an indication that the whole of Singapore could be just as clean and just as stunning. And it is. Singapore City, the capital, is a wonderfully spotless city. Wherever you go you will see no litter anywhere. And the people are incredibly polite. There's some captivating scenery in Singapore as well, but it's not the scenery we are that bothered about really. Number 165 Penang Road is where you need to go. It's not a house. It's the Dubliner. Alright it is a house – a public house. And a very special public house. This is 'home' for all Leeds United supporters in this sumptuous Asian island state. And whenever Leeds are live on the box, you can guarantee a full house at the Dubliner. The support for Leeds over in Singapore is so big that in actual fact they have taken over two public houses. And it was in the Lot, Stock & Barrel where the Singapore branch of the Leeds United Supporters' Club was born back in 2001.

Leeds's penultimate season in the Premiership began with a 2–0 victory over Southampton at Elland Road on 18 August. Thousands of miles away from Elland Road the South-East Asian Whites were gathering in the Lot, Stock & Barrel for a night to remember. A relatively small group of

Singaporean Leeds supporters had been meeting up for live matches on the box for a good few years already, so they decided it was time to approach LUSC and form a branch. Herman Phua sent out emails to all the Leeds fans he knew on the island, and, with the help of some good publicity on the official Leeds United website, leedsunited.com, the Lot, Stock & Barrel was packed. The branch now boasts around 80 members. Talking to the official Leeds magazine *Leeds, Leeds, Leeds* back in July 2002, Herman Phua said, 'My support for Leeds is rooted in the skills of Bremner and Co., and these also enthralled and won the hearts of branch chairman Greg Phua, my brother, and other committee members such as Bradley Fernando, Manojkumar and Lee Chiwi. Revie's great team also motivated Chang Tou Yuen – the branch's merchandise officer – to embark on his passion for Leeds team kits, which has earned him the nickname of "Kit Man". Another very encouraging sign is that the Singapore branch has also managed to catch the eye of many Leeds United supporters around the world. As the team's first official supporters' club in Asia, we attracted new members from neighbouring countries Indonesia, Malaysia, Brunei and Thailand. Also, some fans from as far away as the UK, Malta and Australia have opted to sign up as overseas members after witnessing first-hand the enthusiasm and great atmosphere at the branch's match meets.'

On 30 July 2002, around 20 Singaporean Whites travelled north to Thailand's capital, Bangkok, where Terry Venables had taken his Leeds side as part of their pre-season Far East tour. United beat a Bangkok XI 2–1 at the Rajmangala Stadium thanks to goals by Erik Bakke and Robbie Keane. And LUSCS simply loved every minute of it. For 10 of their members it was even more of a fantastic trip, as they received a treat they never expected from the club. Leeds United FC are only too aware of the support they receive from this part of the world, so as a reward for some of these Singaporean Whites, the club invited 10 members to attend a training session prior to the match at the Rajmangala Stadium. After they had watched their heroes going through their paces, they were given exclusive access to all the players, so they could chat, get their autographs and have photos taken. Gregory Phua had requested this from the club, but wasn't holding out too much hope that the club would agree. He was both surprised and delighted to say the least when LUFC produced the invitation. 'Many of our members have been die-hard fans since the '70s,' said Gregory. 'And we are really happy that a big club like Leeds continues to look after its fans no matter how far away they are.'

Thailand

We all know only too well the catastrophic consequences of the tsunami that struck the region on Boxing Day, 2004. Singapore escaped any damage but large parts of Thailand were hit by mother nature's incredible force. The province of Phang Nga was the worst hit area in Thailand, an area that was completely flattened by the waves and which saw thousands killed. Journalist Eddy Lascelles, who has written for the Leeds United magazine in the past, spent months in the region to help with the relief work, and he is grateful to Leeds United for their small part in putting the smiles back on the faces of a few of the locals at least. 'Part of my work here has included construction at a nearby village which was flattened by the waves,' said Lascelles. 'But mostly I have been helping in schools that have children who have been affected by the tsunami. Either they have lost parents, relatives or friends, or have seen things which, at their age, could have a profound effect on their lives. The long-term damage is hard to judge, it will take a long time for the tourist industries to get back to what they were, and estimates range from two years to 10 years.'

Leeds legend Eddie Gray, however small it may seem in the grand scale of things, donated full Leeds United kits, with Michael Ziff of Stylo also donating sports shoes for the youngsters in this devastated area, many of whom lost their parents in the tragedy.

Japan

Leeds United can say a big thank you to former Irish Whites Ian Harte and Robbie Keane, as well as legend Gary Kelly, for the birth of our fan base in a place called Chiba. Where? Not familiar? Think back to the 2002 World Cup in South Korea and Japan. Or, rather, just think of the latter. Chiba is based south-east of the Tokyo Disney Resort and around 30 miles south from Tokyo International Airport. And if you ask any Irish player that served their country during the 2002 World Cup, they will be able to tell you exactly where Chiba is. Chiba was their temporary home while Mick McCarthy's troops enjoyed their World Cup campaign. With Harte and Co. in town it was an opportunity then to spread the best two words on the planet – Leeds United – across to another part of the world. With the help of Irish Leeds follower Tony Kelly (no relation), Kells, Harty and the proper R. Keane were introduced to one Satoshi Tamura, who has not looked back since. Seven years on, Satoshi has been to 17

Leeds United games. Given the distance he has to travel, not forgetting the cost, that is impressive stuff. His family are yet to be converted, preferring instead to support their local side Jef United Chiba – but he's working on them.

'I travel to Leeds at least once a season,' he says. Coming all that way, it is not surprising that it is not just home games he attends either. 'My favourite match is against Southampton on 19 November 2005. It was the most dramatic comeback I have ever seen. We were 3–0 down after 70 minutes and came back to win. It's impossible to say how I felt when Liam Miller got the winner.'

'Dedication' is the middle name of any Leeds fan, but Satoshi Tamura can boast that he pushes his love for Leeds to even further limits. Costing around £1,000 whenever he makes the long haul west, the one-hour drive to the airport is followed by a 12-hour flight to London, where he meets up with some of the London Whites, including Angela Schofield. It is then a two-hour journey on the train from the capital before he arrives at Leeds City station, totalling 15 hours' travel. And that does not include hanging around for luggage when he has landed at Heathrow, check-in time (usually another two hours prior to the flight) and the comparatively short trip from Leeds City station to Elland Road.

On 21 May 2006, Leeds descended on Cardiff for what we all thought was to be our glorious return to the Premiership and Satoshi was no exception, so he boarded a flight bound for Heathrow. It was to be his 10th Leeds match. But you would actually think that, following his first five matches, he would have given up watching Leeds. Following a 1–1 draw at home to Arsenal in 2002, Satoshi then saw us lose four on the bounce. But no, like all good Leeds fans, he stuck by the team and was rewarded when he attended that great 6–1 demolition of QPR in 2004. He then went on to watch us win four on the bounce and the next match he attended was the Watford game at the Millennium Stadium. Why oh why couldn't it have been five?

Satoshi is doing his best to spread Leeds United's name around Japan as well and has already converted his mate Yoshikazu Yasuda. 'He is a Leeds fan now,' says Satoshi. 'He was a classmate when I was in college. I've bought programmes for him every time I watch a match and in 2006 he bought a team calendar of Leeds! He has not gone to Elland Road yet, but he is very interested in visiting. There are about 800,000 people who live in Chiba, so I have a few more people to convert!' You could just tell them about the chippies in Leeds, Satoshi, which is an added bonus for the 34-year-old whenever he is in the city. 'I like fish'n'chips and there are so many shops in Leeds, and the quality is good,' he admits.

In 2008 Satoshi flew over for two League games and then returned for our ill-fated Play-off Final against Doncaster Rovers. He wrote a diary for the League encounters, for which he always stays with staunch Leeds fanatic Angela Schofield in her London home. It was hardly a vintage year for the Japanese globetrotter, Leeds losing all three of the games and not even scoring a goal, but the Tranmere game, sandwiched in between the Southend game and Wembley, will forever live in his memory. After such a special occasion Satoshi wrote the following, which has been left as close to the original translation as possible:

Tranmere: Home - Saturday, 2 February, fine weather

'I got up at 5am. I am considerably tense, and Angela seems to be too, but is always nervous before a game. We went by car to Kings Cross at 7am, received the tickets for the train from Mark and got the Inter-City at 8.10am to Leeds. We arrive at Leeds on schedule at 10.35. There was snow everywhere but it is likely that the game will be played. I drink coffee in a pub on the station and go to Elland Road by taxi at 11.00. Angela joyfully talks about going in the Chairman's Suite with the driver of the taxi. After shopping in the club shop at Elland Road we went to the ticket collection point of the north-east corner. I hand the souvenir chopsticks I brought over for Tracey, who gives me my ticket. Tracey has been in charge of the tickets since I came for the first time in 2002 and exchanges mail many times, but this time is the first time that we met. She is very charming and looked very pleased when I handed her a present. We went to the Radebe Suite a little before 12.00. Paul Dews, in charge of media, comes a little after and took us on the Stadium Tour. He took us to the pitch, changing rooms and the press conference center in the ground. We meet some excellent players like Allan Clarke and Paul Reaney of former times and had photographs together. I have seen them on the DVD of the FA Cup Final in 1972, but I am really proud and moved to meet them. In addition, a trophy and the autographed shirt of the opponents are displayed proudly, and the rotation of the Players' Lounge lets you feel the history of the club.

Paul introduced Gary McAllister and Jermaine Beckford afterwards. Gary McAllister spoke to us open heartedly even while he was very busy because it was his first match as new manager, and he was very pleased when I presented him with a souvenir. Jermaine Beckford was also very friendly and he was also pleased with the chopsticks I gave him. I requested to him that I wanted him to present a shirt to me that I would put on display in my new home and he answered 'Yes, it would be a pleasure.' Paul then took us to the Chairman's Suite next. It was a lounge, like you would find at a high-quality hotel with the magnificence that I cannot think to be like a football stadium. Mr Ken & Mrs Suzanna Bates meet us in the Chairman's Suite. I have seen them via the internet and the magazine, but to meet them they were wonderful people who were very friendly. An aura drifts around them. The attention that they prepared sushi for a fan coming from Japan was great. The interview on Leeds United TV is prepared in the Chairman's Suite and would be an interview as part of the Greatest Fan in the World campaign that began yesterday. The contents of the interview were ordinary contents such as the process that I became a fan and who was my favourite player, but the interview on TV was the first time for me, and the interview in English was really tense. Angela told me later that I 'seemed to have looked totally frozen.' The interview on TV is over, and Peter Lorimer visits the Chairman's Lounge and I talk pleasantly while drinking wine, and Mr Ken Bates introduces him to me. I have seen him in a column in the match programme, but this is the first time I meet him and have an impression very much of a friendly feeling which can last. Like Allan Clarke and Paul Reaney, I realize they are human beings where their demeanour is soft so as not to give the impression of that they were unapproachable because they were excellent players. I have a very luxurious lunch with the chairman and CEO of Tranmere Rovers, which was lamb for main course. The chairman of Tranmere expresses how unbelievable it was that there is a fan forthcoming to watching some matches every year from Japan. The lunch was luxurious, delicious and the meal seemed to be like in a really high-quality hotel. I eat so much of the meal and feel really happy. In addition, the sushi which the chairman prepared was so delicious, I never thought I would find it that good abroad, and am really moved. After a meal we move to the John Charles Stand and watch the match. My seat is a leather seat next to the chairman! Suzanna talks with the fans openheartedly and really melt into Leeds' hearts splendidly. The great chorus of *Marching on Together* before the match starts and is as impressive as usual and I am glad. And the match cannot make a decisive chance with both sides and the first half was 0–0. During half-time we enjoy coffee and a cake in the Chairman's Suite. Angela and the secretary and chairman take me to the Radebe Suite and Nick 'Peanut' Baines, who is the keyboard player of the Kaiser Chiefs, is in there! I read that the Kaiser Chiefs support Leeds United in the *Leeds Leeds Leeds* magazine and match programme, but I never dreamed I would be able to meet him at Elland Road! He told me that the third album will be announced soon.

Although the start of the second half was good, Tranmere scored in succession in 61 and 69 minutes and Leeds were defeated 0–2. The second goal was scored by Ian Moore, who played at Leeds until last year. After the match, we went back to the Chairman's Suite and had tea and a light meal like a delicious sandwich and a pie. We talked about the impression of the match and the hope of the remaining season. Paul Dews brings the shirt of Jermaine Beckford. He seems to have really worn it in a match and mud is on here and there! I was very moved Jermaine writes his autograph on the back. Really thank you very much for Jermaine, Paul! Gary McAllister comes and talks with Ken Bates afterwards. I think Gary is a really brave person because he undertook the manager's job when the condition of the team is not good enough after Christmas and sudden transfer in a season of Dennis Wise. It may take a little time until a team gets on track, but I think that he will surely accomplish promotion [unfortunately we all know that never quite happened for Gary Mac].

I took a photograph with Ken and Suzanna and left Elland Road. When we leave Ken said to me, 'Bring your wife with you next time.' We return to London by train at 18.40. I remember the dreamlike day while talking to friends Kathey and Julie at the pub in Kings Cross Station. I am very pleased because Ken & Suzanna Bates and so many staff of Leeds United treated me very heartily for only a fan who cannot speak English very well and can only come to watch a match only once a year. I want to visit Elland Road and spend time with friends of many Leeds fans in the future. Last, I want to thank Angela & Chris, who provide a wonderful place to stay whenever I come to the U.K.'

For the record, here are the matches the proud Japanese White travelled halfway round the world to watch:

Date	Opponent	Competition	H or A	Score	Scorers
20 January 2002	Arsenal	Premiership	H	1–1	Fowler
24 November 2002	Tottenham	Premiership	A	0–2	
1 December 2002	Charlton	Premiership	H	1–2	Kewell
4 January 2004	Arsenal	FA Cup	H	1–4	Viduka
13 November 2004	Ipswich	Championship	A	0–1	
20 November 2004	QPR	Championship	H	6–1	Deane 4, Healy, Wright
19 November 2005	Southampton	Championship	A	4–3	Butler, Blake, Healy, Miller
22 November 2005	Burnley	Championship	H	2–0	Healy, Blake
26 November 2005	Millwall	Championship	A	1–0	May (og)
21 May 2006	Watford	Play-off Final	N*	0–3	
3 February 2007	Norwich City	Championship	A	1–2	Howson
10 February 2007	Crystal Palace	Championship	H	2–1	Heath, Blake
29 January 2008	Southend Utd	League One	A	0–1	
2 February 2008	Tranmere R	League One	H	0–2	
25 May 2008	Doncaster R	Play-off Final	N†	0–1	
13 December 2008	Colchester Utd	League One	H	1–2	Snodgrass
20 December 2008	MK Dons	League One	A	1–3	Snodgrass

* Played at the Millennium Stadium, Cardiff. † Played at Wembley Stadium.

And here's his all time Leeds XI with three subs:

Paul Robinson, Gary Kelly, Ian Harte, Simon Walton, Matthew Killgalon, Rio Ferdinand, Liam Miller, Shaun Derry, Mark Viduka, David Healy, Lee Bowyer. Subs: Robbie Keane, Frazer Richardson, Neil Sullivan.

Chapter 11

UNITED FANS BLOWING HOT AND COLD

South Pole

From Japan we'll briefly head south – very south – very briefly – where Craig Nicholls is spreading the name of Leeds United almost certainly further than anybody else, unless anyone knows of a Leeds fan living on Mars! Tent parked up, with Leeds patch firmly sewn on at the front, the adventurous Nicholls visited the South Pole on a two-year stay as part of the British Antarctic Survey Team. Craig was converted into becoming a Leeds supporter by his two nephews, Oscar and Declan Johnson. The two boys and their father Michael Johnson, who is a lifelong Leeds nut, live in Bournemouth now and have made the 10-hour round trip to Leeds on a number of occasions. On one such occasion, Oscar and Declan decided to buy a door plaque for their uncle, who promptly stuck it on his South Pole-bound tent. Far too cold to stick around though, so we'll set off north on our virtual Leeds United World Tour. Where are we off to next then?

Saudi Arabia

Ah, somewhere a tad hotter! A place ex-pat and staunch White David Aldridge knows only too well. David has attended over 500 Leeds games over the years and thought he would be suffering from football withdrawal symptoms once in the desert. But when he arrived in the Middle East, fanatical football fever was just around the corner – Arabic-style. Being almost certainly the only non-Arab in a crowd of 80,000 at the King Fahd Stadium in Riyadh, he sat for four sweltering hours through a vital World Cup qualifying match between Saudi and Uzbekistan. A win for the Saudis would mean qualification to the 2006 Finals in Germany. With Kenyan and Yemeni companions to enjoy the experience with, it was the biggest game the country had been involved in for years – and what's more, it was *free* to get in. Feeling at home in the stadium with everyone wearing white (naturally!), David took in an incredible atmosphere, which he felt was a throwback to the 1980s. 'During that period, following Leeds round the country, I'd guess 95 per cent of UK football fans were testosterone-fuelled males – it is only in the last 15 years that woman have filtered back into the safer and more family friendly crowds. The King Fahd Stadium was a throwback to those days, with the crowd a heaving mass of males, none of them seemingly above the age of 40, due to the rules of Saudi society which do not allow women and men to mix in public. As kick-off approached, the atmosphere cranked up, the aisles and gangways were full, although fans continued to pour in, perching on anything they could to get a view. I even saw the VIP's seating themselves on top of the Royal Enclosure (a bullet-proof executive style box) as they struggled to find space and a view. The atmosphere during the game actually dropped off – presumably through exhaustion. At half-time, the three of us bought 20 water bottles, which we handed out to everyone around us. "A gift from Allah", our neighbours declared. By the end I had been in the stadium for four hours and was drained. If I'd known more than a few words in Arabic they would have carried me out on a stretcher.'

The final whistle blew and the Saudis had made it to Germany, via a comfortable 3–0 victory. The pitch became a mass of white-clad (we like that) Arabs worshipping their heroes and carrying them on their shoulders around the stadium. David and his two buddies left the stadium, walked a short distance across the desert to where their car was parked and then became part of a mad race, fuelled by World Cup euphoria, back to their base. And it really was a mad race home. Music blaring from the cars, people standing on the back of their trucks, supporters flying down the road sat on lowered car windows with just their legs barely inside the car. And they were not just cruising along, they were putting their foot down, barely 5ft behind the car in front and mounting pavements if the road got a little too congested. The team did not do quite so well in the Finals in Germany, although on 14 June 2006 they almost snatched victory against Tunisia before the Africans equalised to make it 2–2 in the last minute. A 4–0 defeat against the Ukraine and a 1–0 loss against Spain completed their World Cup before they headed home.

South Africa

On the pitch – South African-born Leeds Whites:

Name	Joined	Left	Apps	Goals
Gerry Francis	1957	1961	50	9
Ken Hastie	1952	1953	4	0
Gordon Hodgson	1936	1939	86	53
Albert Johanneson	1960	1969	197/3	67
Philomen Masinga	1994	1996	39	11
George Miller	1950	1951	14	1
Lucas Radebe	1994	2005	262	3
Gordon Stewart	1951	1953	11	2

I have delved into the record books and cannot find a Saudi Arabian that has worn our sacred shirt, but at our next port of call, there is a slightly different tale. From South Africa Sergeant Wilko produced the buy of the century – he's been shot and his smile is legendary. Need I say any more? Altogether now – 'Radebeeeeeeeee, Radebeeeeeee, Radebe, Radebe, Radebeeeeeee, Radebeeeeeee, Redebeeeeeeee'eee, Radebeee'ee'ee'ee'ee – LUCAS!!!' A chant fondly known by every Leeds fan alive, so let's just nip into his homeland to say a brief hello to Gary Wepener from Cape Town. A life-long Leeds fan, he names Allan Clarke, Billy Bremner and of course Lucas Radebe as his all-time favourite players. In 2004 he was responsible for taking Leeds right to the very top in Africa. Climbing to the peak of Kilimanjaro, the highest mountain in the continent, standing at 19,335.6ft above sea level, he proudly took his Strongbow Leeds shirt with him and joked, 'At least for one day we were truly higher than everyone else!'

Just before we head off to another part of Africa, it is commonly known that one of the best bands in the world owes South Africa much. The Kaiser Chiefs, who gave a fantastic performance at Elland Road the night before Leeds's Play-off Final with Doncaster Rovers in 2008, are named after a South African football team with a subtle difference in their name, the Kaizer Chiefs. As mentioned above, Howard Wilkinson paid a fee of £250,000 for Radebe to the Kaizer Chiefs in August 1994, not knowing at the time what an Elland Road legend he would turn out to be. In honour of the great man, nicknamed 'The Chief', massive Leeds United fans and band members Andrew White, Nick 'Peanut' Baines, Nick Hodgson, Ricky Wilson and Simon Rix came up with the band's excellent name.

Zimbabwe

Wellington Kufinya (Welly) – what a good lad! His English is far better than my Rhodesian, so for the sake of not mistaking any of the translation of a letter he sent to me for publication in this book, it was simply decided to photocopy the letter in its entirety, which clearly shows his heartfelt love for Leeds United. The letter was written during Leeds's first-ever season in the third tier of English football – season 2007–08, prior to Gary McAllister departing the club. Here it is:

Dear Andy Starmore

First and foremost I would like to give special greetings to you and your family I hope this letter will reaches you in good condition. I have enclosed my photo in my beloved colour. I have reply your question if they is something I have omit but you want it please don't hasitate to contact me at wellyRufie @ yahoo.com.

My letter reads as follows:

A huge fan from Africa.

My name is Wellington Kufinya, I was born in Zimbabwe at Karoi Hospital and it is where I am still live, Karoi is a small Town but have many Leeds fans. I started supporting Leeds from a very tender age. I have been in good times and bad times and I have seen the good times when we were — playing in Europe and now down into the League One football.

Since I started following Leeds I never see live match of Leeds because here in Zimbabwe League one matches are not shown at all, better when we were in the UEFA or Primiership because sometimes Leeds matches were shown as delayed at midnight. Some other fans has charged their mind to quit supporting Leeds but me and others almost 40 to 45 fans we know that we can only appreciate the good if you have seen the bad, one day will be back into the Primiership. So with this type of situation I am planning to set up Members' Club. If there are some fans who can help me to set up, please try by all means to contact me.

I have became Leeds fan because my father always keep me updated with Leeds progress before he passed away in July 2000.

My other hobbies are watching T.V, listening to music and I am also a football player, I have got a football club called Leeds United Supporter F.C, where only Leeds fans can partcipate. If you are not Leeds fan you cant play because we play othe English Supporters club. We are now 5th in that local legue, You know, what we are in the 5th position because we don't have kit we play barefooted also we don't have shirts. All most the club we play aganist, laugh at us that how can you say you are Leeds fans without anything that belongs, sometimes they say join us to fellow their favourite team but we are Leeds till we die.

Also I would like to say to all Leeds fans that please keep up the marvelous support although we have been deducted 15 points that doesn't stop us supporting Leeds, it has give us more power to support the club and this season it has been fantastic. I am sure the lads are go doing the good job to reward the fans.

My favourite players of all the time will be , the first XI are Paul Robbinson, Ian Harte, Radebe, Bridge Rio Ferdinard, Gary McCalister, Lee Bowyer, Gary Speed Olivier Dacourt, Robbie Keane, Alan Smith →

I am more than happy for the appointment of Gary McAlister and I am confidence that he will take us back into the Primiership because he knows everything about football at Elland Road. and he is my player of all the time because he was a quality player and he's probably the best I have ever seen.

Lastly I would like to seek help from loyal Leeds fans that if you have anything that you think can help us with please help us also including any type of sportwear (even old ones) related to Leeds or else you can keep me updated.

If you are willing to help me don't hasitate to contact me. You can easily get me in touch at my email wellykufie@yahoo.com or my postal address is WELLINGTON KUFINYA
                HSE No 888
                SPORTS FIELD ROAD
                KAROI
                ZIMBABWE
                AFRICA.

Yours Faithfully

        Welly

✳ Please let me know if you receive this letter
        WE ARE LEEDS !!!

Chapter 12

KEEPING IT 'REAL'

Malta

On the pitch – Maltese-born Leeds Whites:

Name	Joined	Left	Apps	Goals
Dylan Kerr	1988	1993	9/11	0

From the heat of Africa we head north-west now to another of the world's top hotspots and the beautiful island of Malta. Officially called the Republic of Malta, the island boasts over 50 Leeds supporters and Hilary Attard, who is the chairman of the 'Real Leeds United Regional Members' Club Malta' is undoubtedly the island's number-one White. Flying over at least twice a season, he began his 40-year love affair with the club in the late 1960s after reading an article that fascinated him. In a magazine called *Goal*, Attard read all about how the late, great Don Revie had taken over Leeds United when they were at the foot of the old Second Division and turned them into genuine Championship contenders. 'It was so inspiring,' Attard enthuses. 'It felt like I'd been bitten by the Leeds United bug and I've been infected now for 40 years. I am so proud of this infection that I never want to be healed!' He was already a massive follower of Leeds and so, when Leeds drew Valletta in the UEFA Cup first round in 1979, he could not believe his luck. 'It was an "away" match but I did not have far to go. I was secretary of LUSC Malta at the time and it was a pleasure and an honour to be involved with the squad from their arrival at the airport until they left Malta with a handsome 4–0 score in their favour [Arthur Graham hat-trick and one from Paul Hart]. After the match I accompanied the full squad with their directors to a great dinner dance where they met all the Maltese supporters and my great friend and number-one Leeds fan Gary Edwards.'

Leeds won the second leg at Elland Road 3–0 to go through comfortably 7–0 on aggregate. Alan Curtis, Ray Hankin and Paul Hart again got on the scoresheet. It was the first time Leeds had been allowed back in Europe following their ban after the Paris riots at the European Cup Final debacle against Bayern Munich in 1975. Sadly, they went out 4–0 on aggregate in the second round to Uni Craiova and did not feature in Europe again for another 13 long years. Ever since Hilary Attard's first match at Elland Road, in which Leeds beat Manchester City 2–0 with goals from Ken De Mange (his only goal for the club in his 19 appearances) and Glynn Snodin back in 1987, he has attended around 80 Leeds games – not bad when you live halfway between Sicily and Libya. There are plenty of great memories for Hilary to reflect on but he is very proud to be 'the first-ever Maltese Leeds fan to travel with home-grown Leeds fans to a European Champions League match when we went to Real Madrid in 2001.' He added, 'For me to be at the Bernabeu was a dream come true, as this was a gift to the great Don Revie.'

The Maltese Whites are now thriving, congregating at the Cherry Tree Pub in St Paul's Bay for meetings and live matches on the box. But like the club, it has been a bumpy ride along the way. The Maltese LUSC went bust in 1982 following the relegation to the old Second Division, but Hilary Attard was persuaded to start it up again in 2000. Following internal squabbling between some of the committee members, it folded again. When the members' club was formed, Leeds United chairman Ken Bates proposed to Hilary Attard that they form an LURMC, which Attard duly accepted. 'I promised to help them keep the Leeds United flag flying again in Malta,' said Attard. 'I named it the 'Real Leeds' Malta Fans in order to separate the genuine and occasional Leeds fans. During our Champions League adventure they used to turn up in numbers for all the matches. Leeds United is a quality side so all I need here is quality not quantity.'

Go on then Hilary, give us your all time Leeds XI?

Nigel Martyn, Paul Reaney, Terry Cooper, Billy Bremner, Jack Charlton, Norman Hunter, Peter Lorimer, Allan Clarke, John Charles, Johnny Giles, Eddie Gray. Subs: Paul Madeley, Gordon Strachan, Joe Jordan.

His top three players are Billy Bremner 'for his non-stop commitment,' Peter Lorimer 'for his dynamite shooting' and Allan Clarke 'for making scoring look easy.' Hilary's nephew Rambert is also a massive follower of Leeds, but, whisper it, Rambert's father, Hilary's elder brother, who quite frankly should know better, follows a little club on the other side of the Pennines. Let's leave it there.

Like many Leeds supporters around the world, Hilary Attard's apartment is a shrine to Leeds United, but there will not be too many that have had their photos taken with practically every player that has played for Leeds since 1987. He has also collected every Leeds home programme since 1978, had an article written about him being the number-one Leeds fan on the island in the *Malta Times* and been presented with a memento for his promotion of Leeds United in Malta by the Mayor of Leeds. He has also been very privileged to have received a signed photo of every Leeds United manager except Brian Clough since Don Revie.

Mark Briffa is another fellow Maltese White, taking after his dad Chris, and Briffa Snr owes his love affair with Leeds to one Bobby Charlton. 'Back in the late 1960s all my friends were into Man United and Bobby Charlton. I wanted to be different and knew that Bobby had a brother called Jack who played for another club. I decided to support that club, and the rest is history.' Following Leeds since his terrace debut in a brilliant 2–1 victory with a thunderbolt free-kick from Peter Lorimer at Arsenal in 1973 (Paul Madeley got the other), Chris Briffa recalls a moment of sheer joy in his home town of Sliema. 'I was listening on the radio to the Bournemouth versus Leeds match in 1990 when we won promotion back to the old First Division. When we won I was ecstatic. I then collected my young kids [he has six now – two Leeds – working on the others!], packed them into my car and drove off around the town hooting my horn incessantly. It was a one-car Leeds United celebration!'

And how does Chris Briffa's all time Leeds XI differ from that of Hilary Attard?

Nigel Martyn, Paul Reaney, Terry Cooper, Billy Bremner, Gordon Strachan, Norman Hunter, Peter Lorimer, Allan Clarke, Lee Chapman, Johnny Giles, Eddie Gray. Subs: Paul Madeley, Tony Yeboah, Gary Sprake.

Answer then: two in the XI and two out of the three subs.

Paul Lathey is another true Leeds fan living on the sunny island of Malta. Originally from Horsforth in Leeds, he recalls the moment when his love for the club was cemented for life. 'My first match I went to was Leeds versus Oxford in the mid '80s, but it was the game against Leicester City at the end of the 1989–90 season that did it for me. I was 10 years old and when we won 2–1 I remember jumping with delight. It was the first time I had felt a serious emotion at a game and from that day I was hooked.' He has since been to 'at least 400 games' and still makes the trip over to Elland Road from his exotic adopted home five times a season. One of his pals, who simply goes by the name of 'Tax', did a bit of shirt-swapping at a Leeds match against West Ham United after the last match of the 1999–2000 season at Upton Park. Tax watched as the Leeds players made their way over to the Leeds supporters and they all threw their shirts into the fans' end. Tax was one of the lucky ones to nab one from the air. Feeling ever so grateful, he then decided to offer his shirt in return. As the players left for the dressing room and the fans headed for the exits, Tax's shirt remained a forlorn lonely item on the Upton Park playing surface. Paul Lathey's all-time Leeds XI looks like this:

Nigel Martyn, Gary Kelly, Tony Dorigo, David Batty, Lucas Radebe, Jonathan Woodgate, Gordon Strachan, Eric Cantona, Alan Smith, Gary McAllister, Harry Kewell. Subs: Lee Bowyer, Tony Yeboah, John Sheridan.

Chapter 13

CLOSER TO BORAT BUT HEART STILL IN LEEDS

Azerbaijan

Andy Burniston is part of just six per cent of the 'other' ethnic compositions that make up the country of Azerbaijan. Not really surprising given that it is on the borders of Iran, Armenia, Georgia and Russia, and his place of residence is the Azerbaijan capital Baku, which is situated on the banks of the Caspian Sea. A short boat ride across the Caspian will take you to Kazakhstan, somewhere many people in the past would possibly have been unfamiliar with until British comedian Sacha Baron Cohen made the controversial comedy film *Borat*, which firmly highlighted the country. Now millions more people know exactly where Kazakhstan is. Andy Burniston may not be putting bums on cinema seats, but one thing Cohen and Burniston do have in common is 'putting something on the map'. For Cohen it is a country, for Burniston it is far greater than that – Leeds United. Andy, who works as an operations director for a construction company in Baku, alongside another five Leeds supporters, can often be seen around the humid Azerbaijan capital, proudly displaying his bare back, which has a huge Leeds badge slap bang in the middle of it, with the words 'White Till I Die' across his broad and equally proud shoulders. He has been living on the Caspian coastline for five years but has been travelling for 30, having originated from Middlesbrough, leaving there when he was just 18 months old to grow up in Garforth. Now, several years on, he recollects the good days, the bad days and the downright ugly days following Leeds. One of the first matches he went to see was with his dad and brother Dave way back on 10 December 1966, which Leeds drew 1–1 with Blackpool at Elland Road (Jimmy Greenhoff scoring for Leeds). Billy Bremner got sent off and Alan Ball was in the Blackpool line up. Andy had clearly caught the bug and to this day he still travels over, enduring an 18-hour haul from Baku four or five times a season, and has never lost faith in supporting United.

Andy quickly sums up the 'ups and downs' of the last five decades: 'The 1960s and '70s were fantastic days, the '80s was a period of mediocrity, still some good times with one or two exceptions but mainly poor, and in the 1990s I thought we were back big time. The title party in 1992, which was followed by the Charity Shield, then Cantona is away for pennies to sc*m. Aston Villa at Wembley (Coca-Cola Cup Final) in '96 was a disgrace, we never showed up. A new Millennium, new hope, a dream, then two murders, a court case, pain, hurt and anger. I travelled back for the Play-off Final in 2006 and couldn't get a ticket! Still, here we are, where we are, if we're not where we're supposed to be.' Despite the 2,435 miles between Baku and Leeds, Andy will always be a massive Leeds fan and believes we are all a special breed. 'You're born a White,' he says. 'I was born on 28 April 1956, the day Leeds got promoted back into the old First Division after nine years down [beat Hull City that day 4–1 – John Charles got two, one penalty and Harold Brook also scored a brace]. You can't just "become" a White. When we lost the 15 points everyone said they don't like us. We don't care. It was a kick in the teeth when Gus Poyet went as well, but not so much Wise. He'll never be a coach as far as I can see.'

Andy Burniston recalls one of the saddest days in the life of Leeds United. The date was 5 May 1973, and the name Sunderland has cropped up in this book probably far too often. Andy explains his day out at Wembley, which started with joyous enthusiasm and an expectation that for the second year on the trot the FA Cup would be heading back to West Yorkshire. 'We all went off to Wembley to pick up the Cup, there we were, a full squad of us from Garforth, we had booked in a hotel for the weekend and were there to party. Me and Stevie Leeds, who is like a brother to me, dressed in the finest *Clockwork Orange* gear, bowler hats, eye makeup, the lot. On our way through Wembley there was loads of patter with the Mackems [Sunderland fans]. Not a bit of bother. The game was a blur but even when we went one down we didn't think we would lose it. Even after that double save from Jim Montgomery, we still thought we would win. Sunderland couldn't beat the Super Leeds. When the final whistle went it seemed so quiet. We all looked at each other in silence, then behind us one lad in a mac started to clap and say things like "Well done, a Second Division team, good effort" and all that. That was it for me and Steve. If it wasn't for the fact that Big Keith Trow grabbed our braces there would have been blood spilt. We walked back down Wembley Way, the Mackems couldn't believe it, we certainly couldn't, but again there was no bother. That was until we got to Wembley Station. We were just kicking our heels waiting for a train when around the corner came Arsenal fans ripping the p*** right out of us. There wasn't time to think and a right rumble took place before we ran down to the platform as the train was just ready to leave, jumped on as the police were running to the "battlefield", got off at the next station and got taxis to Kings Cross. Away up the line for the last orders in Leeds. Stevie was working in London and picked up the bags from the hotel the next week.'

Andy, who names Kippax's Dave Talbot, Collar & Lawrence and Eddie Crawly as legends to a man, recalls a happier occasion when he met footballing legend Norman Hunter. 'I first met him as an 18-year-old at a Billy Bremner testimonial dinner at the Wakefield Variety Club. He gave me and my mate Stevie Leeds half an hour of his time when his wife was wanting him to leave to get back for the babysitter. He signed photos, talked the talk and he still stops to speak to us now when I see him at the games. A gentleman and a legend. Didn't get more England caps due to Bobby Moore being Ramsey's blue-eyed boy.'

When Leeds secured their place in the Play-offs at the end of the 2007–08 season with a win at Yeovil Town, Andy summed up how he and every Leeds fan felt at the time. In a handful of sentences, which are pure poetry, this is what he said:

'This is the hour. Now is the time; history is about to be made. From nothing we have become something. From a long sleep we have awakened. From the dead we have returned. Since first we ambled onto Fullerton Park as young men in the post-World War One days, every era of Leeds fans have walked forward carrying the torch of our club. The standards set by Revie have been etched in the concrete and bricks of our stadium and our hearts. Yes, teams and individuals have failed, but true Whites never have. This week, we make new history for the club. The beloved ghosts of the stadium, from the Geldard End to the dressing room, look down on us and this team and they want us to win, to win not just for them for they are in the past, but to win for now, for the present of this club, for ourselves and for the future, for our children. We owe it to them and we owe it to ourselves. We will play with courage, we will defend with heart and voice, we will attack with belief and pride and we will be dignified, honest and ready. We will struggle at times, but we will prevail. We were Leeds back then and we're still Leeds now. I believe we will emerge from this week, and the weeks ahead, filled with pride. Marching on together we're going to see them WIN – for we are Leeds.'

Just before we leave Azerbaijan, Andy names his all-time Leeds XI, which he has no problem in rattling off with instant reflection – with an interesting choice as assistant manager as well:

David Harvey, Paul Reaney, Terry Cooper, Billy Bremner, Jack Charlton, Norman Hunter, Peter Lorimer, Allan Clarke, Mick Jones, Johnny Giles, Eddie Gray. Subs: Paul Madeley, Tony Yeboah, Gordon Strachan. Manager: Don Revie. Assistant manager: Brian Clough.

Ukraine/Russia

The truly global network of Leeds United supporters continues with a short flight over to the Ukraine, and on to another former part of the Soviet Union. Will Sellars, a lifelong Leeds fan, went one giant step further than just encouraging the people of Ukraine to jump onboard the good ship *Leeds United* – he married one! It was 3 October 2002 at the Meteor Stadium, where Nick Barmby's goal secured a 2–1 aggregate win over Metalurg Zaporizhzhya, where not only were Leeds progressing to round two of the UEFA Cup, but there was also love in the air. Will met and instantly fell head over heels in love with Olga, whom he eventually proposed to by Billy Bremner's statue at Elland Road. In 2003 Olga made her very first trip to ER, and although she did not get to see a game, she went on the stadium tour and was suitably impressed, particularly by the history of the proud club. She finally got to stand on the Kop a year later, when just under 20,000 turned up for the pre-season friendly with Valencia (2–2 – Simon Walton and Matthew Spring). Olga found another two Ukrainian Whites back home, Ruslan and Dima, who appreciated trips made by Olga to Elland Road where she took a hefty shopping list for the club shop, which naturally included Leeds United vodka glasses! Ruslan began supporting Leeds in the late 1980s, despite there being very little English League football on the television over there. The few Leeds games he saw were when Leeds were playing in the FA Cup and Ruslan was impressed with the Whites' apparent refusal to ever accept defeat. Dima was transformed into a Ukranian White following our Championship win in 1992.

Russia got a real taste of Leeds United in 1999, when David O'Leary took sides over to conquer both Lokomotiv Moscow (3–0 – Ian Harte pen, Michael Bridges 2, 7–1 on aggregate) and Spartak Moscow (lost 2–1 in Bulgaria – original match in Russia postponed because of frozen pitch – Harry Kewell scored – went through on away goals rule). Many Muscovites were very impressed with the team and the supporters, who famously swirled their shirts above their heads, bare-chested, in freezing conditions. How many clubs have copied that since? Two such Russians instantly became Russian Whites, Alexei and Vitaliy, who come from St Petersburg. They have already made their first trip to Elland Road, flying over for the League game against Preston on 5 November 2005. Sadly for them, though, the game ended up being a sleepy 0–0 affair with very little for Leeds to get excited about in the attacking third. 'The fans support impressed me much though,' said Alexei. Rest assured then that they *will* return to Elland Road.

Chapter 14

VI MARSJERER SAMMEN

On the pitch – Scandinavian-born Whites:

Name	Joined	Left	Apps	Goals	Born
Casper Ankergren	2007	CP	103	0	Denmark
Eirik Bakke	1999	2007	164/32	21	Norway
Thomas Brolin	1995	1997	20/5	4	Sweden
Gylfi Einarsson	2005	2007	15/10	1	Iceland
Tore Andre Flo	2007	2008	5/19	4	Norway
Alf-Inge Haaland	1997	2000	72/20	8	Norway
Gunnar Halle	1996	1999	78/7	4	Norway
Tommy Knarvik	1999	1999	0/1	0	Norway
Teddy Lucic	2002	2003	19/2	1	Sweden
Frank Strandli	1993	1994	6/10	2	Norway

Norway

'Vi marsjerer sammen' and 'Vi er Leeds', translated from Norwegian to English, are two phrases constantly echoed around Elland Road. 'Vi er Leeds' is one you could probably have a fairly good stab at – yes, you're right, it's the title of this book – but 'Vi marsjerer sammen?' This roughly translates as 'Marching on together.' Did you get that one? In fact, what it exactly means is 'We march together,' but it is the closest translation of the most important song on the planet. Anyway, the point is that these two phrases are frequently uttered by followers of Leeds United from right across Scandinavia, where LUSCOS (Leeds United Supporters' Club of Scandinavia) boasts the largest branch of LUSC in the world. Including members from Sweden, Finland, Denmark, Iceland, the Faroe Islands and Greenland, it is an impressive membership to say the least, with just over 3,000 supporters pledging their loyalty to Leeds. And it all began in a little place called Fredrikstad, about an hour's drive south of the Norwegian capital Oslo, way back in 1980.

At just 18 years of age, Arild Bekken and Thorbjorn Lerfald decided it was time that this part of the world got a White makeover. Lerfald you could say was *the* founder member, having noticed an advert in a Norwegian football magazine inviting people to join the first supporters' club in the region for Leeds United.

Lerfald approached the man who had placed the advert in the magazine, but was told by him that because of the large response to the advert, he had changed his mind and decided it was going to be too much to take on.

He was willing to help Lerfald out, though, by handing over the list of 200 names that had contacted him to join a proposed branch. Without hesitation, Lerfald mailed every single person on the list and, together with his friend Bekken, LUSCON (Leeds United Supporters' Club of Norway), as it was known then, was born. All 200 members immediately jumped on board, but at that time it was difficult to get information from Elland Road, so to keep in touch with their favourite football team was not exactly the easiest of tasks. There was no Sky television in those days and live football was something that only really happened in major Cup Finals or internationals, so Bekken and Lerfald worked tirelessly to keep their members informed as to what was happening at Elland Road.

They gathered information from the club, including any news on transfers and particularly match reports and then manually wrote and printed newsletters, which they sent out to all the members. For all their hard work, membership in those days cost just 30 kroner, or £2.50 in sterling. The branch grew and grew and at one stage, when the club were enjoying their run to the semi-finals of the Champions League in 2001, membership rose to almost 4,000. And one such member, who will never jump ship like some have since the club slipped from being one of the top four sides in Europe, Svend Anders Karlsen-Moum can thank founder member Thorbjorn Lerfald for his undying love for the Yorkshire club. Lerfald has a son called Fredrik Lerfald, and it is Svend's friendship with Fredrik since kindergarten that has led to his long and never-ending adventure with Leeds United.

'When I was eight years old, I had my first trip to Leeds with his family,' explained Svend. 'I saw Leeds beat Wimbledon 4–0 and I still remember that very well. Gary Speed and Gary McAllister both scored two goals and one from "Macca" was a terrific free-kick. Since then my relationship with Leeds United has only grown.'

Dedication is part of the vocabulary of any Leeds United supporter and Svend typifies such passion in quantities way beyond the call of duty. The list of tasks that Svend carries out for LUSCOS is quite unbelievable and only someone with an undying love could perform so many duties purely for his own enjoyment. He writes for the branch magazine, which is called *The Peacock News*, writing stories on junior players, new signings and members, and he also has his own column. He writes most of the stories for the very impressive LUSCOS website (www.luscos.com) and is the spokesperson to the media for the branch. He is responsible for getting people gathered around Scandinavia together on match days and events, and he is also the guide on some of the trips the branch make to Elland Road. You would think that because of all this, Karlsen-Moum must be of a fairly mature age, taking all this responsibility on, but no, he is only 25 years old and has been an active member within the branch since the age of just 16.

'I remember my first-ever task for the supporters' club,' he said. 'It was to do an interview with Mark Viduka just after he signed, on their pre-season tour in Sweden. I was dead nervous but the Duke is a fantastic man and it went great. We had a four-page story on him after that. I went on the board of LUSCOS in Autumn 2005, aged 21. All the other board members are a lot older than me though, and it's not that often to have board members this young. But hey, I'm in for it with my heart, so why not? Everything I do for LUSCOS is unpaid, I do this because I like to. The only person who gets paid is the editor of *The Peacock News*, Sverre Robech, because of all his time with the magazine.'

Svend and his friend Trond Kasin, who is also passionate about Leeds, took their dedication one step further when they applied for and got places at Leeds Metropolitan University. Sadly, they stayed just one year due to finances, and it just happened to be the year that saw relegation from the Premiership at the end of the campaign.

'We got our season tickets and we got accepted at Uni. Unfortunately, we picked the wrong season to move over, but it really was fantastic to go to Elland Road for every home match and shout out our hearts every time. I'm the screaming kind of guy whilst watching Leeds, I get excited – happy and angry. We were in the Kop, of course. I don't believe I've been more proud of being a Leeds fan than when we played our last few matches of that season [2003–04]. I went to the Reebok Stadium and watched us get relegated, but I was damn proud to be a Leeds supporter that day. The following weekend we filled up Elland Road against Charlton and we showed that this club is made by the best fans in the world. I'm so proud to be a part of that, whatever division and wherever we go.'

Since Svend and his friend returned to their native country they do not see Leeds as often as they would like, but they still make the massive effort of organising trips to Elland Road from Norway, which is no mean feat. He continued, 'A standard weekend trip goes from Friday till Monday. If you live around Oslo you can fly directly to Manchester airport, which takes just under two hours. But there are lots of flights, especially the cheaper ones, which go to London, Newcastle or Leeds/Bradford. They often go via other airports, though, which makes the journey longer.

'Norway and Scandinavia is a big place, so people far from Oslo have to fly from their place to Oslo first or find flights from their place to somewhere in the UK, so on an average basis I would say it usually takes half a day to travel one way. We usually go over on the Friday, explore the city and then on match day we have our regular way to Elland Road from the hotel, which means a visit to Peter Lorimer's pub the Commercial Inn. I believe you will find Norwegians in that place on a match day all the time. After the match we go out for a meal and enjoy ourselves.'

One way of getting a lot of members together and members from many other supporters' clubs throughout Norway is a football tournament held in Oslo, which LUSCOS has entered since its inaugural year in 1991. The Scandinavian Whites have won the tournament twice – in 1996 and 1998 – and there is an overall League table of all the clubs, with LUSCOS standing proud in second place. With 58 teams having been involved stretching back 18 years, LUSCOS are sitting just two places behind leaders Exeter City in the all-time table, which is a great credit to the branch.

Here is the full all-time table (please note how far down Man Utd are!):

Pos	Team	Pld	W	D	L	F	A	Pts
1	Exeter City	93	64	16	13	212	- 55	208
2	Celtic	86	50	27	9	179	- 55	177
3	**Leeds United**	**93**	**51**	**16**	**26**	**184**	**-107**	**169**
4	Arsenal	85	49	20	16	166	- 91	167
5	Wolverhampton Wanderers	86	48	15	23	200	- 90	159
6	Nottingham Forest	77	44	21	12	164	- 68	153
7	Liverpool	86	45	16	25	178	-107	151
8	Manchester City	77	39	14	24	139	- 98	131
9	Queens Park Rangers	76	36	18	22	158	-102	126
10	MK Dons (tidl. Wimbledon)	65	34	18	13	109	- 56	120
11	Birmingham City	66	31	10	25	109	-104	103
12	Everton	67	32	6	29	104	- 84	102
13	Man Utd	74	27	12	35	131	-121	93
14	Tottenham Hotspur	60	26	9	25	84	-119	87
15	West Ham United	65	23	11	31	106	-132	80
16	Burnley	60	22	13	25	91	- 81	79
17	Derby County	58	23	8	27	85	98	77
18	Scarborough	45	20	14	11	96	- 58	74
19	Stoke City	54	17	14	23	68	- 76	65
20	Macclesfield Town	47	19	6	22	68	- 83	63
21	Luton Town	44	17	11	16	70	- 70	62

Pos	Team	Pld	W	D	L	F		A	Pts
22	Southampton	45	16	7	22	73	-	76	55
23	Barnet	41	15	6	20	89	-	86	51
24	Newcastle United	40	15	6	19	77	-	75	51
25	Blackburn Rovers	31	15	5	11	50	-	39	50
26	Crystal Palace	54	13	11	30	66	-	124	50
27	Leicester City	29	13	4	12	64	-	70	43
28	Norwich City	40	11	6	23	48	-	126	39
29	AFC Wimbledon	19	11	5	3	30	-	10	38
30	Woking	25	11	2	12	42	-	42	35
31	Aston Villa	31	8	9	14	42	-	69	33
32	Chelsea	35	9	6	20	32	-	66	33
33	Ipswich Town	51	10	2	39	48	-	157	32
34	Accrington Stanley	10	9	1	0	39	-	11	28
35	Cheltenham Town	20	7	3	10	18	-	20	24
36	West Bromwich Albion	22	6	4	12	15	-	50	22
37	Middlesbrough	21	6	3	12	44	-	52	21
38	Sheffield Wednesday	22	5	5	12	26	-	42	20
39	Bolton Wanderers	19	5	3	11	18	-	37	18
40	Portsmouth	10	4	1	5	10	-	9	13
41	Rushden & Diamonds	12	2	3	7	10	-	20	9
42	Tranmere Rovers	6	2	1	3	10	-	14	7
43	Stockport County	12	2	1	9	11	-	28	7
44	AFC Bournemouth	16	1	4	11	17	-	44	7
45	Dagenham & Redbridge	7	2	0	5	9	-	11	6
46	Charlton Athletic	3	1	1	1	3	-	3	4
47	Sunderland	9	0	3	6	10	-	18	3
48	Millwall	5	1	0	4	4	-	20	3
49	Brentford	9	1	0	8	1	-	17	3
50	Torquay United	12	1	0	11	4	-	39	3
51	Scunthorpe United	10	1	0	9	6	-	49	3
52	Hull City	3	0	1	2	4	-	6	1
53	Rochdale	3	0	1	2	1	-	8	1
54	Wigan Athletic	6	0	1	5	2	-	14	1
55	Coventry City	6	0	1	5	0	-	21	1
56	Fulham	9	0	1	8	0	-	28	1
57	Leyton Orient	2	0	0	2	0	-	4	0
58	Cardiff City	3	0	0	3	0	-	11	0

Third place was never good enough for one famous Scandinavian Leeds United supporter, however. He now resides in London and when he was in his prime, travelling the globe year in, year out, he would arm himself with racket and ball and practically blow away anyone who dared to stand in his way on a tennis court, particularly for two weeks of the year in the south of the capital. Every year at the end of June and the beginning of July Wimbledon welcomed one of its greatest stars in Stefan Edberg, and on three occasions he walked away with the big prize as Men's Singles Champion.

Other famous Scandinavian Whites include Tore Pederson, the former footballer who donned such shirts as Blackburn, Wimbledon and Oldham Athletic, and Frode Estil, who was the World and Olympic Champion in cross-country skiing. Per Gessle is another from the Nordic countries – he of Roxette fame, who is now a solo artist and has released a total of seven solo albums. There is no doubting who is the funniest of the Scandinavian celebrity Whites, though. It has to be the famous commentator Bjorge Lillelien. Lillelien was the voice behind the hilarious commentary when Norway famously beat England in a World Cup Qualifier in 1981. The Norwegian White simply could not hold back his overwhelming feelings of emotion that his national side had beaten England, and, almost losing his voice, came out with, 'Lord Nelson! Lord Beaverbrook! Sir Winston Churchill! Sir Anthony Eden! Clement Attlee! Henry Cooper! Lady Diana! Maggie Thatcher! Can you hear me Maggie Thatcher? Your boys took one hell of a beating – a hell of a beating!' It was 2–1.

On the subject of famous Scandinavian Whites, Jostein Flo also comes into this category. He is the brother of former Chelsea striker Toré Andre, who, of course, ended up wearing a Leeds shirt himself, scoring on his debut against West Bromwich Albion in a 2–3 Championship Elland Road defeat in January 2007. Toré retired from football during the 2007–08 season, and I am sure every Leeds fan would wish the popular striker a deserved rest from the game. His brother Jostein played for a number of clubs including Sheffield United, and on one occasion, before they were due to play Leeds at Bramall Lane, he was told by his boss Dave 'Harry' Bassett that he would be up against David Wetherall. Flo then left Bassett flabbergasted when he turned round to his boss and named Wetheralls' birthplace, his birthday, how many games he had played and how many goals he had scored. Flo then felt the wrath of Bassett's tongue, when the gaffer found a copy of *The Peacock News* in his bag!

It is an enormous following from the Nordic regions and here are a few tales from these passionate Scandinavian Whites. When Leeds visited Norway in 1997 and played against Steinkjer, Frode Resve took the opportunity to watch his very first Leeds United game live. 'I remember that I was excited to see Alf-Inge Haaland and Gunnar Halle play for Leeds. But I was a bit disappointed when Haaland was injured and couldn't play the match. I was also excited to see how good they were. Were Leeds able to run over the Steinkjer team that was strengthened with the best players in the region? The stadium was crowded that day. Let me assume that there were 1,500 supporters there, mostly Leeds supporters. Supporters came from all around the country. Some had travelled over 1,000km to be at the match. I went there with my father and brother, but at the stadium I met many of my friends. I think that all my friends that are a little interested in football were there. I can't remember very much of the match, I think that Leeds won 6–0 or something. But something burned in to my memory forever – Lucas Radebe. He changed my opinion about him as a player. Before that day I thought that he was an ordinary player, but he was so good. He stopped every ball and man that came near him. He was good with his head, with his feet and read the game very well. I will never forget Gary Kelly that day as well. He was so passionate and enthusiastic. I don't remember if he was captain or not, but he pushed his teammates to perform 110 per cent despite it being a training match in pre-season. I think that Rod Wallace scored a few goals. I didn't take any pictures, and I regret that to this day. Almost all my friends that are Leeds supporters (and supporters of other English clubs) often play *Championship Manager* and *Football Manager* on the computer. These kind of games increase the interest of English clubs. I play regularly with some of my friends and I can say that this keeps us up-to-date on tables, new players, injuries *et cetera*.'

Frode's all-time Leeds XI plus three subs is as follows:

Nigel Martyn, Gary Kelly, Tony Dorigo, David Batty, Lucas Radebe, Chris Fairclough, Gordon Strachan, Lee Bowyer, Lee Chapman, Gary McAllister, Gary Speed. Subs: Ian Harte, Rod Wallace, Tony Yeboah.

Terje Hagen enjoyed his first experience watching Leeds in the flesh in 1991, when the Whites travelled down to Wimbledon for a game that turned out to be a goalless affair at Selhurst Park. Leeds were top of the League at the time, but it is his first visit to Elland Road that sticks in the mind more, as he explains, 'It was Leeds against Manchester City in March 1993. We won 1–0 with a goal from David Rocastle, which was one of the two goals he scored for us. I was pretty excited, even though I was on my own. My wife and I had a holiday in London and I took the train up to Leeds and back. I met some Leeds fans on the train going back to London, who thought that the result was good but not the match. I didn't agree but it was my first game in Leeds so any game would have been good for me! I don't remember exactly when I started supporting Leeds but I do remember it was the year we won the League in 1974, and I remember that bad European Cup Final versus Bayern Munich in 1975. From that moment on there was never any doubt what my team was going to be. I went to the Chelsea game the season we were relegated and the atmosphere was brilliant, even if we were at the bottom of the table. About 30 Norwegians travelled together to Elland Road for this match and with the drawn result [1–1, Jermaine Pennant scoring], we were hoping that the bad days were over and the table-climbing had started. Since Chelsea is one of the 'hate' teams, it was electric when we scored and had the lead during the break. We could feel relief when we talked to people in the city that night and thought the good days were to come.'

Terje is maybe a little shy and prefers not to sing at matches, but that is not to say he is not as passionate about Leeds as those who *do* sing. 'I don't sing but I get chills down my neck when I hear *Marching on Together* from the terraces, even at home in my TV-chair. And at the few games I've been to I almost get tears in my eyes. I think it's a good song for singing and it's our own. No other team has the same song, that's important for our fans. It's a bit like in Norway when Leeds go away as well. You become a bit more 'crazy' at away games. You are a gang together and make a bit of noise to have fun to make the trip worth it in a way. In Norway at home matches you are more afraid of what the neighbours think when they see you yelling and shouting and singing, rather than in away matches where you normally don't meet people that you know. But, of course, there are fans that have to see games and support the team anyway and they are very important to the club. The club and players should be more aware of them and take notice and appreciate them.' Of course, any trip for Terje to Leeds is hardly a 'home' game for him, and he describes his occasional Elland Road jaunts as being both wonderful and at the same time strange experiences. 'Normally in Norway when you see the name "Leeds" it's about football, but staying in the city with Leeds signs everywhere, it is a strange feeling. To be there and see that Leeds was more than football and see that not everybody in Leeds were football fans was strange. Back home in pre-season just before the 2005–06 season, I was in Haugesund [Leeds lost 1 0] and it was very nice to see all those "middle-aged" men, like myself, in Leeds shirts and scarves, not only at the game but in the whole of the town. Even the day after the match I met some English Leeds supporters many miles inside the country admiring the mountains and waterfalls. They told me they have been to every Leeds game since the mid-1970s. And they were interested in the nature as well. It's extremely inspiring to meet these kind of supporters.'

And as for his all time Leeds side, with three on the bench?

Nigel Martyn, Paul Reaney, Ian Harte, Billy Bremner, Lucas Radebe, Norman Hunter, Gordon Strachan, Allan Clarke, Peter Lorimer, Tony Currie, Harry Kewell. Subs: David Batty, Eddie Gray, Jimmy Floyd Hasselbaink.

Arne Flatin should definitely go and see Leeds much more often. In fact, he should never miss a match. Alright, he has only been to five games, but he is yet to see Leeds lose. A lucky omen? Possibly. He is a bit of a celebrity himself in his native country as well, working as a live radio commentator covering Norway's Premier League games for the Norwegian Broadcasting Corporation NRK. He is also the chief of the newsdesk for NRK in Aalesund. He began supporting Leeds in the mid-1970s and in 1991 his dream was fulfilled, making the trip over the North Sea for his first live game, at home to Liverpool. It is not very often Leeds get the better of the red part of Merseyside, but with 'Lucky Arne' in tow there was always a chance. And sure enough, a Steve Hodge goal was enough to separate the two sides in what was to become Leeds's Championship season. 'It was fantastic,' reflects Arne. 'I was travelling with a friend who is a Liverpool supporter. He was the only one in the stand who didn't cheer the Leeds goal. We got tickets from a man who knows Lee Chapman, so on my ticket it's printed L. Chapman! I've still got that ticket today. The whole day was like a fairytale for me. At the age of 26 my dream of watching Leeds live was finally fulfilled. My first Leeds away game was also against Liverpool in the same season. I went with the same Liverpool-supporting friend, who got tickets in the Liverpool Kop. I'm glad I didn't have to cheer about a Leeds goal [the match ended 0–0], as I was standing among thousands of Kopites!'

So why Leeds in the first place Arne? 'At the age of 10 I saw Leeds star Peter Lorimer shooting a penalty straight through the net and I was also fascinated by the all-white strip. It just started from there really. It's very frustrating living so far from Elland Road but there are many Leeds fans in my area, so every time they are shown live on the television I send out an email to my Leeds friends and we often see the matches together. I remember going over to watch Leeds against Ipswich in a mid-week match in 1995. It was a tremendous game under the floodlights and we won 4–0 with Yeboah getting a hat-trick; Gary Speed got the other one. I spent the night at Peter Lorimer's pub. Early the next morning it was strange. I was the only guest up and he served me breakfast!'

Based on the players that he has seen, either live or on television, here is his Leeds XI with three subs:

> Nigel Martyn, Mel Sterland, Frank Gray, Billy Bremner, Gordon McQueen, Paul Madeley, Peter Lorimer, Allan Clarke, Ray Hankin, Tony Currie, David Batty. Subs: John Lukic, Eddie Gray, Duncan McKenzie.

Borge Nordal went one better than his Norwegian compatriot when he too stayed at Lorimer's Commercial Inn pub. Flying over for the QPR match on 1 May 1993, which ended in a 1–1 stalemate (Steve Hodge scoring for Leeds), Borge had what you might call a real 'up and down' trip. In the end he describes his visit to Leeds as a 'great trip' but as he explains it was not the best of starts. 'My first time in Leeds a lot of things happened. I was mugged by two guys and on the same day there was a terror bombing alarm going off in a hotel close by. We stayed at the Hilton and some guy on the street outside tried to sell us cheap Rolex watches, so it was an interesting first day for a young man of just 14. The mugging took place just across the street from the Hilton. I had no idea that there was a thing called 'travel insurance' and even less idea of the meaning of it, so I went around with all my travelling cash on me. I had some shopping bags as well with a new pair of shoes. I had no intention of giving away anything. One of the guys was standing in front of me and the other at my back. The one in front showed me a knife and spoke very fast. So I didn't have to pretend very much to make the impression of a stupid Norwegian that didn't understand them. I then stood there while he was getting more and more aggressive, pondering my next move. I was considering the possibility of beating both of them, but changed my mind about that because they were much older and looked strong. So I just ran as fast as I could, and that was pretty fast. I ran straight over the main road, which I remember as being four lanes, and I then went into the hotel and got hold of an enormous porter. He must have been the biggest and broadest man in the world. I was pretty shaken, so he came running back out in the street with me. When the guys saw us they ran for it, so I didn't lose anything, but I made a stupid and hazardous decision! I was lucky.

'Later the more positive side of the trip was going to the Commercial Inn. I played snooker against Peter Lorimer and Paul Reaney. I got a prize after winning a competition and was awarded the prize by Peter Lorimer and Sir John

Charles. I got a picture of this and for a young Leeds fan this was a great moment. To be standing there amid two of Leeds's all-time greats was amazing. The whole trip was a bit like Christmas Eve when you are really young. Everything from the smells, the people, the stadium – it was all so extraordinary. It was massive and to be at the stadium was so immense. Because everything was so new it was all so overwhelming. I travelled to Leeds once with Eirik Bakke's cousin. We went to Thorp Arch and watched the team train before the game against Portsmouth the season we were relegated. I met the whole team, as well as Eddie Gray and Kevin Blackwell. After the game against Portsmouth I was also in the players' lounge with Dominic Matteo, Eirik Bakke, Scott Carson, Alan Smith *et cetera*, which was a great moment. I also met and spoke with Chris Fairclough, John Charles, Paul Reaney and, of course, Peter [Lorimer].'

It was a bit of an 'up and down' trip for his first away game as well, although there were no muggings or potential bombs going off for that one. 'We were off to watch Blackburn versus Leeds, which was a Christmas game during the 1993–94 season. We travelled on the bus from Leeds with all the English Leeds supporters, singing all the way. It was a great atmosphere on the bus, but when we got to Ewood Park, the game was postponed due to a waterlogged pitch. When we got this sad news, some of us went to a pub close to the ground and it was crowded with Blackburn supporters. There was just five of us Leeds fans, which made it quite intimidating, but it was fine in the end. Everyone was disappointed that the game was postponed. We had some pints and talked with the Blackburn fans and then went back to Leeds.'

So, given his close encounters with some of Leeds' greatest players, it would be interesting to find out what his all-time Leeds XI is, plus three subs.

'I have to look at my era as a fan,' he says. 'From 1987 to the present. I haven't been part of the time when Bremner, Sniffer, Lorimer, Gray, Hunter and Charles *et cetera* were playing for Leeds. So for me the two outstanding players are Alan Smith, for his tenacity and dedication to Leeds until he left for Man Utd, and Gary McAllister for his football brain, beautiful passes and distribution.'

Here we go then, with the 29-year-old insurance worker's 14. Smith, you will notice, for his desertion to the dark side, is relegated to the bench:

Nigel Martyn, Gary Kelly, Tony Dorigo, David Batty, Lucas Radebe, Jonathan Woodgate, Gordon Strachan, Gary McAllister, Lee Chapman, Tony Yeboah, Gary Speed. Subs: Alan Smith, Rio Ferdinand, Mark Viduka.

Kjell Skjerven took his love for Leeds United to new levels by actually upping sticks from his Norwegian roots in a small town called Vik i Sogn to move to the city of Leeds for one whole season. Achieving a lifetime's ambition, he attended every game, home and away, during the 2004–05 season. And, of course, he was to experience his 'ups and downs' during that campaign as well. 'I took 10 months' leave to fulfil my dream of seeing Leeds for every game for one season, and the biggest 'up' was without a doubt Lucas Radebe's testimonial game. Also beating QPR at home 6–1 was great, with Brian Deane scoring four of them [David Healey and Jermaine Wright getting the other two]. Going down to Plymouth was also brilliant [won 1–0 via an own-goal], not in terms of playing against a good team but because the fans didn't stop singing all the way through the match. As for a 'down', losing 4–0 at home to Sheffield United was awful. I had a Norwegian friend of mine who came over to visit me for that game and afterwards we hardly spoke a word to each other! I remember the awful ground in Brighton. It reminded me of a Second Division ground in Norway. And the hostile reception in Cardiff. I remember Wolves because of all the police in the streets. And not to mention all the terrible results we had that season. We lost against big teams [!] like Brighton, Gillingham and Rotherham. The funniest thing for me that season was at Burnley when Brian Dean had a good chance but his shot went for a throw in!'

And his all time line up?

Nigel Martyn, Gary Kelly, Tony Dorigo, David Batty, Lucas Radebe, Dominic Matteo, Gordon Strachan, Gary McAllister, Lee Chapman, Tony Yeboah, Harry Kewell. Subs: Mark Viduka, Lee Bowyer, Gary Speed.

Chapter 15

VIKINGS, BENT REFEREES AND THE BENELUX CLAN

Iceland

A little further north and a little colder, Thorleifur Leó Ananìasson is flying the White flag in Iceland, where again the support is quite incredible. Iceland's scenery all over the country is simply awesome and the Leeds following over there is also quite staggering. The country is about the same size as the American state of Ohio and has a tiny population of just 288,000 people. Its highest peak is Hvannadalshnukur, which is 6,500ft above sea level. It has the largest glaciers in Europe. In fact, 11 per cent of the country is covered by glaciers. Some amazing landscapes include more than 10,000 waterfalls and countless hot springs. And the coastline is dotted with more than 100 fjords. The language the Icelanders speak is fascinating. Although the majority speak perfect fluent English, they also still speak the language of the Vikings (Old Norse). When new words are needed, they simply coin words that are combinations or modifications of old words. And have you ever wondered what former Leeds midfielder Gylfi Einarsson's father is called? It is easy to work out, once you know the system. The country is alone in upholding this Norse tradition, the custom of using patronyms, rather than surnames. If, for example, Einar has a son named Peter, the son's name is Peter Einarsson (Peter Einar's son). If Einar has a daughter whom he names Margaret, she becomes Margaret Einarsdottir (Margaret Einar's daughter). Members of the same family can therefore have different last names, which often causes confusion to foreigners. If you are looking for someone in the phone book, you look them up by their first name. So now you know Gylfi's dad's first name!

Leeds fans are quite literally scattered all over the world, but you would probably guess that there are no more than a handful of Icelandic Whites. This remote Viking land could not possibly harbour such fanatical support for our club, surely? Wrong. Thorleifur is from the north of the island, from a place called Akureyri. But all over Iceland, including the capital Reykjavik, there are around 500 members of the Icelandic branch of LUSC. The Ölver sports bar in the capital is where the branch hold their meetings. Once inside this establishment you would think you were just across the road from Elland Road, having good old John Smiths Yorkshire bitter readily available. Thorleifur told the official Leeds United magazine *Leeds, Leeds, Leeds* back in April 2003, 'In Iceland the support for Leeds United has grown through the years. In 1998 we set up a supporters' club here. It had 156 members but come 2002 that number had risen to 426.' The branch organises trips to Elland Road once or twice a year but, sadly for Thorleifur, he is yet to visit the ground. 'I have only been to England once, in 1999, when I stayed in Grimsby on business. I was invited to two matches, the first of which was at Old Trafford for Man Utd versus Aston Villa. The lowlight of that trip was to be so close yet so far from Elland Road. The highlight was to hear the sigh from the fans at Old Trafford at half-time when the score from West Ham versus Leeds was announced – Leeds were winning! And later when I returned to Iceland I was able to tell people 'I have pissed on Old Trafford!' My second game was at Highbury, Arsenal. My highlight there was to see former Leeds player John Lukic, Arsenal's reserve goalkeeper, warm up. And the lowlight was to see David Seaman, knowing that he was a player that we let slip from our youth system. Given the choice, rather than Man Utd or Arsenal, I would definitely have rather have seen a Leeds Reserves match!' The Viking Whites have their own website which, if your Icelandic language is up to scratch, you can find at *www.leeds.is*.

And now, at last, we are heading off to a warmer climate.

Greece

May 1973 was a bad month for all concerned with Leeds United, but at least something great came out of it. We all know what happened in the infamous Cup-Winners' Cup Final when Leeds faced an AC Milan outfit in the Greek island of Salonika. Not only were Leeds up against the Italians, we were also up against a bent referee. After making some diabolical decisions, Christos Michas was censured after the game by the European footballing hierarchy and subsequently never refereed again. It did not alter the fact that he had single-handedly won the game for the Italians, though, as Leeds were cheated out of the trophy. So Leeds travelled home empty-handed, when it should have been time to make room for another piece of silverware in the Elland Road trophy cabinet.

That particular Cup never did make it to Elland Road, but, in a strange roundabout way, a blessing in disguise took place in Salonika.

The locals were also incensed with the man in the middle during that Cup-Winners' Cup farce and decided to take sides and get behind Leeds. The referee denied Leeds three blatant penalties. Leeds totally outplayed the Italians that night and the only goal of the game came via a highly dubious Milan free-kick. When Milan emerged victorious, they were advised not to do a lap of honour, given the hostility towards them and the referee from both Leeds fans and the local Greeks following the final whistle. From that night, the Hellenic Branch of LUSC was born – albeit 26 years later! Costas Karberis is now general secretary of the Hellenic branch of LUSC, which was formed back in 1999. Each year they take part in a six-a-side tournament with supporters' clubs of other European teams, such as Lazio, Bayern Munich and Real Madrid, as well as English clubs: Liverpool, Everton, Arsenal and 'that lot'. Members such as Nikos Sarros, Dimitris Karpouzas, Costas himself, his brother George Karberis, Dimitris Theorharis, Harry Gougoulitsas, George Lioris, Perikles Gerasopoulos, John Bouhros, Socrates Karpouzas, Harry Kouzis and Panagiotis Maragos have all represented Leeds in past tournaments. And the most impressive statistic regarding LUSC Hellenic? It is the oldest of all foreign supporters' clubs in Greece. Chelsea, incidentally, have a supporters' club over in Greece now, which amazingly is just a couple of years old.

Karberis and Co. meet up at the Bulldog in Athens whenever Leeds are live on the box. One ex-pat, Jon Nuttall, recalls the time when Leeds surprised everyone and played in a mid-season friendly during the 2004–05 campaign away to Iraklis Thessaloniki. Many of the Hellenic Whites boarded a train to Iraklis, which was a seven-hour journey. On arrival they quickly found out where the team were staying and made their way to the hotel. They were thrilled to get their photos taken with Peter Lorimer as well as some of the players in the hotel reception. Manager Kevin Blackwell also made an appearance and was more than happy to chat to the locals. The team boarded their coach, bound for the ground, and the Hellenic Whites were about to order a few taxis when Blackwell asked them if they'd all got tickets for the match. 'No,' came the answer, at which point Blackwell produced a handful of complimentary tickets. After Leeds had battled out a 1–1 draw with Iraklis Thessaloniki (Paul Butler finding the net for Leeds), the Greek Whites wanted more photos and autographs, so waited by the team coach. Blackwell was again happy to chat to them, talking about the game. That was that then? No. The Hellenic Whites, who were clearly in awe of their heroes and wanted to make the most of a rare opportunity to mix with the players, then went back to the hotel again, by which time Jon Nuttall was beginning to feel slightly embarrassed. On apologising to Blackwell that it looked a little OTT from his Greek friends, the gaffer gave them another surprise. He disappeared for five minutes before returning to give everyone a handshake and a Leeds pin badge each. He was indeed a top bloke.

Belgium

Tom Vanoirbeek, his girlfriend Evi Dekens, Kristoff de Bruyne and Dirk de Maesschalck take their passion for Leeds United to new levels, setting off on their mammoth journey to Elland Road, or wherever Leeds are playing for that matter, in the very early hours of the morning. Living in St Truiden, Belgium, near the German border, it is hardly surprising their trips to watch Leeds begin in the pitch dark. There is a strong contingent of Benelux Whites, including members from Holland and Luxembourg and ex-pat journalist Martin Banks. Their journey begins with a drive to Calais, where they board Le Shuttle at 10.20am. Once on English soil, they put on a Leeds CD playing all the Leeds songs in the car, putting them in the mood for 90 minutes of White action. The journey back, if Leeds have won, is fairly comfortable to endure, but should Leeds come second, arriving home at no earlier than 2am the following morning makes it feel like the longest journey on earth. 'It's a hell of a journey,' says Tom. 'But I'm already looking forward to the next one.' That's the spirit Tom.

Chapter 16

THE EDWARDS VIEW PART II

Gary Edwards and I share the same birthday, 28 March, although I have to say I'm seven years his junior (sorry mate!). It was two days prior to his 10th birthday that he made his debut on the Elland Road terraces. Another coincidence is I was brought up in Blackpool and was a junior member of LUSC Blackpool before moving away. And who was Gary's first match against? Blackpool!

There is, however, a massive difference between the two of us. My passion for the club is enormous but I could not class myself as a superfan, which he undoubtedly is. As the song goes 'we've had our ups and downs', and Gary Edwards has seen it all. The glory years of the late 1960s and early 70s, the travesties of not having won more silverware during that time, the glum years of the 80s, the title in 1992, the rapid rise to Champions League semi-final status in 2001, the fall from grace once more, the attempted rebuilding process under the guidance of the two KBs, chairman Ken Bates and manager Kevin Blackwell, the stewardship of both Dennis Wise and Gus Poyet, the arrival and departure of one of Elland Road's favourite sons Gary McAllister and the new recruit in the gaffer's seat, Simon Grayson.

The dramatic rapid fall from grace from being one of the top four teams in Europe to relegation in the space of two years, and relegation again, had many people pointing the finger at ex-chairman Peter Ridsdale. Gary Edwards is not arguing against that.

'Although not entirely to blame, Peter Ridsdale should have taken responsibility for the financial situation at Elland Road at that time. I was invited to one of the chairman/supporters' meetings he held in the midst of the crisis. I'd met with Ridsdale on many occasions, but on this final occasion he seemed agitated and very uncomfortable. We'd been told by PR man David Walker to keep what we heard in the room between ourselves and not to "feed the press", who were gathering outside. Believe me, there was nothing to tell anyone! To put it bluntly, Ridsdale talked a load of sh**. He accepted no blame whatsoever for the present predicament and in effect, put all the blame on the manager at the time, Terry Venables, and the previous manager, David O'Leary. In fact, he referred to Venables throughout the discussion as "the manager", never once using his name. He said he regretted "deeply" his comments in which he had said that he would sooner have £9 million in the bank than 10,000 supporters. I asked him if it was true, that he was hoping and praying that Newcastle wouldn't come in at the final hour with a £9 million offer for Woodgate. He said that it was true and that if they [Newcastle] hadn't have come in for him, then they [Leeds] would have found the £9 million [which Leeds desperately needed to ward off creditors *et cetera*] from somewhere else. My immediate follow-up question of "So why the hell didn't we then?" was met with a dismissive shrug of the shoulders. He also told us that the £9 million sale of Woodgate would definitely be the last transfer of that type of figure anywhere in football, including abroad, for at least five years [Beckham's transfer from Manchester United to Real Madrid blew Ridsdale's statement clean out of the water]. I suggested to him that at least it meant we wouldn't be selling anyone else then? He just laughed and said "it was nothing to do with me". Good riddance Ridsdale, God help whichever club he's at!'

Having seen everything for more than 40 years makes it tough to single out the highest single achievement, but Gary does so nonetheless.

'The highest point of watching Leeds is difficult to pin-point, but I think winning the League Championship in 1974 and manchester united getting relegated the very same season will take some beating. Watching Leeds at the beginning of that season was an absolute privilege. It also saw the team at their very best. They went 29 games unbeaten and to see the look on the opposing fans' faces each week was brilliant.'

And the other end of the spectrum?

'Getting relegated in 1982 was hard, so too was coming so close in 1987 to promotion and FA Cup glory. Losing in extra-time against Charlton and also in extra-time against Coventry in the FA Cup semi-final was very disappointing. Ironically, during the 1980s the support was second to none. Towards the end of the '80s Elland Road's atmosphere was great. Visiting supporters were penned into the lower South East corner and completely intimidated by Leeds fans in the Lowfields, South Stand, the Geldard End and even Section B in the West Stand. Alan Ball once described it as a "cauldron of hate" when he came as Portsmouth's manager. Sadly, the Leeds directors didn't quite relish the atmosphere and as we turned into the '90s they set about splitting large groups of Leeds fans up and eventually leaving Elland Road, for the most part, resembling a cemetery. The Leeds directors were responsible for killing the atmosphere at Elland Road. Consciously splitting large groups of vocal supporters up to create a "family atmosphere". I'm all for families and youngsters attending games, that's how I started, but it should be arranged in such a way as not to interfere with the overall atmosphere. When I started going without my dad, I would go in the "boys' pen" in the Lowfields Road for three bob. There were a few dads about but it was mainly all young lads together. The noise at the ground was electric at times as we young un's would watch (and sometimes join in) in awe as the chanting all round the ground would encourage the white shirts on the pitch. Supporting Leeds in the '80s, particularly away, was something special. So too was the fantastic support the team received in Europe during the UEFA Cup in 1999, 2000 and 2002 and the Champions League in 2001.'

The following in the 1970s was also quite phenomenal; although, as Gary explains, it was marred by trouble week in, week out.

'In the 1970s violence was commonplace. I was once travelling on a service train to a Wolves away match with half a dozen of the lads. I can't remember why we didn't go on the "special", but anyway when we pulled up at Dewsbury station, hundreds of man utd fans got on. They noticed us straight away and believe it or not they were calling us Yorkshire bastards! We barricaded ourselves in the compartment with seats but when the train pulled up at Huddersfield, twice as many more of them got on. Another couple of stops further on, Stalybridge, we decided to get off. We charged at one of the doors and fought our way through them, they were a little taken aback as we exchanged punches before jumping off the train, which was now pulling out of the station.

'I got a good hiding at Maine Road on Boxing Day 1975. It used to be about a two-mile walk back to the coaches in those days and if you wandered from the main pack of Leeds fans you could be easy pickings for the hundreds of City fans following behind. Two other lads and me did just that, and about 20 City fans suddenly surrounded us, one of the lads ran off, the other was a midget. Despite being two years older than me he was only about 4ft tall. He started crying and thinking he was only about seven years old, the City fans turned their attention to me. I received a couple of severe kickings before a group of Leeds fans appeared around the corner.

'The 1976 pre-season tournament in Amsterdam was another hairy time. Four teams were in the tournament, Leeds, Ajax, Anderlecht and Mönchengladbach. During the first game, some Leeds fans set fire to the Dutch national flag. This didn't really help the relationship between our Dutch hosts and us and fighting continued throughout the game and during the second game two days later. Outside the Leeds end afterwards we encountered continuous fighting all the way into the city centre from Ajax fans, bikers and large numbers of the Chinese and black communities. Several of both sides finished up in hospital. We've had some right ding-dongs at Chelsea, West Ham and Tottenham, as well as across Stanley Park with Everton and Liverpool. Newcastle was always a guaranteed rumble, the same at Sunderland. Derby fans always had a brave attempt at the Leeds fans that always heavily outnumbered them. It was similar at Burnley. Stoke fans used to ambush us as we passed a graveyard near the coaches. Middlesbrough fans used the same tactics. In fact, looking back, there wasn't many grounds where it didn't kick off.'

It is fair to say that Leeds United had a reputation for causing trouble in the 1970s and '80s, but there are two clubs that are worse – two sides that continue to cause mayhem on many occasions, and it appears that neither club is concerned with cleaning up its act. Cardiff City, the ever-so-insecure Welsh outfit, who have an enormous bag of King Edwards on their shoulder, and Galatasaray, a club that is so despicable it is hard to describe such vile supporters, who should simply be banned from anywhere in the world.

Gary sums up these two disgraceful sets of football fans perfectly.

'Cardiff first. […] tension [between the Welsh and the English] rose to the fore like I have never before witnessed, during and after the Cardiff/Leeds FA Cup clash at Cardiff in January 2002. To make matters even worse it wasn't just the Cardiff fans, it was the police as well. Charging officers attacked dozens of Leeds fans in the coach park and the treasurer of the official Leeds United Supporters' Club was attacked and badly injured by police dogs. I asked a policeman what was going on and after covering his shoulder badge up so I couldn't read his number he told me "F*** off, you shouldn't be here." Many other Leeds fans were called "English bastards" by the police, and after complaining to the South Wales police I received a letter from a Superintendent Twigg (which I still have). It was merely a token gesture and the couple of letters I received made it pretty clear that it would be nigh-on impossible to prove anything but I was to "feel free to pursue the matter further if I so desired." After the game, led by a totally deplorable Sam Hamman, the Cardiff fans swarmed the pitch and raced across to taunt the Leeds fans. When Leeds fans reacted angrily and began scaling the fence to confront the Welsh fans, police attacked them with batons. All the time the police video cameras were trained only on the Leeds contingent, while thousands and thousands of Cardiff fans caused havoc unrecorded and ignored by the police. Had this riot occurred at Elland Road, there is absolutely no doubt whatsoever, Leeds would have been kicked out of the FA Cup instantly. Three months later Cardiff were fined just £20,000.

'Another club who seemingly do as they like is Galatasaray of Turkey. When Leeds met them in the UEFA Cup semi-final it was totally unbelievable. There has been trouble at several European games, involving a number of English clubs, staged at Galatasaray, but apparently they remain immune to punishment. I arrived in Istanbul on a plane full of Leeds fans at around 11.45 the night before the game. As our coach was been escorted by siren-blasting police vans, news began filtering through to people's mobile phones that there had been some trouble in the centre of Istanbul. Reports then followed that there had been fatalities, but how many was unknown. When we arrived at our hotel we learned that two people, both from Leeds, had been killed in the trouble. As about a dozen of us moved from bar to bar, closely followed everywhere by a police van, we picked up additional news on the killings, but as yet no one knew for sure what had happened or who the two Leeds fans were. All the time we were out, everyone's phone was going off with calls from home to see if they were ok. We returned to the hotel at around 7am (still followed by our yawning escort), had a quick shower and returned to the reception to try and find out some more on last night's incident. When the names of the two Leeds fans were announced I was stunned. Kevin "Spag" Speight was a good Leeds fan and I'd had more than one beer with him on our European travels. Christopher Loftus was another top supporter and only a few years previously I had attended his brother's wedding. I was sat in a chair in the lobby trying to take it all in when our organiser, Mick Hewitt, told us all that our party of 50 was under "hotel arrest" and we would not be allowed to leave until shortly before tonight's kick-off, under escort. We found out later that Leeds fans all over the city had been confined to their hotels. Despite our protests that we couldn't possibly have had anything to do with the disturbance, a heavily armed police force remained outside the hotel all day. We were told that as a goodwill gesture there would be a reduction in the beer price at the bar. It was easy to contain our excitement. By 1pm the bar had run dry and a phone call to the local brewery resulted in a lorry full of beer dashing through the traffic and replenishing our supply.

'On our way to the match our coach was completely surrounded by police vans, cars and bikes. However, our escort mysteriously disappeared as we drew near to the ground and we were pelted by bricks, stones and bottles and hundreds of crazy Turks banged on the side of our coach, many demonstrating the familiar "finger across the throat" gesture. When about the fourth brick came flying through our window, some of us had had enough. The back door was opened and we jumped off the coach screaming at the Turks. To our amazement they backed off and many of them scattered. Baton-wielding police

Author Andy Starmore and Jack Charlton in April 2009.

Russell and Harry Starmore in Leeds kits.

The Isle of Man Leeds fans just off the boat.

Paul and Sandra Morley from the Isle of Man.

Jermaine Beckford looks down on five die-hards at the Seabourne Pub, Bournemouth.

Bournemouth and Leeds fans.

John Sullivan and his daughter, Kaelin Rivillas, from Port Laoise.

David Flanagan and Paul Talbot with the certificate from Leeds United, Port Laoise.

John Nugent from Port Laoise with Lucas the Kop Kat.

Paul Murphy (in Leeds shirt) and the Irish Whites.

Peter Lorimer (left) and Colm O'Hara, Port Laoise.

The Hampshire Whites celebrate victory over Preston in the Play-off semi-final second leg in 2006.

LUSCNA in California.

Ian and Regina Bloom with their daughter Laura in Brazil.

Steve Richardson and his son Aiden of the Pennsylvania Whites with Eddie Lewis.

Andy Pinder from Kansas with Dave Prutton.

London Whites with Satoshi Tamura.

Satoshi with Jermaine Beckford.

Satoshi Tamura Japan fun run.

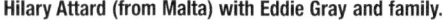

Ken Bates (Leeds chairman), Mrs Bates, Satoshi Tamura and Angela Schofield.

Hilary Attard (from Malta) with Eddie Gray and family.

A posh Russian white.

Peruvian Leeds fans currently living in Canada.

Wellington Kufinya (Zimbabwe).

Norwegian Whites.

Svend Anders Karlsen-Moum (left) and Rune Roalsvig (who produce a Norwegian Leeds magazine called *The Peacock News*).

Svend Anders Karlsen-Moum with Leslie Silver (former Leeds chairman).

Scandinavian Leeds fans.

Andy Starmore, Frank van Grunsven (Holland) and Gary Edwards.

Leeds fans boarding a blue, yellow and white plane for a European match.

Leeds fans on a train to an away match.

The Leeds end at the Millennium Stadium for the Championship Play-off Final against Watford, 2006.

The crowd at Wembley for the League One Play-off Final on 24 May 2008 against Doncaster, lost 0–1.

appeared from nowhere and ushered us back onto the bus. On our way to the stadium in the coach we had to endure a barrage of missiles, all watched by smiling policemen. Once inside the ground around 600 Leeds fans [many others had been grounded in England and refused permission to travel] began to make their presence felt. Me and Webby unfurled my large flag and it was greeted by boos and whistles from the home supporters – it read, "Hello Hell, We are Leeds!" The Leeds team emerged from under a tunnel of police riot shields wearing black armbands; the Galatasaray team refused to wear them. Not only that, but they also refused to hold a minute's silence, claiming afterwards that the incident wasn't football related. As their own mark of respect, the Leeds fans turned their back on the pitch for a minute's silence. As the Turks continued throughout to throw the odd missile and drag their fingers across their throats, the police surrounding us simply laughed at us. It was unreal. The game was a complete non-event and afterwards we headed for our coaches, escorted by our smiling police friends. As Leeds fans boarded their coaches, ours was nowhere to be seen. After about an hour, with the rest of the coaches long gone we were still stood waiting for our coach. We were still surrounded. A police tank drew alongside us and after a discussion with one of our escorts it was revealed that our coach had refused to come back for us. He had called us "Loco!" for jumping off the back of the coach and said he would not carry us again because "we were dangerous" – absolutely unbelievable! Ten minutes later we boarded a police coach, which had about half a dozen officers on board. On our way back to the hotel one of the lads was chatting with one of the coppers, when he took hold of his high-velocity machine gun. Everyone on board ducked as Palmer swung round with the gun and began pointing it out of the window, "Come on, ya Turkish bastards!" he shouted. All the time the owner of the gun, who was still in his teens, smiled affectionately. Palmer then gave him back the machine gun and was allowed to take his pistol from its side holster. With both hands firmly clenched around the handle he repeated his war cry to the Turks walking by. "Yes, this is me!" he snarled. I swear, all the police on board never batted an eyelid.

'Reading the newspapers the next morning, it became all too apparent that the Turkish people and media in general weren't that affected by the murders of the two Leeds fans. Pictures of Kevin's uncovered body were splashed all over the pages. The next day we were still under hotel arrest but we'd had enough and a dozen of us escaped through the hotel restaurant's back door. We went on a boat trip around the harbour and we were wearing Leeds shirts, but there was no mention of the incident two nights earlier. It was as if nothing had happened.

At the time, I personally wanted the game to go ahead. I felt very angry and wanted the Leeds players to take revenge on the pitch. However, in hindsight I feel that the game should not have been played. The players were obviously deeply affected on the night. Peter Ridsdale handled the whole affair with great dignity at the time and even on our next trip to Istanbul against Besiktas in the Champions League. He met every one of the arriving Leeds fans at the airport and thanked them for coming.'

Of course, Cardiff City and Galatasaray are held in a high degree of contempt by Leeds United supporters, and, come to think of it, any decent football fan, but it is 'that lot' from the other side of the Pennines that will always remain way ahead in the dislike stakes. And Gary is no different to anyone else who follows the Whites – in fact, he probably is different. He hates them so much, those words 'Manchester United' have not passed his lips for more than 30 years and you can bet your life on him never uttering them ever again in his lifetime.

'I hate manchester united,' he says (in the written words only!) with simple but effective venom. So, go on then Gary, we all hate them, but in your particular case – why?

'It's difficult to pinpoint any one particular reason for my hatred, but it certainly isn't jealousy. We [Leeds] used to beat them almost every time we played them in the 1960s and early '70s and I hated them then. I think it's a combination of their arrogance and attitude. Seemingly, everything has to revolve around them. Very few, if any, penalties are awarded against them, and can anyone explain to me how they win the Fair Play Trophy as often as they do? A survey once revealed referee Mike Riley's obvious love of the club with an amazing detailed account of his last 10 or so games in charge of manchester united. On the other hand, any referee who dares to cross Ferguson and his merry men will feel the full force of the FA (that's the Ferguson Association, a much higher body than the Football Association). I'm a big fan of Her Majesty the Queen and I have a large portrait of her hanging in my lounge, but when she knighted Ferguson I immediately took her picture down and placed her in a cupboard under the stairs. She remained there for two weeks and after the second week I opened the cupboard door. Her eyes flickered as she was exposed to the bright light, I told her I still wasn't happy and I closed the door and left her there for a further week. She'll think twice in future, before doing anything as stupid.

'When Gordon McQueen & Joe Jordan went to manchester united I was slightly annoyed and upset. Our manager at the time was Jimmy Armfield. Jimmy was a brilliant manager but was a bit of a soft touch with the players. His assistant Don Howe was the one who laid down the rules and told the players what was expected of them. When Howe left, it wasn't long afterwards that McQueen and Jordan went across the Pennines.

'I still blame Howard Wilkinson for the Cantona saga. Wilko, in my opinion had lost his marbles by this time anyway, but to give our rivals the missing ingredient that they needed was certifiable. It is often said that "one man doesn't make a team". This disproves that theory. manchester united were going absolutely nowhere, until the French one [who once lied to Leeds fans, telling us he loved us] joined them. Ferdinand was never really Leeds and is just a greedy bastard and good riddance. When Ferdinand, I refuse to call him by his first name ever again, joined "them" we were told by the "Truth Doctor" [Ridsdale] that we had only bought Ferdinand as a "stop gap" to compensate for Jonathan Woodgate's absence. I, along with all the other "donkey ear"-wearing Leeds fans, believed him. That is why it was devastating to see Woodgate given away to Newcastle. I was disappointed when Batty had "an affair" with Blackburn and Newcastle before getting his brain back and returning to Yorkshire. I was saddened by his departure. I still feel that Wilkinson should have stood his ground and refused to sell him. We had just won the League and he [Wilko] was in a strong position but he allowed good old Bill Fotherby to offload Batty and replace him with none other than Carlton Palmer! I was so disgusted whenever I saw the red rose of Lancashire over Batty's left tit on the Blackburn shirt that at times I couldn't eat my tea. Batty didn't get a very good reception at all whenever he came back to Elland Road. It got steadily worse as time passed as well, and it reached boiling point once at Elland Road when he played for Newcastle. He went over the top and left Gary Speed writhing in agony. The angry chants of "F*** Off Batty! F*** Off Batty!" seemed unreal. I was upset when Noel Whelan was sold but not half as disappointed as Whelan himself. I didn't want to sell David Wetherall, and again the player himself didn't want to go. Another player who clearly didn't want to go was Vinnie Jones. One player always guaranteed a great reception was Jones. He's the Top Man as far as Leeds fans are concerned. He always gave the "Leeds Salute" whenever he played against us after his transfer, and he's got a Leeds tattoo on his leg! Another ex-Leeds player familiar to the "Leeds Salute" is Noel Whelan. It was really comical watching Boro fans get wound up as he saluted Leeds fans who were singing, "Whelan is a Leeds fan, nah nah nah nah!" Chris Whyte received a standing ovation as he did a lap of honour after his side, Rushden & Diamonds, had been beaten at Elland Road in the FA Cup a few years back. David Wetherall is another player still in Leeds fans' hearts. One of my old favourites and a good friend of the Kippax Branch, Gary McAllister, always got a bad reception.

Hasselbaink gets what he deserves. Obviously Ferdinand got some stick, as did Cantona, but they go without saying.'

We have digressed somewhat. What about when Gordon Strachan came to his senses and *left* Manchester United to come and play for us?

'Gordon Strachan was brilliant for Leeds, there is no doubt whatsoever about that. Most Leeds fans took to him almost immediately (the younger fans in general) but a hardcore of fans (myself included) took a little more persuading. I remember before the first game of the 1991–92 season, he wrote in the newspapers, "There is only one United on this year's Championship trophy and it is not us". I, along with many others, felt a bit miffed. He was supposed to be a Leeds player now, what was he playing at? Anyway, as we all know Leeds United won the Championship and Strachan lifted the trophy. It was a slow process, Strachan went from very red to red, red to pink, pink to pale pink, very pale pink to off white and finally off white to WHITE, but he was still on probation. If he'd made any more references to his old employers we'd have turned on him. I needn't have worried.'

Another club that hates Manchester United as much as Leeds do is Liverpool, and, as Gary explains, Leeds and Liverpool have a kind of bond that stretches back some 40 years.

'Back in 1969, Leeds won their first League title by getting a vital point at Anfield in a 0–0 draw in the penultimate game. After the game, as Leeds celebrated with the Leeds fans, the Liverpool Kop began chanting "Champions! Champions!" in honour of Leeds United. Revie sent the Leeds team to the other end and the scenes were quite unbelievable. The Liverpool fans continued to chant and applaud the victorious Leeds team. Although not quite as friendly these days, a fairly close affinity between the clubs still exists. There were reports that at the end of the 1991–92 season, during the Liverpool game with manchester united, the Kop were again chanting the Leeds name, as we won the title, the same day, at Sheffield United. Don Revie and Bill Shankly were always very close and so too were David O'Leary and Gerard Houllier.'

In 1979 Liverpool visited Elland Road already crowned champions, but they had to beat Leeds on a Friday night to overtake us for the record amount of points (two points for a win in those days). Two goals from David Johnson and one from Jimmy Case inflicted a 3–0 defeat on our boys, at the same time stealing our proud record of 67 points, upping the record to 68. The Leeds faithful returned the 10-year-old compliment by applauding the Liverpool side after the game as they did *their* lap of honour.

Chapter 17

FROM OSS TO BEESTON

BYPASSING PSV

On the pitch – Dutch-born Whites:

Name	Joined	Left	Apps	Goals
Jimmy Floyd Hasselbaink	1997	1999	84/3	42
Willem Korsten	1999	1999	6/4	2
Robert Molenaar	1997	2000	60/5	6

Holland

Dutch football has always been one to admire over the years. Ajax had a fantastic team in the early 1970s, winning the European Cup three times in a row between 1971 and 1973. Feyenoord and PSV Eindhoven have also walked away with Europe's biggest club prize. And in the mid to late 1970s the Dutch national side were without doubt the best team in the world, undeservedly coming runners-up in both the 1974 and 1978 World Cup Finals. There is no doubt they should have been crowned champions of the world in both West Germany and Argentina – the hosts winning on both occasions. The Dutch support is also fanatical, so if you were born in Holland and live near PSV Eindhoven, chances are you are going to become a PSV fan or at least support another Dutch outfit. Frank Van Grunsven, however, has far too much sense for that. Glued to his Dutch television way back in 1972 in his home town of Oss, a small place near Nijmegen, Frank watched Leeds United beat Arsenal to claim our only FA Cup triumph to date. He instantly fell in love with the white shirt and has followed Leeds ever since, insisting he has 'never looked back.' A few years after Sniffer Clarke rattled the back of the Arsenal net for that glorious winner, Frank went to his first match, as he explains. 'I went to see Leeds against PSV Eindhoven in a pre-season friendly in Holland in 1979. In the ground I met a Leeds supporter from Bedford, Jimmy Urquhart, who became my pen-pal for several years. I later went to England for the first time as a 16-year-old and stayed at his parent's home for the Easter holiday period and went to see Leeds versus Liverpool [0–0] and

Birmingham versus Leeds [2–0 to Leeds – Derek Parlane and Kevin Hird with a penalty]. The Liverpool match was my first match at Elland Road, which will always be very special to me. I will always remember standing in a packed Geldard End. What an experience. Since then I've been to around 65 games, including some fantastic matches in terms of atmosphere: the Charlton Play-off second-leg match in 1987 at Elland Road [1–0 to Leeds – Brendan Ormsby scoring], the 1–0 win against Man Utd at Elland Road in 1997 with David Wetherall scoring, and the Champions League semi-final first leg against Valencia in 2001 [0–0]. I went to the Valencia match with my girlfriend Louise and ordered tickets via Eric Carlile, the secretary of the supporters' club, but the demand for tickets was so high the chances of getting two were very slim. I still booked our trip to Leeds, though, because I desperately wanted to be in Leeds for this match even if it meant watching the game in a pub. Luckily I got a phone call from Eric and he had sorted tickets out for us. To say I was a happy person is an understatement. The Norwich game after we became League Champions in 1992 was also an electric atmosphere. I've sadly lost touch with Jimmy Urquhart now and often wonder what he's up to these days.' You never know Frank, he might be reading this right now.

A typical journey from Oss to Elland Road is quite a bit faster now than it used to be. Frank used to take the ferry from Rotterdam to Hull, but in the last decade has been opting for the Eurostar from Brussels to London, then the train up to Leeds. 'It used to take us about 12 hours,' he says. 'But with the new fast speed tracks it now takes about nine hours from my hometown to Leeds station.' Frank has a nine-year-old son Clay, who is yet to be introduced to Elland Road (just a matter of time), but Frank has already done his fatherly job of teaching his offspring to support the only 'United' that counts. 'All his friends at school support either PSV Eindhoven or Ajax but he sticks with Leeds,' says a proud dad. 'But I have been devastated with the state of the club in recent times, it really hurts. And every week I have had to explain to him the situation at Leeds. To see the disappointment on his face when I tell him we've lost again is hard to watch. Leeds fans have suffered a lot over the years but the support has always been fantastic. The last 25 years Leeds fans have been confronted with all sorts of successes and even more disappointments, much more than any other team I think. Only the most fanatical supporters stay and Leeds still have loads of them.'

Frank attended a few of the European matches under David O'Leary, including our Champions League qualifying second-leg tie against TSV 1860 Munich, which he was lucky to come away from in one piece. History dictates that there has never been any love lost between German and Dutch teams, so Frank had to do some explaining to get out of a sticky situation. He retorts, 'In Munich four of us went to a pub packed with Munich fans before the match. They didn't have any problems with English fans but when they heard we were Dutch some Germans suddenly became aggressive. We had a lot of talking to do to convince them we didn't support Ajax or Feyenoord but only Leeds. A lucky escape that time. After the match we celebrated the win [1–0 Alan Smith – 3–1 on aggregate] in style with Gary Edwards and his mates. A very good night out in Munich was had by all.' The following season, when Leeds played PSV home and away in a UEFA Cup fourth-round tie [0–0 away, lost 1–0 at ER] Frank van Grunsven and his fellow Dutch Leeds supporters went to both legs, but they had some more explaining to do at Elland Road. 'The matches against PSV were very special for me as I only live 40km from Eindhoven and loads of my mates support PSV. Both matches in Eindhoven we went on a packed train from Oss with many PSV fans and our group of Leeds fans. The match at Elland Road we travelled with the PSV supporters' coaches from Holland. When we arrived in Leeds we had to escape the police escort to get into the Leeds end. The funny thing was that we had tickets in the South Stand only a couple of yards from the away supporters. After the match when the police cleared the South Stand our little group refused to leave because we wanted to join the PSV supporters in the south-east corner. The police really didn't understand what we were talking about and when we showed our passports and explained to them we were Leeds fans from Holland and we had travelled with the Eindhoven fans they finally agreed with a little head-shaking. Against Belgrade in Heerenveen [14 September 1999 – UEFA Cup round one first leg – won 3–1 with two goals from Lee Bowyer and one from Lucas Radebe] a small coach-load of Leeds fans led by Roy Coles (Collar) stopped in my home town. They had spent the night in Antwerp and because Oss was en route between Antwerp and Heerenveen they made a stop in Oss and we all joined them to spend part of the afternoon drinking together. I can remember that the local landlord was a very happy and proud man to have Leeds United supporters from England in his pub. On another European occasion I went on a pre-season tour in Germany with another lad. Leeds played two matches but we never saw the second match because of some wrong information as to where the match was taking place. We arrived at an empty ground and had to return to Holland.'

Frank has clearly had some good times watching Leeds United, as well as plenty of heartaches along the way, as we have all had, but as he and so many of us will agree, it is not just about the football with Leeds, it is also the fans' bonding and togetherness that surely cannot be beaten at any other club. It might sound a bit tacky and a bit of a cliché, but it really is one massive family that sticks together through very thick and ultra thin. Frank cannot agree enough. 'Every trip to Leeds is special for me. Leeds United is not only the football. I love the city of Leeds and its people.

I love the nightlife in Leeds and we've had some good fun over the years in many different venues. All these years we've always stayed in the Crescent Hotel in Beeston. We've known the landlord, Walt Philips, for more than 25 years and he really has become a friend to us. There were times that we tried to book our stay in the hotel only to hear that he was closed for his holiday, but he still allowed us to stay in his hotel. We were the only people in the hotel and of course we always thanked him for this special hospitality. Many times he shook his head because of us. He's sold the hotel now and retired but we still meet up for a drink when we go to Leeds. Some people in Leeds think we're fools to support Leeds all the way from Holland and others have loads of respect for us. Back in Oss, everyone knows I support Leeds United. When I was younger everybody knew me as the lad with the radio as whenever Leeds were playing I had to listen to the match on BBC radio. I've also got some Leeds United tattoos and many people react to them while I'm on holiday. Of course, everybody thinks I am English so many are amazed when I tell them I am from Holland and support Leeds United. I am proud to be a Leeds supporter.'

When Kevin Speight and Christopher Loftus were murdered in Istanbul prior to our match against Galatasaray in a UEFA Cup semi-final tie in 2000, tensions even reached Oss, as Frank explains, 'There is a big immigrant Turkish population in my home town. After Leeds lost the semi-final they started celebrating in the town centre. I hated it. I even got stuck in a traffic jam between all their cars after the match and I can tell you that I was not a happy person. I was really devastated after the killings in Istanbul. Tension stayed for some weeks and even resulted in a mass fight with Turkish supporters in our city centre.'

On a much better note, Frank names Billy Bremner as his all-time favourite player, and here is his all-time XI with three subs, a manager and an assistant manager – once again it's an interesting line up:

David Harvey, Paul Reaney, Mel Sterland, Paul Madeley, John Charles, Billy Bremner, Peter Lorimer, Gordon Strachan, David Batty, Tony Yeboah, Eddie Gray. Subs: Jack Charlton, Vinnie Jones, Allan Clarke. Manager: Don Revie. Assistant manager: David O'Leary.

Just before we depart from these Dutch shores, there is a similar website to that of the social network site Facebook in Holland called Hyves. And there is a specific Leeds United Hyves, which has around 100 members. If you would like to join up and your Dutch is up to scratch, here is the link: http://leedsunited.hyves.nl/

Chapter 18

BACK TO BLIGHTY VIA DODGY SOLENT

Isle of Wight

Dodgy boat journeys, kidnapping, press passes in Sofia and a bottle of vodka ensure that the Isle of Wight Branch of LUSC will always have a tale to tell. The branch are based at Cowes, a town that since 1826 has had a proud tradition of staging one of the biggest annual sailing weeks in the world today. Every 12 months, in excess of 1,000 yachts take part in all sorts of competitions throughout Cowes Week, with a staggering 8,000 competitors in all. So, given the island's rich tradition in the boating world, it's not surprising to hear that at the Isle of Wight Branch of LUSC have a tale to tell about travelling across the Solent.

It was Boxing Day 1990 and the alarm clocks were ringing at around five o'clock in the morning for five die-hard Leeds United fans. They did not really need an alarm clock, however. They woke to the sound of lashing rain and howling force five winds. At 11.30am that morning Leeds United Football Club were playing at home to Chelsea in their first season back in the top flight since they had been promoted seven months earlier, and the Isle of Wight Whites were not about to miss out on this one. A big problem was the fact that there were no ferries running at that time of the morning and the fans were not about to don swimming trunks. Luckily, or unluckily given the extreme weather conditions, a friend offered to take them over on his 20-foot RIB. As well as the wind and rain, the Solent was freezing cold and the prospect of what in the end was a terrifyingly nervous journey led to one member returning to the comfort of his own bed! Gary Antill, Rich Newbury, Andy Hillier and Dave Cox, however, were willing to take what was a big risk in such a small boat. A journey that would normally take around 25 minutes in good weather took 45 minutes, and it was three quarters of an hour that must have felt like three quarters of a day before they finally made their destination in Southampton.

Holding on for dear life, they were thrown all over the place, with the ice-cold water saturating everyone on board. This was in pitch darkness! Thoughts of sitting at a crowded Elland Road for the festive fixture against one of United's fiercest of rivals at this stage were a million miles from anyone's mind, but they finally docked at Southampton and the relief was palpable. After the fans were picked up in cars for what must have seemed like a tame four-hour journey to Yorkshire from the south coast, they got their reward for such dedication. Goals from Mel Sterland, Mike Whitlow and two from Lee Chapman helped Leeds to a sterling 4–1 victory over the Londoners before Messrs Antill, Newbury, Hillier and Cox boarded a nice warm cosy ferry on the return trip from Southampton to home. Antill remarked, 'The boat owner later told us it was the roughest weather he had ever taken the boat out in!'

A normal wind-free, rain-free, dark-free, freezing-free, dodgy boat-free journey from Cowes all the way to Elland Road will now take around four and a half hours in total, but a few years ago, back in the 1980s and early 1990s, it was hardly the quickest of routes to see Leeds, as Antill explained, 'The service is now much improved from those days when a trip to Elland Road from Cowes would involve a 30-minute drive to catch the 5am car ferry to Portsmouth, which then took 40 minutes, before we had to wait for an hour and a half until the car hire depot opened and then it was a four and a half hour drive to Leeds – that is seven hours and 10 minutes altogether! After the game, we would drive back to Portsmouth, drop the car off and get the 11pm car ferry back to the Island and get home around 12.30am. Thankfully, those days are long gone but it was the "norm" for about six or seven years.'

In 1995, following the demise of the old postal branch of the supporters' club, the Isle of Wight Branch was born. Antill became secretary, Newbury the chairman and Dave Hallett the treasurer and on board came members from other parts of the Isle of Wight, Southampton, Portsmouth, Blandford, Abingdon and Oxford. The branch, in terms of numbers, has grown over the years and it now boasts 65 members, and there have been other moments of madness involving the Islanders, although perhaps not as death-defying as that infamous Boxing Day boat trip. On 4 November 1999 one member, who wants to remain slightly anonymous, going simply by the name of 'Macca', got a little carried away on a trip to the Russian capital, when Leeds were due to play Lokomotive Moscow in a UEFA Cup second-round second-leg match.

Russia's favourite tipple – vodka – was top of Macca's list of things to buy once they had landed and to show some of the locals that the Leeds fans had come in peace and simply wanted to have fun, watch Leeds win and fly home again, Macca offered to share his bottle with a couple of Muscovites. So far so good, despite the fact that the conversation between Macca and the two locals was not exactly flowing, given that Macca knew no Russian whatsoever and the two Russians knew about as much English as a newborn baby! The vodka *was* flowing, however, and it is amazing what a few gulps of the hard stuff can do – everything appeared to be just fine until the bottom of the bottle was reached, in fairly quick time to boot. Macca cracked a smile which was a cross between a Peter Kay smirk and someone who had just been given a very large shot of laughing gas, before attempting to say goodbye in broken Isle of Wight/Yorkshire/Russian. 'Nowt wrong we'em Rushkies' no doubt he thought to himself as his two new foreign friends disappeared, but Macca was about to get a little shock from two other locals, who were not quite so hospitable. As he began the relatively short journey to the Lok Stadium, the vodka took its toll and he promptly tripped up and fell over. Two Russians helped him up but they were not about to wish him an enjoyable match and say goodbye. No, instead they decided to take him behind some iron gates and hold him as a 'hostage'! He did finally make it to the ground to watch Leeds triumph 3–0, courtesy of two goals from Michael Bridges and a penalty from Ian Harte, but only because his mates had to empty their pockets of dollars and pay the locals to retrieve their ever-so-slightly tiddly fellow Leeds compatriot.

Macca retold his story to all and sundry on the way back to the Isle of Wight, so it was understandable that just a few weeks later, when Leeds played their next UEFA Cup match in Bulgaria against Spartak Moscow, that Rich Newbury and Kevin Hunt were a little edgy when they found themselves sat in the Moscow end. On 2 December 1999 they were sat in the Georgi Asparuhov Stadium, home of PFC Levski Sofia, where the game had been switched to after the original match, due to be played in Moscow, was called off at the last minute because of a frozen pitch. The authorities did not want to risk another cancellation in Russia. Messrs Newbury and Hunt kept a low profile, but it was difficult to contain themselves when Harry Kewell put Leeds one up after 13 minutes. By half-time Spartak had equalised through Schirko and the two Isle of Wight Whites had had enough – it was time to leave. As they exited the Moscow end, they made their way over to the Leeds supporters in what was an understandably small crowd of just 6,000, given it was in a neutral country. They never made it to the Leeds end though, instead stopping right next to one of the goals and parking their backsides next to two press photographers. They remained there for the whole of the second half and, despite Leeds going down 2–1 in the end (Leeds were later to win the second leg 1–0 and progress on the away goals rule) Newbury and Hunt had an evening they would not forget in a hurry. As the final whistle blew, an official came over to where Newbury and Hunt were sitting. They fully expected a reprimand and a slap on the wrist, but instead, to their amazement, they were given a press pass each for the post-match press conference. Among newspaper, TV and radio reporters from Russia, England and other countries around Europe, the Leeds manager at the time David O'Leary answered questions from all and sundry, including Messrs Newbury and Hunt!

Chapter 19

SOUTH COAST WHITES

On the pitch – Southern-born Whites:

Name	Joined	Left	Apps	Goals	Born
Mark Beeney	1992	1998	45/1	0	Pembury, Kent
Jason Blunt	1995	1995	2/3	0	Penzance
Thomas Burden	1948	1954	259	13	Andover
Frank Butterworth	1945	1945	2	0	Wokingham
Alfred Dark	1922	1922	3	0	Keynsham
Mervyn Day	1984	1992	268	0	Chelmsford
Frank Dudley	1949	1950	71	27	Southend
John Faulkner	1969	1969	4	0	Orpington
Steve Guppy	2004	2004	2/2	1	Winchester
John Mahon	1931	1935	84	23	Gillingham
Nigel Martyn	1996	2002	273	0	Bethel, nr St Austell
Alan Noble	1922	1924	63	4	Southampton
Paul Peterson	1969	1969	3/1	0	Luton
Ivan Sharpe	1920	1920	1	0	St Albans
Matthew Spring	2004	2004	6/9	1	Harlow
Eric Stephenson	1934	1939	115	22	Bexleyheath
Ian Westlake	2006	2009	33/19	2	Clacton

Bournemouth and Hampshire

Let us take a nice *smooth* crossing over the Solent then for our next port of call – Hampshire and Dorset. You would not really expect too many Leeds supporters living on the south coast now would you, but think again. The south is littered with Whites. I can vouch for that. I have lived in Bournemouth now for nearly 30 years. When I first moved to the area I felt a little isolated. I knew of no other Leeds fans in Bournemouth at all. Not so now. Thanks to fellow Bournemouth-based Whites like Adie Farnell, Matt Chiverton, Nick Spooner, Dave Bowes, (Clitty) Clive Thompson, Stuart Lewis, Jason Mesout, Peter Poole, my brother Barry (Baz) Starmore and of course my eldest son Ben Starmore, whenever Leeds are live on the box and we are not heading north, it is a short walk down the road to my local, the good ole Malt and Hops, for a few scoops and the usual nail-biting 90 minutes of footy.

All around the Bournemouth area there are loads of Leeds supporters. The night Leeds lost in the Champions League semi-final second leg in Valencia, the game was beamed live to TV but on an obscure channel. Only one pub in Bournemouth was showing it and when a few of us turned up we were gobsmacked at the number of Leeds fans, practically all wearing Leeds shirts, that had also turned up. There must have been around 250 people, all eyes glued to the telly. I never imagined there were that many Leeds supporters in Bournemouth. I was shocked and at the same time even more proud that wherever you go, it seems, you will find hordes of Leeds fans. It was such a great feeling and I dared to imagine what it would be like if we had won that match and were heading to another European Cup Final. The place would have erupted. We would have gone mental. Simple as. Sadly, we all know what happened and it was a 'heads down' slow walk home with sentiments of 'what if?' wafting around our heads.

Matt Chiverton, who was a regular down the Malt and originates from Rothwell in Leeds, is the same age as Alan Smith and his claim to fame is that he played against him in a school match. Matt scored twice. Smith scored none. Matt's team won 3–0, and he says, 'that was great but look where he is now and look where I am!' At least you have never worn a silly red shirt though Matt! The game against Arsenal when we survived the drop in 2003 was sheer drama and so emotional, and quite a few of us that were watching the game down the Malt, all wearing Leeds shirts, including a converted Leeds fan from Peru, Julio Arnedo, who was staying at our house, went completely mental. Julio and I swapped shirts before he flew home, so I now have an Alianza Club Lima shirt and Julio is the proud owner of a Leeds United shirt, spreading the Leeds name across South America. Following that Arsenal game we were close to being in a spot of bother, given that there were many Gooners watching as well. They were still going for the title and we effectively killed that off, handing it to you know who. That was an unfortunate irrelevance. We were safe. That was all that counted. And we were jumping round like loonies. A year on we were never going to repeat such an act. Same pub, same people, except Julio, who was back in his native Peru, different horrible outcome. Bolton away, 4–1 down and doomed to the Championship. I remember looking at Matt, not saying a word, and suddenly feeling my eyes welling up. It was time to walk out of the pub for a quiet moment. I remember sending a text to Gary Edwards and telling him I thought I was too old to cry.

A few years prior to this, under the guidance of one David O'Leary, Leeds were going places – or so we thought. And a live game against Derby County was being beamed by satellite to the Malt and Hops. Taking up our usual table we got talking to another lad we had never met before. He was clearly a football fan. I told him I thought Leeds were on the verge of becoming the biggest force in English football and were about to dominate the game for the next 10 years. He was not totally convinced. Sadly, he was right. During our conversation I turned round to him and asked him what he did for a living. He told me he used to be a professional footballer. Oh, I thought. So I asked his name. 'Ted MacDougal' he replied. I felt a bit of an idiot not recognising him. After all, he played alongside Billy Bremner for Scotland and once scored nine goals in an FA Cup tie for Bournemouth, which to this day is still a record in the FA Cup anywhere. He also briefly played for another club, but we won't go there.

Going back to the animosity Leeds fans receive from AFC Bournemouth supporters, stemming back all those years ago to that glorious scorching May Bank Holiday in 1990, I think I've done my bit to attempt to build a few bridges between the two clubs. Whenever the Leeds result is announced on the loudspeaker system at the new Fitness First Stadium and we have come second, 19 years on the Bournemouth fans still let out a huge cheer. But down the local there are a number of 'Cherries' fans that talk to me about Leeds in a now strangely affectionate way. Terry Sowle, Max Frampton, Carl 'Gonzo' Hannah, Dave and Nicky Holland, Andy Fry, twins Chris and Martyn Jones (CJ and MJ), Debbee Houghton and Mark Barrett are all staunch Bournemouth fans and travel all over the country watching what can only be described as less than exhilarating football. But fair play to them. At least they are loyal fans, and anyone reading this book can relate to that.

On 6 November 2007 Leeds returned to Bournemouth for the first time since the 1990 sun-drenched riots. It was a tense time for Bournemouthians and the authorities were worried that Leeds were coming to town again. A massive police operation ensued but, prior to the game, I organised a photo shoot at Bournemouth's Fitness First Stadium which made a few people in the seaside town stand up and take note. On contacting AFC Bournemouth they were only too pleased to allow 17 of us, both Leeds supporters and Bournemouth fans, into the ground for a group photo with both sets of supporters wearing their respective colours. This was then published in the local *Bournemouth Echo* in an attempt to show that both sets of fans can stand side by side in harmony. Of course, Leeds were far louder on the night of the match than the hosts, but I hope this little gesture proved that the vast majority of Leeds fans simply love their football and their club and are not out to cause trouble at the drop of a hat.

In fact it was interesting that after the 3–1 win for Leeds that night there were a total of 14 arrests, and, guess what, they were all Bournemouth fans!

During the Play-offs at the end of the 2005–06 season, a few of us, including 'Gonzo', decided to travel across to the other side of Southampton to meet up with the Hampshire Whites for the second leg of our Play-off semi-final showdown with Preston. There were about 45 staunch Leeds fans inside the Bridge pub in Woolston, and I introduced Gonzo to a number of them, including Danny Martorana. When I gave Danny and Co. two clues about the team Carl supports – 1990 and where do I live?! – Danny began to wind Carl up unwittingly. Carl had promised me that he would behave himself, even though his feelings for Leeds are not exactly favourable (the bridge-building is a slow process!). In the end he did, but I could sense that at times he was ready to lash out, which wouldn't have been the wisest of moves. Leeds scored the first goal against Preston and then a second, and at the final whistle, following our glorious 2–0 win, Carl was the only person in the pub still sat down and with a stern look on his face, clearly showing no joy whatsoever. Why did he come? I've no idea.

I could not believe my bad luck in 1990. I had gone through a separation with my partner and we had sold our house. This all happened in 1989. A year later in January 1990 two mates, Rich Swift and Matt Cadby, and I set off for what was to be a fantastic trip around the world for a whole year. The problem for me was that this particular year was the year we had all been waiting for, for eight bloody years! By the time 5 May came along on the south coast, in the town I lived in, I was 12,000 ruddy miles away in Perth, Australia. Not only that, but when the match was on, there was no internet in those days, no satellite TV and no way at all of finding out the result as it was unfolding. I had to wait a whole day before I found out through the *Western Australian Gazette* that we had actually done it. And, what is more, I could not believe my eyes when on the front page of this paper, the national paper for that side of Australia, there was a picture of riot police in Bournemouth. I looked twice, but mainly to reassure myself that the result was 1–0 to us. To make sure we *were* up. I sank a few tinnies that night!

On the other side of Bournemouth is another staunch and hugely dedicated Leeds supporter, Dave Bowes. Dave is a member of the Hampshire Whites and once gave Adie Farnell and I a lift to 'An evening with Leeds United' in November 2005. We'll come back to Dave in a minute but for now, along with loads more Hampshire Whites, including Dave 'Wimpy' Clements, Mark Chivers, Mark Smith and Phil Townend, we were to enjoy a great night. We all got to meet the manager Kevin Blackwell, former legend Peter Lorimer, another former legend Ian Baird (although I'd had the pleasure of meeting and interviewing Bairdy before – top man) and chairman Ken Bates. Bear in mind this event was around 260 miles south of Leeds and almost 200 fans turned up. To me it was staggering and it filled me up with immense pride. The evening was a huge success, with Lorimer telling tales of when he was playing in the legendary 1960s/70s side, Ian Baird explaining that Howard Wilkinson once sent Vinnie Jones off in a training match for doing one-armed press-ups in the centre of the pitch and Ken Bates discussing the benefits of the members' club. Kevin Blackwell filled you with confidence with his obvious enthusiasm and his sheer love for the club oozing through with genuine authenticity. Sadly, his tenure at the club did not lead to success, but it was not for the want of trying. Following a question and answer session with the floor, the four guests signed autographs and posed for photos.

The following day we all went to what I have to say is the best Leeds United match I've ever attended. It was at Southampton. We were awful in the first half and found ourselves 3–0 down against a very ordinary Saints outfit with one Dennis Wise in their midfield. What was happening? The night before had given us a belief that Leeds were on their way back. Kevin Blackwell had filled you up with a confidence that Leeds were not going to be staying in the Championship for much longer. And then 45 minutes of football later the wheels seemed to have come off the rails in such dramatic fashion. Now was going to be a test of his management skills. The half-time team talk would have to be the best interval 'chat' of his managerial career to date, if Leeds were going to get anything from this game. I had a quiet, sombre pint with Gary Edwards at half-time. As we headed back to our seats, though, I put my hand on Gary's shoulder and said 'you never know mate, we might win 4–3!' I have always been the eternal optimist, but turning the game around looked way beyond us at that point. To make matters worse we had not even pulled a goal back in the opening 25 minutes of the second half, although we were starting to play a bit. With 19 minutes left Paul Butler headed home his first goal for Leeds. Surely a mere consolation at this point? Six minutes later, Robbie Blake slotted home another for Leeds. Hang on a minute, what's going on? We can't come back from three down with 19 minutes left, surely? Minute number 84 and one part of St Mary's went absolutely nuts when Leeds were awarded a penalty. In front of a delirious, gobsmacked United faithful David Healy blasted the penalty beyond Niemi in the Southampton goal and would you believe it – it was 3–3. The confidence in the Leeds players and the support on the terraces linked up beautifully and you could sense that 3–3 was not going to be the final outcome. This was going to be a day to remember. A special match that fans present would be talking about 10 years from now. 'Were you there at Southampton in November 2005?' That is what supporters will be saying. The support was so immense that day, I am convinced we just sucked that ball into the Southampton net for the winner. The statistics will tell you that Liam Miller found the back of the net following a low cross from Rob Hulse. What the statistics will not tell you is that it was cause for the Leeds fans to erupt into sheer euphoria. The whole end was like one massive group hug jumping on a giant trampoline. The final whistle blew. The Leeds players hugged. Then they came over to our end. The mutual appreciation society had gone into overdrive. The Saints fans disappeared quicker than Dr Who's Tardis. We had just witnessed a quite astonishing 90 minutes of football. All the way back to the train station it was impossible to rid yourself of a permanent silly grin. We hugged any Leeds fans we saw on our 'oh-so-happy 20-minute walk', before stopping for a couple of celebratory beverages in a pub just around the corner from the train station. It was half filled with Southampton fans and half filled with Leeds, but there was never a hint of any confrontation. To be fair to the Saints fans, they took the enormous amount of stick in their own pub very well. Chants of '3–0, and you still don't win' were ringing around the pub. I'm not so sure we would be quite so hospitable if another team had done the same to us in the centre of Leeds. And I am pretty sure we would not have been singing that in a 'home' pub just down the road at Saints' arch rivals Portsmouth. There was another occasion at St Mary's that my son Ben remembers vividly. 'At St Mary's we beat Southampton 1–0 with Lee Bowyer scoring,' says Ben. 'I went with Dad and we only had one ticket. We tried for two hours to get hold of another but couldn't. With just five minutes to go to kick-off and standing outside the entrance, Dad gave me the ticket and said 'look, you go mate'. Just after he said that this bloke was walking past us holding a ticket in the air and asking if anyone wanted a ticket. I thought my Dad was going to bite his arm off! The game wasn't really that good and was 0–0 with three minutes left before Bowyer scored. I got flung in the air four rows forward but I didn't care. We'd won!'

Go on then Ben, even though you are just a 22-year-old whippersnapper, tell us your all-time Leeds side, with subs:

> Paul Robinson, Gary Kelly, Ian Harte, Billy Bremner, Lucas Radebe, Rio Ferdinand, Vinnie Jones, Rod Wallace, Alan Smith, David Batty, Harry Kewell. Subs: Tony Yeboah, Jonathan Woodgate, Gary McAllister.

Defiant Bremner Lifts Spirits

I got into journalism when I started writing for the *Bournemouth Evening Echo* back in 1991. It was hardly glamorous stuff, covering Brockenhurst (who?) in the Wessex League every Saturday afternoon for a tenner, but, you have got to start somewhere. And I soon found out that I was not the first person to work for them who supported the mighty Leeds United. Former director and general manager of the paper Mike Emsley has been a massive Leeds nut since 1954. He takes up his own story.

'It goes without saying, as a Leeds fan for so long, I've had great elation but a fair degree of heartbreak too. My great hero was of course John Charles, whose talents took us into Division One. Then I was fortunate enough to experience the Revie years following a period of mediocrity after Big John's departure to Italy. Elation covers three League Championships and I was present at Wembley in 1968 when we won our first major trophy, beating Arsenal in the then League Cup Final. However, I was also there in 1970 when we played Chelsea off the pitch and only drew 2–2 and in 1973 versus Sunderland. I couldn't get a ticket for 1972 even though I had a season ticket, but got to Molineux to see us lose the double the following Monday by losing 2–1 to Wolves. We all know that Billy Bremner was a formidable individual, who, I recollect, after the Wolves game really pepped me up by a simple gesture even though we had just failed to win the double that night. I must have been looking so forlorn, wearing my Leeds scarf and stood alone outside the ground, not even knowing where I'd abandoned the bus to take me back to Leeds, when the Leeds team coach pulled out of the stadium. Terry Cooper was on the back with his broken leg in plaster and Billy caught my glance through the bus window. Despite his own disappointment, and that of the whole team, he clenched his fist in a defiant gesture to me to raise my spirits and pick me back up, meaning we would come back fighting the following season. It was a gesture which typified Billy's indomitable spirit.

'Unfortunately, I did get a ticket for the 1996 Wembley debacle against Aston Villa. I worked in newspapers, *Yorkshire Post*, *Barnsley Chronicle*, and in 1979 I became an estranged Leeds fan when we had to move south to Southampton and ultimately to Bournemouth, where I held the position of director and general manager of the *Daily Echo* in Bournemouth. As a result of my position and being a football nut, I was able to provide some sponsorship from the *Echo* for AFC Bournemouth where we had a hospitality box and sponsored at least two home games each season. I got to know the then manager Harry Redknapp and the MD, the late Brian Tiler [ex-Rotherham and Aston Villa] very well, even being invited to travel on the team coach to Crystal Palace one year where Bournemouth beat Palace, Wright and Bright included.

'As you can imagine, I was keen to sponsor Leeds matches at Bournemouth, which we did in 1988–89. This was one of the late great Billy Bremner's last matches before being sacked and was an uneventful 0–0 draw. The Leeds chairman Leslie Silver and chief executive Bill Fotherby were actually causing me to doubt Billy's future during a conversation with them in the bar after the game. Incidentally, the Leeds assistant manager was a certain Norman Hunter. We had actually sponsored the Bournemouth versus Rotherham game a couple of years earlier, which clinched the old Division Three Championship for Bournemouth, and Norman was then the Rotherham manager. I invited him to come into our hospitality suite for a drink after the game and he brought his whole team in! The *Echo*, through my influence, were therefore the sponsor of the Leeds match on May Bank Holiday in 1990. Bournemouth had to win to avoid relegation and, of course, if Leeds won they were promoted as champions. I invited friends down for the game from Leeds and had nine sleeping at our house, who were all to enjoy the game as guests of the *Echo* along with some local business contacts. As the capacity of the Bournemouth ground, Dean Court, was around 10,000 there were obviously many thousands of Leeds fans who travelled to Bournemouth even though they did not have tickets. Consequently they created mayhem, wrecking the Holiday Revival pub on the sea front on the Friday night before the game and almost drinking Bournemouth dry over the weekend.

'Unfortunately, their behaviour wasn't something I could be proud of as a dyed-in-the-wool Leeds Loiner and staunch fan. Riot police and horses were brought in to try to control them, but they damaged loads of cars in the car park behind the stand and the game then took a back seat to all the violence outside the ground and in the town. Although delighted that we were up via Lee Chapman's head, I was quite ashamed by the behaviour of the masses and was subjected to much criticism within the local community as my Leeds United affinity was widely known. I wrote to Leslie Silver asking if he was prepared to acknowledge how my great day had become almost a day of shame and to demonstrate some regret to the town of Bournemouth about the mayhem caused. I didn't receive a reply. Even now there are still negative references in the local media and in conversations to the visit to Bournemouth of Leeds United back in 1990 and I still get stick as a Leeds fan. However, I never hide my affinity.'

Mike feels quite smug that his all-time Leeds XI is exactly the same as voted by fans, where awards were dished out to the players, on a lavish night at Elland Road on 10 April 2006. Here's his line up and his explanations for why he chose the players:

Nigel Martyn

He narrowly shaded the unfairly much-maligned Gary Sprake. Gary was a wonderfully agile and exciting goalkeeper who made far fewer howlers than are often attributed to him, and his contribution to the success of Revie's team must never be underestimated. However, Nigel got my vote over him because he was such a consistent performer and, unlike Sprake who occasionally might display his fiery Welsh temperament and smack somebody, Nigel was always so cool, though I still feel Sprake commanded his box better and took responsibility for taking crosses more than Nigel Martyn.

Paul Reaney

'Speedy Reaney' was an unsung player who worked so hard at his game. He was a hard-tackling defender first and foremost but, probably because of his schoolboy years as a forward, became an exciting, athletic, overlapping full-back before they came into fashion. I never saw George Best have a good game against Leeds and that was down to Paul Reaney, who was also a master at goal-line clearances behind both Gary Sprake and David Harvey. He was unlucky to break a leg before the 1970 World Cup in Mexico as I believe he could well have gone on to win the number of England caps which his consistency deserved, rather than the three he was actually awarded.

Terry Cooper

'Chopper', or 'TC', transformed himself from a reasonable winger to a wonderful attacking full-back. He was fearless in the tackle but going forward he had great dribbling skills. I have seen other contenders such as the highly consistent Grenville Hair [had Leeds been a top side in the 1950s then he would surely have been a full England international] and Tony Dorigo, but TC has to be the man for the number-three shirt, and I will never forget his goal at Wembley in 1968 when Leeds won their first major honour.

Billy Bremner

Quite simply the heart of Don Revie's great team and a world-class performer. This man led from the front and was capable of doing just anything. Great passer of the ball, regular goalscorer of crucial and often spectacular goals and, despite his size, what a tackler! For me, after John Charles, quite simply the best ever for Leeds.

Jack Charlton

I saw Jack playing in the mid-1950s when he was somewhat lacking in direction but quite obviously a talented individual, as was demonstrated by interest in him from some top clubs. I was happy to watch Jack at centre-half with John Charles at centre-forward! Once Jack settled under Don Revie's management, his talent blossomed and was an integral part of Leeds' formidable defence, yet he also became a prolific goalscorer with his height at set-pieces. A great character to have in our team and, of course, a World Cup hero under Alf Ramsey. I cannot imagine what Jack would have felt like playing under Sven Goran Eriksson!

Norman Hunter

If Bobby Moore had not been around, Norman would have won far more than 28 caps for England. Formidable in the tackle, he was the perfect cover when Big Jack went up for set pieces and when TC left his full-back position. Also, what a dream left side with TC, Norman and Eddie Gray! There was no more consistent performer than Norman, who was also an integral part of Don Revie's jigsaw.

Peter Lorimer

The chant as he ran up to take free-kicks was '90 miles an hour' so I shudder to think what 'Hot Shot' would have done with today's lightweight balls. Peter developed into a hard-working right-sided player, with an often underestimated degree of dribbling skill, and was scorer of the most spectacular goals to lift the crowd. When he received the ball within 40 yards of the goal, the crowd held its breath. On a slightly sick note, Leeds were interested in signing Asa Hartford, a top-class midfield player from West Brom, who eventually went on to play for Manchester City and also became a regular with Scotland. He failed a medical when about to sign for Leeds because a hole in his heart was detected and the transfer fell through. On Asa's next visit to Elland Road he was in the wall as Lorimer ran up to take a free-kick and the 'Scratching Shed' chanted 'Aim through the hole in his heart.'

Allan Clarke

'Sniffer' was something akin to a hired assassin. He was the man to back to be where the goalscoring opportunities fell. A natural goalscorer, he was the final piece in Don Revie's jigsaw when he was signed in 1969 after our first Division One Championship win, to play alongside Mick Jones, and they complemented one another so well. Hardworking Mick and Ice Cool Allan. He could also handle himself when the going got tough.

John Charles

What can I say! The finest all-round footballer I have ever seen. The best centre-half in the world and the best centre-forward. A great example to impressionable youngsters. He was never booked or sent off and let his feet and head do the talking. He dominated games with his sheer skill and athletic ability. I have never seen a footballer with the all-round skills of Big John who, of course, also became a great hero playing for Juventus in Italy. With John in your team, anything was possible and today I cannot begin to think what he would be worth in transfer terms.

Johnny Giles

Signed as a right-winger, he assumed midfield responsibility with Billy Bremner when Bobby Collins broke his thigh against Torino. Thus was established a wonderful midfield pairing. Giles had so much vision and skill in killing a ball and drilling 30 or 40 yard passes around the field and he also scored many goals. He was a penalty-kick expert and, in short, a truly wonderful player. He could also look after himself on the field.

Eddie Gray

A genuinely nice guy and a naturally gifted footballer. If it hadn't been for his terrible luck with injuries, I sincerely believe Eddie would have been revered on the field more than George Best and would have won far more than 12 Scotland caps. He could make a football talk as he waltzed around opposing defenders, and who could forget what he did to David Webb at Wembley in 1970.

Substitutes

Mike considered Mick Jones, Tony Currie, David Batty, Gordon McQueen and many others, but in the end settled quite readily on the following three:

Bobby Collins

Don Revie signed Bobby from Everton in 1962 when we were sliding towards relegation to the Third Division. Almost single-handedly he inspired the team to avoid relegation and the following season Revie put in youngsters like Sprake, Hunter and Reaney to be brought along by Collins. I am sure Billy learned so much from him and I really struggled not to find him a place in the first XI. His contribution to Leeds United's rise should never be forgotten.

Gordon Strachan

Howard Wilkinson's equivalent of Bobby Collins. Wilkinson built a team around Strachan who, again, was an inspirational figure all over the field. A marvellous player with all the skills who led us out of Division Two to the Championship of the then Division One.

Paul Madeley

Superb athlete and loyal club servant who could be slotted in to almost any position. Probably would have won more than his 24 England caps if he had been less of a utility player. 'Rolls Royce' was a most suitable nickname.

A truly immense line up indeed, with of course dear old Billy Bremner in the heart of the midfield. We could have done with him on 13 February 1971, as Mike Emsley reflects.

'We suffered one of the most humiliating defeats in FA Cup history when we lost 3–2 in the fifth round to Colchester United. We had a team of internationals but went 3–0 down and, despite fighting back, could not save the game. I recollect that the only stars missing from our line up were Billy Bremner and Eddie Gray, who may have made a difference. The same evening I went with my wife and some friends for a meal at the Brown Cow at Whitkirk. Imagine my surprise when I looked across and saw Jack Charlton and his wife sat with another couple. The team must have flown back, which was quite unusual in those days, to allow Jack to be out in Leeds by around 8pm. To say his face looked like thunder would be an understatement and he must have been really good company that evening, as he hardly appeared to converse at all. Needless to say, discretion prevailed and I didn't go over to ask him about the match!

'After that shock we did, of course, make amends big style by winning the Centenary Cup Final the following year. However, in 1973 came Sunderland and our humiliating defeat at Wembley. Although I was a season ticket holder in the old Paddock, I couldn't get a ticket for the Final, as had also been the case the previous year for the Arsenal match. However, through a chap I'd met on holiday the previous year in Majorca I was able to get two tickets, as he was a referee with the Kent FA. Our disastrous day started when we left my brother-in-law's home, also in Kent at New Romney, to drive to Tunbridge Wells to rendezvous with our ticket supplier. Fifteen miles into our journey, the clutch went on my brother-in-law's car and we had to limp back to Romney and set off again in my car to meet our rendezvous time. We just made it and transported our supplier and his son to Wembley, where 20,000 Leeds fans were outnumbered by 20,000

Sunderland fans plus 60,000 neutrals, who were all cheering for the underdog, Sunderland. After suffering complete humiliation on the field and hassle from those seated around us throughout the game, we set off back to Romney, whereupon the son of our ticket contact was violently sick in the back of my car. Therefore we drove back to Romney via Tunbridge with the aroma of vomit in the car and reflected on our perfect day! I remember when, years later, Ian Porterfield got sacked as manager of Chelsea and I was admonished by my wife for saying it served him right for scoring that goal against us in 1973. Believe it or not, to serve as a constant reminder of that awful day in 1973, my son actually met and married a girl from Sunderland. To make matters worse, her address was Wembley Road!'

Nowadays the *Bournemouth Echo*'s main editor, Neal Butterworth, is a follower of the dark side.

Lost Vehicles, Flying Burgers and 53–0

Who was that member of the Hampshire Whites I was going to come back to? Ah yes, Dave Bowes, who lives in Bournemouth. You could say he has seen a few places on this planet of ours. Starting life in Scarborough, he moved on to Hull before his work took him to London, Eastern Europe, Asia and eventually…Bournemouth! A die-hard supporter if ever you saw one, holding a season ticket throughout the dark days of the 1980s, Dave Bowes has not only been to a few places through his work, but he has also been to a few places watching Leeds as well.

As a 15-year-old, living on an estate just outside Hull, Dave's first away trip was not that far away, as he explains. 'I started going regularly when I got a job when I was at school. My mum worked in this local hotel as a waitress and I got a job there cleaning the car park every Sunday. I think I got paid about £4.50 for a whole day's work and all that money was spent on going to watch Leeds. I used to go with the Hull Whites then. My first away game was against Leicester City and it was in the old Filbert Street. After the game we parked in the wrong place and we ended up getting a bit of a hammering. We were in a transit van and we used to put a mattress in the back to make it a bit more comfortable. We had a couple of lads who would take turns driving and then we would all pile in the back. Going to school on the Monday was a bit of an interesting one with a black eye and a thick lip! A lot of people say they can remember their first match. I remember the occasion and I remember more about walking into Elland Road and standing on the Kop. I thought that this place is just enormous with all these people in it. I was about seven or eight and my old man took me for my birthday. I was just awestruck by the whole thing. I had seen them in the 1972 FA Cup Final on the TV when I was six, so it was either 1973 or '74 when I went to my first match. We went in the car and we had all the scarves hanging out of the window and everything. I can't even remember who we played, I think it might have been Leicester. I know we won. I think it was 2–1. I was more gobsmacked by the whole scenery and the ground. The football did not mean much really. There I was with all my mates and the atmosphere got me really hooked on it all. My real big time watching Leeds was right the way through the '80s. And then I moved to London in 1992 but I was still going regularly. During the 1980s I was going home and away every week. When I moved to London I was still going to most of the away games. Then in 1994 I moved to Eastern Europe and it became really tricky. I then moved to Asia and I linked in with the Singapore Whites. They are quite a thriving branch and it is a brilliant place to watch football. They show live Premiership games and I was there from 1998 to 2000, so it was a good time for us. It comes on at about 10 o'clock at night over there.'

A law-abiding upstanding member of society, Dave Bowes, in his younger days, did have one or two brushes with the law, although it has to be said through no fault of his own. In 1989 on one such occasion the score was Leeds 53, the Nottingham boys in blue 0! Confused? Take up the story then Dave:

'When Howard Wilkinson had been appointed and we played Nottingham Forest in the FA Cup [on 28 January 1989], we got beat at the City Ground [0–2] but that was when Forest were really flying high. It was a real test for us. We were still in the Second Division, so could we go to a First Division club and hold our own? We did and we played well despite losing. On the bus leaving the ground, one of the lads was banging on the window as you do and he had a signet ring on. It just caught the window right and the window shattered. The police came on the bus and asked who did it and we told them not to worry about it. But the police said 'no, we want to know who did it because we want to charge them'. The bus driver then told the police that the lads on the bus would have a whip round and pay for the window and he was fine with that, but the police still wouldn't have any of it. So they arrested the whole bus – all 53 of us! They probably had about 10 coppers on the bus and they took us all down to Nottingham police station. They processed us all. All this manpower for a broken window that we'd all agreed to pay for! We knew we weren't going to get done because what could they charge us for? They let us all go at about 11.30pm without charge. But I remember that all the way through the evening 53 Leeds fans locked up in cells weren't just singing Leeds songs. There was Englebert Humperdink's *Please Release Me, Let Me Go* and then we sang *The Great Escape*. We had all these prison songs going on for about four or five hours. The police kept coming up to us and banging on the doors telling us to shut up. Every time they did that we just sang louder! I remember going to Brighton away in the FA Cup in the previous round [won 2–1 – two goals from Ian Baird]. My mate took his burger out of his bun and used it as a frisbee. It hit this policewoman right smack in the face. We had to use real negotiating skills to get him away. We pleaded with her that it was purely an accident, but it was a beautiful shot! We got there at half-time, late as usual. We parked our van up on a hill behind the Goldstone Ground. After about 10 minutes of the second half I tapped this guy on the shoulder and said to him "look at our van". The police were impounding it and they took it away. We just thought how are we going to get back to Yorkshire? What are we going to do? After the game, we thought bugger, we don't know where our van is. So we were walking round the other side of the Goldstone Ground and we bumped into some of the Leeds players. We were telling them that we'd got to go and look for our van, that it had been impounded somewhere. So the players, including Glynn Snodin, turned round and said they'd help us out. They jumped on their bus and started giving us loads of their beers. Good lads. We had to go and rescue the van from the police compound. I remember a guy called Rowan Akers doing a somersault down the high street (a mixture of booze and good spirits having won). We found a pub, and eventually got our van back at about 9 or 10pm for the long drive home!'

San Siro Sing-Song

On 8 November 2000 a very special night occurred in Leeds United's history. In the cauldron that is the San Siro Leeds were up against one of Europe's giants, AC Milan, and the game ended in a 1–1 draw with Dom Matteo scoring 'a spiffingly good gooaaal'. But it was not the scoreline and the fact that David O'Leary's side had performed brilliantly yet again in Europe, or the fact that we had knocked Barcelona out as a consequence, it was the events after the match that everyone remembers. Dave Bowes witnessed the sing-a-long with players and supporters first hand. 'After the game in the San Siro it was just awesome because the players were joining in with the singing on the pitch. They came out of the dressing room and they were just joining in. It was just a real bond with the players. You just felt actually yes, they're just part of us. You felt completely united. That was probably the most Leeds "United" I've ever felt. As fans and with everything that was going on, you just felt completely as one. The way that they were doing what they were doing and pitching in with the singing and all the rest of it really tugged at the old heart strings. Dominic Matteo was doing a lot, he was getting really stuck in and Smithy was conducting a lot of it as well. It was just such a surreal experience because I did not think I would ever see something like that. I know Richard Jobson quite well, who is a really nice bloke, and when he used to play for Leeds [October 1995 to October 1998] he'd get us into the players' lounge, so we were interacting with the players, but in a way it disappointed me because they don't share the same passion as us supporters. They don't have the same sort of drive for the shirt that we all do. If you think about it logically, then you would think well of course they don't because they're paid to do a job and that's it. But when you talk to them and realise this, it's disappointing, so I didn't like that. But then when I saw what happened in the San Siro I thought, actually, this is what it's all about. There was that real bond between us and them. Superb.' Dave adds, 'Certain clubs have got character and certain cities have got character and then there's some really boring clubs. For example, Fulham will never ever do anything original, they'll always just follow. I think places like Celtic, Liverpool, Leeds and the Geordies, they've all got something unique. There's a real passion about these clubs and the cities. The people that go to watch Leeds have got real character. They're different. Leeds will always create things and others will follow. I seem to remember it was us (the fans) that started taking our shirts off at half-time and singing. Now loads of clubs do it. We introduced sock tags in the 1970s and clubs followed. Lots of songs we've sung, other clubs have copied. I think it's down to the characters that watch Leeds. They're genuinely interesting people who come up with something different. When you're at home it can be a bit boring but when you're away, you're all together, the numbers are good and you just feel terrific. And it inspires a bit of creativity and a bit of passion. I think sometimes when you're watching a lot of crap on the pitch you just have to cheer yourselves up another way!'

When Dave Bowes moved to work in Finland, he simply had to teach one of his employees the error of his ways and with it managed to convert some naive Scandinavians to support the team from the correct side of the Pennines.

'I had a load of guys who worked for me who didn't know what football was, so they were Man Utd supporters! I said to them "look, I don't want any Man Utd supporters working for me". One lad came to work in a Man Utd shirt and

I took it off him and I burnt his shirt in front of him in the office. I let him go home so he could change his shirt. I came home to England the following week and bought him a Leeds shirt to replace it. I shouldn't really have burnt his shirt, but he got the message that wearing a Man Utd shirt wasn't right!

'In Finland saunas are very popular. We had a big sauna in the office, so I got everybody in the office, all the lads and lasses, to go in the sauna. In Finland, whether you like it or not, it's always a naked sauna. I was telling them all in the sauna all about Leeds and Man Utd. Our office was right in the middle of Helsinki and this was the middle of winter. Freezing cold outside and ice on the pavements. I was teaching them songs and I started with a simple one, which was *Stand up if you hate Man U*. So it ended up with 20 people coming out of the sauna and then going out into the streets of Helsinki (still naked!), running around singing 'stand up if you hate Man U'! The police followed us all around when we were doing this and just started singing with us!'

Chapter 20

LEEDS WITH A CAPITAL L

On the pitch – London-born Whites:

Name	Joined	Left	Apps	Goals	Born
Patrick Agana	1991	1991	1/1	0	Bromley
Wayne Andrews	2007	2007	2	0	Paddington
Jermaine Beckford	2006	CP	79/16	54	London
Frederick Blackman	1914	1919	46	0	Brixton
Lee Bowyer	1996	2002	257/8	55	Canning Town
Jeff Chandler	1979	1980	23/5	2	Hammersmith
Leon Constantine	2007	2008	2/5	2	Hackney
Tony Currie	1976	1978	124	16	Edgware
Michael Duberry	1999	2005	67/11	4	Enfield
Ugo Ehiogu	2006	2006	6	1	Hackney
Rio Ferdinand	2000	2001	73	3	Peckham
Danny Granville	1998	1998	11/3	0	Islington
Vince Hilaire	1988	1990	49/4	7	Forest Hill
Bradley Johnson	2007	2007	21/3	3	Hackney
Vinnie Jones	1989	1990	51/2	5	Watford
Darren Kenton	2007	2007	16	0	Wandsworth
David Kerslake	1992	1992	8	0	Stepney
Neil Kilkenny	2007	CP	54/3	5	Enfield
Marlon King	2004	2004	4/5	0	Dulwich
Ernie Langley	1952	1952	9	3	Kilburn
Stephen McPhail	1996	2003	72/34	3	Westminster
Jody Morris	2003	2003	11/1	0	Hammersmith
Kevin Nicholls	2006	2006	14/1	0	Newham
David O'Leary	1993	1994	10	0	Stoke Newington
Paul Reaney	1962	1977	737/12	9	Fulham
David Rocastle	1992	1993	19/15	2	Lewisham
Sam Sodje	2009	2009	7	0	Greenwhich
Alex Stacey	1927	1933	51	0	London
Graham Stack	2006	2007	12	0	Hampstead
Neil Sullivan	2003	2006	110	0	Sutton

Name	Joined	Left	Apps	Goals	Born
Imre Varadi	1989	1992	23/6	6	Paddington
Ray Wallace	1991	1993	5/2	0	Lewisham
Rod Wallace	1991	1997	222/35	66	Lewisham
Curtis Weston	2007	2008	3/8	1	London
Chris Whyte	1990	1992	146/1	6	Islington
Stan Wilcockson	1934	1934	4	0	Poplar
George Wilkins	1949	1949	3	0	Hackney
Jermaine Wright	2004	2005	38/2	3	Greenwich

London

Right, an hour and a half up the M3 then and, ah, the capital of England. Home to the 2012 Olympic Games. Home to the Queen of England. Home to the second-best football stadium in the world, Wembley (after Elland Road, silly!). Home to Beefeaters, the Houses of Parliament, 10 Downing Street, Wimbledon, Harrods, St Paul's Cathedral and erm…Wormwood Scrubs! Yes, Wormwood Scrubs. I know what you are thinking. Of course, Buckingham Palace is a tourist venue that attracts millions from around the world 365 days a year. Wembley Stadium knocks socks off any football stadium in the world today (still second best, though); although it should do, given the amount it has cost to build – £904 million in the end. Strawberries and cream and the inevitable umbrellas are par for the course at Wimbledon, the biggest tennis tournament on the planet attracting a world-wide audience of millions. Harrods, the Houses of Parliament, 10 Downing Street and St Paul's Cathedral are all places of interest regularly visited by enormous numbers. But Wormwood Scrubs? Well, you could argue that it is not going to be high on the list of tourist attractions in most travel agents' brochures. But, if you are a Leeds United fan, and you are in the Big Smoke for a Leeds United match, forget all the above frequently visited places and head down to the Scrubs for a pre-match beverage – you could do far worse. I cannot imagine that being a resident at such an establishment is a whole bunch of fun, but as long as you are on the right side of the wall, the Scrubs has a very firm place in its heart for Leeds United Football Club.

It all began in the early 1980s. There was a shortage of prison officers in the south of England and in particular at the Scrubs. So it was time for the authorities to address the situation. Prison officers in the north were offered a decent financial incentive to up sticks and head south. So a number of officers from Armley Jail in Leeds took up the offer. Dave Everett, Dave Beale, Geoff Kates, Mike 'Tomo' Tomlinson and Jack Jenkinson were all early members of what was originally known as the 'Wormwood Scrubs Branch' of LUSC. In our Championship season of 1991–92 the branch changed its name to the 'West London Branch', but the facilities at the extremely hospitable Scrubs social club are still being used on a regular basis by branch members and visiting Leeds fans today. In 1996 12 officers were having a quiet pint after coming off a hard shift patrolling the inmates, but their cosy little beverage was about to change somewhat and they were about to get a bit of a shock. Every Leeds fan that attended would really rather forget about that dreadful afternoon when we played against Aston Villa in the Final of the Coca-Cola Cup. Did the side turn up that day? It was all going so well prior to the match. The atmosphere was electric. It was our first Cup Final for 23 years and we had a half-decent side, or so it seemed. But then the match kicked-off. Only Frank Gray's son Andrew played well for Leeds that day in a match where we were second best all over the park. It is easy to sum up our performance that day. One word – awful! Never let it be said, however, that our supporters do not know how to turn what had been a very forgetable afternoon's football into a memorable night. Back at the Scrubs, these 12 officers were probably talking shop about this murderer and that burglar, when all of a sudden the place was literally taken over by around 300 Leeds supporters determined to have a good time despite our heartache only a short time ago. Mike 'Tomo' Tomlinson said, 'I overheard one of the officers at the bar muttering, "Where the bloody hell have this lot come from?!"' They stayed until the early hours of the following morning!

A Milan T…ale

'Leeds Jack' (Jack Jenkinson), as the treasurer of the branch is known in Kilburn, is a die-hard fanatic of the club. He lives and sleeps in his Leeds shirt and wears the colours with immense pride. He also has a love for a certain Yorkshire ale. Let us just go back to the Dominic Matteo San Siro experience for a moment. If you were there, on 8 November 2000, the sing-song between players and supporters after the match is something that will always live in the memory, and as if the night could not get any better, for 'Leeds Jack' and the West London Whites, it did. On leaving the magnificent stadium, heads held high, surely a drop of ale was on the cards? Unfortunately, however, with the paranoid Italian police insisting that all watering holes were shut for this match, it would be hard to find an open bar. Not for 'Leeds Jack'! After a short train journey away from the San Siro, Jenkinson and his mates from the West London Branch took a chance and got off at a remote little place in the pitch dark. In the distance Jenkinson could see a small light shining brightly. It was coming from a building that turned out to be a bar – an open bar! And that was not the end of the fans' joyous discovery. In they piled and, as soon as they stepped foot inside, Jenkinson's eyes lit up at the site of 'Tetley's Export' on draught. The night could not be any better! At first the slightly nervous landlord was not best pleased, but he soon realised that there wouldn't be any trouble and 'a good night was had by all.' As the rest of the West London Whites say, 'only Jack could find a pub in Milan that sells Tetley's!'

There are other London Whites scattered around the capital, one such fan being Angela Schofield. As loyal a supporter you could ever wish to meet, Angela can be found sat in her season ticket seat every other week at Elland Road, come rain or shine. And she's been to a fair few away games as well. Back in November 2005 was the incredible 4–3 victory on the south coast at Southampton, which has already been described. It was a simply amazing match, coming back from three down with less than 20 minutes left. Sure enough Angela was there, with her friends Bob Hinchcliffe and Simon Barrie. They too, like all of us, were going through the heartache of us playing some diabolical football in the first half, going in at the break 3–0 down. What was happening? For this trio, it was all a little too much to take. Two seasons before, just down the road at Portsmouth, we had been humiliated 6–1 in the Premiership and there was an air of familiarity about this match. They were not prepared to stick around and watch a repeat of that awful day. Southampton had cruised to their three-goal advantage and we did not look like we could hit a barn door. Messrs Schofield, Hinchcliffe and Barrie promptly left the building to find solace in a nearby boozer. They then lost each other outside the ground, so Angela dived into the nearest pub to watch events unfold on Sky TV.

'There were a few other Leeds fans that also left,' says Angela. 'We were all watching Sky Sports in the pub and we pulled a goal back to make it 3–1. Then it was 3–2 and by this time I'd necked a few more vodkas to numb the pain. When it went to 3–3 quite a few Saints fans had started to stream into the pub. Then this guy came running in on his mobile and said it was 4–3 to Leeds. Everyone started doing a "Let's go f'ing mental" chant in the pub. The strange thing was I kept getting complete strangers at our next away game at Millwall telling me that I should be leaving, as it was still 0–0. But I was there when we scored – own-goal but still 1–0 nevertheless – so there!'

Broken Sofas, Women's Magazines and Harvey to the Rescue

A stone's throw from the capital are the Essex Whites, who all come together for matches from towns such as Wickford, Chelmsford, Colchester and Harlow. They recently formed their Leeds United Regional Members' Club with chairman Paul Downer at the helm. Despite having been born in Berkshire, Downer was bitten by the Leeds bug at the tender age of just five after he watched on TV Allan Clarke's wonderful diving header against Arsenal to lift the 1972 FA Cup. Another hooked White on board. As he was growing up in the home counties people used to ask him why he supported Leeds. He used to retort, 'Because I'm from Reading!' His nickname was always simply 'Reading' but in 1986 he upped sticks to travel east and began studying in Essex, where he has lived ever since. On 27 August 1983 he went to his first Leeds match which was at home to Newcastle United, unfortunately going down 0–1, but it is a day he will forever have etched in his memory. 'It was a dream come true and I will never forget the atmosphere with over 30,000 there [30,806 to be precise],' he says. Exactly 20 years later he took his son James Downer along to *his* first match, ironically also against Newcastle United. Again it was not a win for Leeds, but at least there were Leeds goals and it was not a defeat. Mark Viduka and Alan Smith were on target in a 2–2 draw on Sunday 17 August 2003. They almost did not make it, however, as Downer Snr explains: 'On the way up we got hit up the back of the car while stationary on the A1. I was quite concerned about the accident but James was more worried about missing the match! He needn't have worried, we got there just in time.'

Paul Downer's wife-to-be at the time found out exactly what being a Leeds fan is all about when she joined him to watch on TV Tony Yeboah's fantastic hat-trick against Monaco on 12 September 1995 to sink the Frenchmen. Downer: 'When Yeboah scored his third my joy meant that I nearly hit the ceiling as I leapt up. However, as I landed I went straight through the sofa. She then knew what it's like to be a Leeds fan as I was still going mad despite being stuck for the remainder of the game!'

On the present state of affairs at Elland Road, Downer is happy with the current hierarchy. 'I feel the club is in good hands now. If I ran my company like the Ridsdale regime I am sure I would end up in jail. We may be in Division One but I would rather watch players who show the same passion and love for the club as the fans rather than watch so-called superstars on stupid money fleece the club. Ken Bates is getting the finances right and without him there would have been no Leeds United.'

On naming his favourite players in a Leeds shirt, Downer Snr replied, 'I have a number of favourite players, generally number fours and number nines – Bremner and Batty, Baird and Viduka. I also liked Lorimer and Strachan, and keeping with tradition, Douglas and Beckford now!'

Fellow Essex White Peter Drew names Arthur 'Lightning' Graham as his all-time favourite Leeds player and goes on to name his all-time XI, with subs, manager and assistant:

Nigel Martyn, Frankie Gray, Mel Sterland, Jon Woodgate, Rio Ferdinand, Arthur Graham, Eddie Gray, Johnny Giles, Peter Lorimer, Allan Clarke, Tony Yeboah. Subs: Carl Harris, Scott Sellars, David Batty, Gary McAllister, Lee Chapman. Manager: Don Revie, Asst: Sgt Wilko.

He may name Martyn in goal and there is clearly nothing wrong with that at all, but he also has a special mention for another great goalkeeper for Leeds, David Harvey. 'I was at an away match in Ipswich,' he says. 'The only Leeds fan standing all alone in the Churchman's Stand, the home end. I was just 13 years old, and songs of 'your going home in an Ipswich ambulance' were aimed at me. Then there's a crowd surge and I'm squashed against the railing and fall back and hit my head against the concrete terracing. Next thing I'm semi-conscious being lifted over the crowd by the police. Ipswich fans were calling me a drunk – I was 13! I'm put on a stretcher behind the goal and look up in a daze as a voice says "you alright mate?" and there's David Harvey staring down at me. The game was going on but he came off the pitch behind the goal to show his concern. What a great guy and a great 'keeper! The Ipswich fans then started their ambulance chorus as I was carried away. I managed to find my way home still half-conscious and emptying my stomach at regular intervals. Still, the upside was that Eddie Gray had scored the only goal of the game.'

On a trip some years later at Notts County Drew was only too glad to be *among* the hordes of Leeds supporters, as everyone watched County fans being shown the exit door one by one. 'It was a hot sunny day and some of the home supporters gathered on the fence segregating the fans. Leeds fans started chanting "who's the w***** on the fence". One Notts County fan reacted by going crazy and tried to scale the fence, getting himself arrested in the process. Focus then moved on to the next nearest County fan, with the same result. On the third attempt there was too much laughing among us to be able to chant coherently at the next victim!'

This book is certainly not sexist, but Peter Drew's Norwegian wife did not do the fairer sex any favours when, on her first outing to Elland Road, she enquired as to whether there was a shop at the ground. Initially Peter thought things are looking up, but as he finishes the story he explains, 'I asked her what she wanted to buy. "*Bella*" she replied. I then had to explain that the idea was not to spend a fortune on a ticket and then read a magazine during the game. At my youngest son's first game at Elland Road, my eldest son Kristian, now 14, was getting excited with the pre-match atmosphere, but Alexander, now 12, looked bored and ready for a sleep, so much so that a kindly steward in the South Stand took pity on him and came over and offered to fetch him a duvet and a pillow!'

The club seem to be heading in the right direction at last after a period of uncertainty and downright disastrous in-house management. Peter, who does not get to as many matches these days as he would like to due to running a youth football team called Boxford Rovers, could not agree more and is now excited about the future of our great club. 'The club appears to be in a healthy state for the first time in a long time. In the days of Leeds Sporting I used to attend the analysts' meetings in London, meeting with Peter Ridsdale, David O'Leary and Stephen Harrison. The club always boasted how it kept players' wages below 49 per cent of turnover and finances were run efficiently, then things changed. This would have been after the season we were defeated in Istanbul. We "lived the dream" (or attempted to) and, as a result, were left holding worthless share certificates. A tight hold on the finances appears to be in place now. There is a strong playing squad and, of course, the fan base is omnipresent. Leeds are not a fashionable club any more, but the fans are dedicated, committed and do their utmost to ensure their offspring keep the faith. It's a lifetime commitment and maybe beyond.'

Just before we move on to another staunch Essex White, Peter reflects, 'I remember Paul Hart giving me his "Hand of Peace" sweat band once before a match against Ipswich. Later that evening Jimmy Saville [from Leeds] was wearing one on BBC's *Jim'll Fix It*.'

Talking of Ipswich, it is not really such a shock that many of the Essex Whites' first glimpses of the glorious white shirts in action live came at Portman Road, and such is the case of John Bowgen, whose debut on the terraces came in the glorious Championship season of 1973–74 on 8 December 1973. 'I was nine,' says John. 'Mick Jones, Allan Clarke and Terry Yorath scored the goals in a 3–0 win. We went on to win the League, of course. I remember Sniffer's goal well. He cut in from the right and drilled a left-footed shot low into the corner. He tried to do the same thing later in the game, but only managed to twist his knee and was carried off. Apart from the goal, the other clear memory is of the players in the tracksuits with their names on, years ahead of time. I have clear memories of the FA Cup games against Ipswich in 1975 as well. I went to Portman Road on 8 March 1975, aged 11. The crowd was 38,010. That's still their record attendance now. I stood behind the goal in their North Stand, and remember hearing a Leeds song, so I looked around and their home end was full of Leeds scarves. I went to both replays at Filbert Street later in the month [after the initial replay at Elland Road – four matches in all, eventually Leeds going down 2–3 in the third replay]. God knows where my mum got the money to take me and my Ipswich fan brother. Nowadays I see more Leeds shirts in Essex than any other club, other than Man United, Arsenal, Chelsea, West Ham and Ipswich. I have been at the local gym with three people in there wearing Leeds gear. I saw Matt Heath in there, too, but he was in Colchester colours! I can understand the 40-year-olds like myself, but I am always amazed when I see teenagers in Leeds colours. I think in a strange way, our recent troubles and history of bad luck, controversial goals and referees, has only added to our brand. I think we all like the underdog. I must admit, I thought relegation from the Championship was the end of the world, but when you are watching a match, it doesn't matter what League you are in, or who you are playing, you love your team, and you want them to win. It's no different. I would imagine that watching a mid-table Premiership team, like Blackburn or Middlesbrough, can get pretty boring. Their fans know already that they are not going to win anything next year. The 2007–08 season, every single minute of every single Leeds game was important. It is easy to see why our fans are so passionate. Even before I got home after the Play-off Final at Wembley, I was getting excited about the following season.'

John concludes with his number-one White and all-time XI:

'Billy Bremner is my all-time favourite player. I had a number four sewn on to the back of my yellow shirt as a kid, even though I played up front. My greatest team is this: Nigel Martyn, Paul Reaney, Terry Cooper, Billy Bremner, Jack Charlton, Norman Hunter, Peter Lorimer, Allan Clarke, John Charles, Johnny Giles, Eddie Gray. Subs: David Harvey, Paul Madeley, Gordon Strachan, Gary McAllister, Mark Viduka. Manager: Don Revie. Assistant manager: Eddie Gray.

'Paul Madeley doesn't hold a position in my greatest-ever Leeds team, but only because of his versatility. Like Revie said, "He would be one of the first names on my team sheet", so deserves special mention. He is a Leeds legend.'

Keith Sanderson is the secretary/treasurer of the Essex Leeds United RMC and has only been following the Whites for a relatively short period, going to his first match at the end of the doomed 2003–04 season, watching Leeds draw 3–3 with Charlton Athletic, before being relegated to the Championship. Keith reflects on what was a fantastic atmosphere but one full of heartache. 'It was a full house and the Elland Road faithful were awesome. It was Alan Smith's last Elland Road game for the club and he was carried around after the game by the Kop crowd for some considerable time. It was a great day for me personally irrespective of the fact we were on our way down to the Championship. I will never forget the crowd were chanting "We're going down but we'll be back". They omitted to mention which year!' He adds, 'Leeds are a long-established club, with a great history, world known and players remembered from all decades, but probably the club is best known for its passionate supporters from youth to maturity.'

There is no questioning Keith's favourite player of all time: a certain youngster who began his life with Leeds United at the youthful age of just 15 and is still at the club now. 'I admired Peter Lorimer as a youngster and he is the reason, having been born in Coventry and brought up in Benfleet, Essex, I chose to support the club from an early age.'

Chiltern

Hector McFarlane moved away from his West Yorkshire roots in 1988 to take up his new job in Wellingborough. He eventually ended up in Milton Keynes, and it was there that his love affair with Leeds United really took off. 'While I was living in Bradford I was the proverbial armchair fan who was just happy to support the team by listening to the local radio stations or through the local press,' he says. 'I wasn't interested in actually attending matches, but when I left Bradford it was then that I began to miss my Leeds United fix. I simply couldn't get excited about listening to match reports about Northampton Town, Luton and Watford, and at the same time Wilko's revolution was beginning to gather steam. One of my biggest regrets is that I never took up the offers from a work colleague, Chris Ward, who at this time was a season ticket holder. During the successful Championship campaign in 1991–92 Chris often offered to drive me up to selected home games and sort me out with a match ticket. Once we were League champions I finally started to listen to Chris and found out what was required to be a season ticket holder. I would drive up on the day of a match or make a weekend of it, but after a few months I began to get a bit bored with the journey and started to miss a few games. In November 1992 I saw a small advert in the home programme against Glasgow Rangers. It read '*A minibus travels from Luton to all home games, picking up at MK Coachways – anyone interested can contact Terry Campbell*'. This was my first contact with the Chiltern Whites. Since 1992 I've now been to over 600 games and I think the best match I've been to we actually lost! It was the Deportivo game in Spain in the quarter-finals of the Champions League. I was quietly confident that since we had a 3–0 lead from the first leg it was unlikely that Deportivo could overturn the deficit. However, I vaguely remember them in a previous Champions League game that season overturning a three-goal deficit in less than 45 minutes and winning 5–3 on aggregate. On the night, when the score was 2–0 to them, I remember searching out my fellow Chiltern Whites in the crowd and asking them to hold out their arms to see how shaky and nervous they all were. The whole experience was fantastic and the fact that we actually qualified for the semi-finals and Arsenal went out on the same night made it even sweeter.'

Hector remembers an excellent victory at Newcastle United on 17 April 1995 when the magnificent Tony Yeboah grabbed the winning goal to inflict on the Geordies their first home defeat for 18 months. Recalling an amusing song from the opposition, Hector says, 'We were a goal up and then Newcastle equalised. Their supporters started to sing "You're not singing anymore", but then somehow Yeboah broke away and scored the winner for us. I remember seeing Yeboah reeling away to celebrate when the Toon Army's song turned into "you're not singing any…SH*T!" Just as we started our goal celebrations a small coin passed me and hit another of our members, Stephen Ricketts, and cut his lip. Steve picked up the offending coin and started gesturing to the police, showing them the blood on his lip. They didn't seem all that interested and did nothing apart from take the coin away. I was in trouble with our own members once. We were playing a midweek game against Leicester City and our group had arrived a little earlier than expected so we were looking for a place for a quick drink before the game. Myself and Terry Campbell were leading the way and we saw a bar with some bouncers at the entrance. Terry and I had just got past the entrance and were heading towards the bar when Paul Radnall, who was in our group, caught up with us. Paul was showing some Leeds United colours and the bouncers became a little dubious. He asked if we were all together. I didn't say anything but I suppose my body language gave the impression that we'd never seen him before. Before we got served Terry got to my better nature and we decided that it wasn't fair to leave Paul by himself so we reluctantly left the bar and went in search of another one. I got loads of stick for several weeks after that.'

Norwich

Norwich is probably most famous for Nicholas Parsons hosting *The Sale of the Century* ('it's the quiz of the week'), East Anglia's bumbling early morning spoof DJ Alan Partridge, as well as cook (and on the odd occasion tipsy) Delia Smith. The latter, of course, is a life-long Norwich City supporter and board member who famously once went onto the Carrow Road turf at half-time disappointed with the lack of vocal support by Norwich fans and in a slurred and comical manner said, 'Come on City, let's be 'avin' you.' Leeds, of course, have played there many times.

Marcus Oldbury played in a very surreal football match when he wore the Canaries' colours in an FA Youth Cup tie *against* Leeds United in 1993. The Leeds side contained the likes of Noel Whelan and Jamie Forrester and went on to beat Manchester United in the Final (oh what joy!), and Oldbury felt very strange trying to overturn Leeds at Elland Road, the very club he has adored all his life. 'I had to bite my tongue during the match,' said Oldbury of the second-leg semi-final, when any altercation between himself and any Leeds player took place simply because he did not want to have a go at anyone wearing a Leeds shirt. Oldbury, as a 17-year-old at the time, ended up on the winning side on the night as Norwich beat Leeds 2–0 but, following Leeds' triumphant 4–1 victory at Carrow Road in the first leg, it was not enough to knock United out and Leeds won 4–3 on aggregate. Oldbury had been to Leeds twice before with his dad, once to have a look at the magnificent stadium and secondly for a trial with United. He obviously impressed as Leeds offered him schoolboy forms, but the assurance of a more permanent apprenticeship at Norwich City was taken up partly because of Oldbury's father's advice. Oldbury was a cultured midfielder but in the end never made it to the first team at Carrow Road and made just 13 appearances for AFC Bournemouth in the professional game before he enjoyed a very successful non-League career, dominating the midfield with the kind of determination associated with many players that have worn the white of Leeds United. Now, at the age of 35, he is still going strong on the non-League circuit, but his thoughts and spirit are always with Leeds every Saturday afternoon, or whenever Leeds are kicking a ball in anger. Living on the south coast now he says, 'It frustrates me massively that I can't get to see Leeds, especially when they are playing on the south coast, but I'm always there in spirit.' One solution: hang up your boots Marcus, you know it makes sense!

Just before we head off back to Yorkshire, here is a list of Leeds players who were born in the Midlands:

Name	Joined	Left	Apps	Goals	Born
Ian Andrews	1988	1988	1	0	Nottingham
Aaron Baker	1927	1927	2	0	Basford Green
James Baker	1920	1925	208	2	Basford Green
Ian Bennett	2005	2005	4	0	Worksop
Harold Bridgett	1909	1913	14	2	Stoke-on-Trent
Henry Bromage	1905	1911	152	0	Derby
Brian Caswell	1985	1985	9	0	Birmingham
Lee Chapman	1989/92	1995	171/4	78	Lincoln
Malcolm Christie	2008	2009	4	1	Stamford
James Clapham	2007	2007	12/3	0	Lincoln
Allan Clarke	1969	1977	361/5	151	Willenhall
Fred Croot	1907	1919	227	38	Rushden
Ernest Depear	1948	1948	5	0	Spalding
Shaun Derry	2003	2007	75/3	3	Nottingham
Carl Dickinson	2009	2009	7	0	Swandlincote
Albert Duffield	1920	1925	211	0	Owston Ferry
William Dunderdale	1938	1939	4	0	Willingham-by-Stow
Willis Edwards	1924	1939	444	6	Alfreton
Anthony Elding	2007	2008	4/5	1	Boston
Merton Ellson	1920	1921	37	8	Thrapston
Chris Fairclough	1988	1994	232/9	23	Nottingham
Grenville Hair	1950	1963	474	2	Burton upon Trent
John Hampson	1913	1919	74	8	Oswestry
Gary Hamson	1979	1985	142/10	4	Nottingham
Dan Harding	2005	2005	21	0	Gloucester
Peter Harrison	1949	1951	67	9	Sleaford
Ernie Hart	1920	1935	472	15	Overseal
Matt Heath	2006	2007	57/2	4	Leicester
Steve Hodge	1991	1993	34/33	10	Nottingham
Eddie Hodgkinson	1946	1947	2	0	Ilkeston
Cyril Hornby	1930	1935	89	5	West Bromwich
Darren Huckerby	1999	2000	14/42	6	Nottingham
Julian Joachim	2001	2001	13/18	2	Boston
Seth Johnson	2001	2004	47/12	4	Birmingham
Simon Johnson	2000	2004	4/8	0	West Bromwich
Mick Jones	1967	1973	308/5	111	Worksop
Charlie Keetley	1927	1934	169	110	Derby

Name	Joined	Left	Apps	Goals	Born
John Kilford	1958	1961	23	0	Derby
Roy Kirk	1950	1951	39	4	Shuttlewood
David McAdam	1948	1949	24	0	Hereford
Geoff Martin	1960	1960	1	0	New Tupton
George Mason	1920	1922	66	5	Church Gresley
Danny Mills	1999	2003	133/8	4	Norwich
Fred Mills	1934	1938	70	2	Hanley-on-Trent
Ron Mollatt	1951	1954	17	0	Edwinstone
Stan Moore	1931	1934	83	0	Worksop
Harry O'Grady	1932	1932	9	2	Tunstall
Brendan Ormsby	1985	1989	57	7	Birmingham
John Oster	2004	2004	8	1	Boston
Carlton Palmer	1994	1996	128/2	7	Rowley Regis
John Pemberton	1993	1996	56/12	0	Nottingham
Michael Ricketts	2004	2005	13/16	2	Birmingham
Lee Sharpe	1996	1998	32/5	6	Halesowen
Harry Sherwin	1921	1924	107	2	Walsall
Len Smith	1922	1925	33	0	Birmingham or Worcester
John Turner	1935	1937	14	0	Worksop
Ben Underwood	1928	1930	6	0	Alfreton
Russell Wainscoat	1925	1931	226	93	East Retford
Don Weston	1962	1965	78	26	New Houghton
Andy Williams	1988	1991	35/26	5	Birmingham
Gary Williams	1987	1989	44/1	3	Wolverhampton

Chapter 21

ALMOST HOME VIA VAMPIRES AND DISCOVERIES

On the pitch – Yorkshire-born Whites outside Leeds:

Name	Joined	Left	Apps	Goals	Born
Mickey Adams	1987	1989	88/1	3	Sheffield
Michael Addy	1962	1962	4	0	Knottingley
Len Armitage	1920	1923	53	14	Sheffield
Thomas Astill	1908	1911	1	0	Sheffield
Ian Baird	1985 & 1987	1988 & 1990	190/2	57	Rotherham
Lawrie Baker	1923	1925	11	0	Sheffield
Leonard Baker	1923	1924	11	0	Sheffield
Ron Barritt	1950	1952	6	1	Huddersfield
Mick Bates	1964	1976	151/37	9	Doncaster
William Bates	1907	1909	15	0	Yorkshire
Rod Belfitt	1963	1971	104/32	33	Doncaster
Harold Brook	1954	1958	106	47	Sheffield
Tony Brown	1983	1990	24	1	Bradford
George Brown	1935	1936	41	21	Bradford
Victor Brown	1931	1931	1	0	Bradford
Eddie Burbanks	1953	1953	13	1	Doncaster
Ted Burgin	1958	1961	59	0	Sheffield
Danny Cadamarteri	2004	2004	0/1	0	Cleckheaton
Terry Caldwell	1959	1961	22	0	Wakefield
Terry Carling	1956	1962	6	0	Otley
Dick Coope	1920	1920	2	0	Pudsey
Terry Cooper	1963	1974	340/11	11	Brotherton
Will Copping	1929 & 1939	1934 & 1942	183	4	Barnsley
Andy Couzens	1993	1996	21/11	2	Shipley
Cyril Coyne	1944	1946	26	0	Barnsley
Richard Cresswell	2005	2006	31/13	11	Bridlington
Nigel Davey	1964	1974	20/3	0	Garforth

Name	Joined	Left	Apps	Goals	Born
Fabian Delph	2006	CP	47/7	6	Bradford
Roger Eli	1982	1985	1/1	0	Bradford
Harry Fearnley	1941	1949	29	0	Morley
Neil Firm	1976	1982	11/1	0	Bradford
Joseph Firth	1928	1934	75	25	Glasshoughton
Mark Ford	1993	1997	39/3	1	Pontefract
John Forrest	1952	1958	121	37	Rossington
Jamie Forrester	1992	1995	8/2	2	Bradford
Alan Fowler	1927	1934	15	8	Rothwell
Chris Galvin	1968	1973	11/5	2	Huddersfield
Colin Grainger	1960	1961	37	6	Wakefield
Dennis Grainger	1945	1947	40	6	Barnsley
Andy Gray	1995	1998	16/12	0	Harrogate
Simon Grayson	1988	1992	3/1	0	Ripon
Harry Green	1930	1934	19	4	Sheffield
Brian Greenhoff	1979	1983	74/4	1	Barnsley
Jimmy Greenhoff	1963	1968	128/8	33	Barnsley
Jack Hargreaves	1934	1945	48	11	Rotherham
Ralph Harrison	1949	1949	2	0	Clayton-le-Moors
Paul Hart	1977	1982	223	20	Golborne
John Hawksby	1959	1964	45	2	York
John Hawley	1978	1979	39/3	17	Withernsea
Gerry Henry	1938	1946	47	5	Hemsworth
George Hill	1920	1920	8	0	Dronfield
Tom Hindle	1945	1948	46	2	Keighley
Geoff Horsfield	2006	2006	12/3	2	Barnsley
Roy Ellam	1972	1973	19/2	0	Hemsworth
David Harle	1985	1985	3	0	Denaby
Terry Hibbitt	1964	1971	63	11	Bradford
George Hill	1920	1921	8	0	Sheffield
Tom Hindle	1943	1948	46	2	Keighley
George Hutchinson	1955	1957	11	5	Castleford
Arthur Hydes	1930	1938	137	82	Barsnley
Ray Iggleton	1948	1955	181	50	Hull
Tony Ingham	1947	1950	3	0	Harrogate
Mark Jackson	1995	2000	15/8	0	Barnsley
Eric Longden	1928	1930	28	7	Goldthorpe

Name	Joined	Left	Apps	Goals	Born
Richard Jobson	1995	1997	26	1	Hull
Bill Johnson	1923	1931	73	0	Sheffield
Chris Kamara	1989	1991	17/7	1	Middlesbrough
Matthew Kilgallon	2003	2006	86/9	3	York
John Lambert	1923	1923	1	0	Greasborough
Eric Longden	1929	1930	28	7	Rotherham
Peter Maguire	1987	1987	2	0	Holmfirth
Jimmy Mann	1971	1972	4/1	0	Goole
Cliff Mason	1961	1962	33	0	York
Lee Matthews	1995	1997	0/3	0	Middlesbrough
Don Mills	1951	1952	37	10	Bramley
Norman Morton	1945	1946	2	0	Barnsley
Peter Mumby	1987	1989	3/5	1	Bradford
Jon Newsome	1989	1994	73/15	3	Sheffield
Albert Nightingale	1952	1956	135	48	Thryburgh
Ben Parker	2004	CP	15	0	Pontefract
Bill Parry	1938	1938	8	0	Denaby
Alan Peacock	1964	1967	65	31	Middlesbrough
John Pearson	1987	1991	67/60	12	Sheffield
Sam Powell	1921	1925	28	7	Rotherham
David Prutton	2007	CP	49	4	Hull
George Reed	1924	1931	150	3	Altofts
Don Revie	1958	1961	81	12	Middlesbrough
Frazer Richardson	1999	2009	145/28	5	Rotherham
Keith Ripley	1954	1957	70	15	Normanton
Harry Roberts	1925	1937	87	2	Crofton
Paul Robinson	1997	2003	117/2	1	Beverley
Jimmy Rudd	1949	1949	18	1	Hull
George Scaife	1936	1939	9	0	Bradford
Scott Sellars	1983 & 1992	1986 & 1993	90/6	14	Sheffield
John Short	1946	1948	63	19	Gateshead
Carl Shutt	1989	1993	66/41	24	Sheffield
Albert Sissons	1925	1927	31	1	Kiveton Park, Sheffield
Alf Smelt	1920	1921	1	0	Rotherham
Barry Smith	1952	1952	2	1	South Kirkby
Glynn Snodin	1987	1992	102/14	13	Rotherham
Ian Snodin	1985	1987	55	8	Rotherham

Name	Joined	Left	Apps	Goals	Born
Mel Sterland	1989	1994	143/3	20	Sheffield
Ernie Stevenson	1951	1952	16	5	Rotherham
Bob Taylor	1951	1951	11	0	Rossington
Arthur Tillotson	1920	1920	2	0	Hunslet
Bobby Turnbull	1925	1932	215	46	Middlesbrough
Chris Turner	1989	1989	2	0	Sheffield
Peter Vickers	1951	1956	21	4	Doncaster
Albert Wakefield	1942	1949	50	23	Pontefract
Simon Walton	2004	2005	29/9	3	Sherburn-in-Elmet
Fred Waterhouse	1920	1920	2	1	Horsforth
Bobby Webb	1951	1955	3	0	Castleford
David Wetherall	1991	1999	232/18	18	Sheffield
John Williams	1948	1950	1	0	Doncaster
Ken Willingham	1947	1948	36	0	Sheffield
James Wilson	1928	1930	4	0	Garforth
Billy Windle	1947	1947	2	0	Maltby
Basil Wood	1920	1922	56	2	Wortley
Jon Woodgate	1997	2002	138/4	4	Middlesbrough
Frank Worthington	1982	1982	35	15	Halifax
Barrie Wright	1962	1964	8	0	Bradford

Yorkshire

Here is a good question for you. Who was the first Yorkshire captain to tour Australia? No, not John Hampshire. No, not Brian Close. Geoff Boycott (the 'true' Yorkshireman who supports the dark side)? No, not him either. Give up? Right, it was James Cook. Who? Who said anything about cricket? We are talking about Captain James Cook, who navigated his ship HM Bark *Endeavour* halfway around the globe to discover the east side of Australia. What an adventure that must have been. Cook was born in 1729 in Yorkshire and now you can find a fantastic mini-version of his famous ship, built with almost completely authentic parts, anchored permanently in the town of Whitby. There is someone else who also has connections with the seaside resort whose imagination turned into a bloodthirsty nocturnal set of adventures. Bram Stoker is the author who wrote his classic horror masterpiece *Dracula* in the Royal Hotel on the western side of Whitby. And, of course, Whitby is another place where many a Leeds fan resides.

They have endured and enjoyed some amazing adventures of their own. 'Scunny', Graeme Smith, Glenn Stamp, James Wales, Terry Graham and Kev Howard are just a handful of die-hard Leeds fans living on the Yorkshire coast, and they attend most games year after year. There are another 47 members in the Whitby Leeds United Regional Members' Club. And like Bram Stoker's world-famous book, which has since been adapted many times for cinema-goers to cower in their seats, these Whitby Whites have suffered their fair share of scary moments of their own watching Leeds United. The majority of them attend nearly all the home games and meet up at Whitby Rugby Club every first Thursday of every month, and every now and again they organise a special evening. One such event was in the early part of 2007. 'We had a raffle for a signed Leeds shirt and ball,' says club secretary Graeme Smith. 'We had a pool and darts knockout tournament, enjoyed a big breakfast and had a damn good drink. Our aim is to gather Leeds fans together and give the club the best support we possibly can. Even though we are not in the top flight, we will be back.' Club chairman Kev Howard recalls an occasion during the 1990–91 campaign when a Whitby supporters' coach caused the M1 to move along slower than a one-legged, visually impaired tortoise. 'We were watching a somewhat adult film on the coach video and the tailback behind us, with other vehicles trying to peek at the screen, brought the motorway to a practical standstill!' Moving swiftly forward to the present, having held a season ticket on and off since the 1970s, what's his opinion on the members' club? 'I believe it has given the tickets back to the fans,' he enthuses.

Going back to the dark days of the 1980s, James Wales owes his lifetime love of Leeds to former Whites midfield maestro John Sheridan. 'In 1988 he took me round the ground and gave me his Euro '88 Ireland shirt because they had no Leeds shirts in the club shop at the time,' he said. 'He told me to support Leeds, so I did! I then went to watch us beat Bradford 1–0 at Elland Road. I was able to get into the players' lounge afterwards and had my photo taken with David Batty. Walking into the ground that day as a seven-year-old was amazing.'

Susan Piper remembers the first match she went to see with her dad when she was two months short of her 11th birthday back on Wednesday 5 September 1973. 'We beat Wolves at Elland Road 4–1 [Lorimer got two – one a penalty – Jones and Bremner the others]. I felt so excited about seeing my heroes like Billy Bremner, Peter Lorimer and Gordon McQueen. I felt very grown up as well. It's the nearest football team to where my family come from and so supporting Leeds has been in our blood for generations. Leeds are my club and I am fiercely proud. To be a Leeds fan is to be a martyr, everyone hates us. Leeds are and always have been very unpopular. It's interesting seeing the winces on many people's faces when I tell them I'm a fan. Nowadays I live on the south coast but travel to Leeds as often as possible, some seasons not missing a home match. Season 2007–08 we visited all new grounds so it was like being on tour. Bremner is my all-time favourite player. He hated losing, and had a volcanic temper. One of the most enduring memories of Bremner is his unscheduled lightweight bout with Kevin Keegan at the 1974 Charity Shield. Bremner's midfield partnership with Johnny Giles was indisputably the engine room, which turned Leeds into the most formidable machine in British football. He was an inspirational footballer. He was a small man in civvies but a giant on the football pitch. He was not just instrumental in Leeds' success back in the '70s, he was the leader of the pack. People talk about his ball-winning skills, but there was much more to his game than that. He was a superb passer of the ball, scored some great goals and always rose to the occasion.'

Susan, who is a cardiac physiologist, understandably knows plenty of fellow Leeds supporters given her numerous years on the terraces, one of whom is staunch White Ralph Wainwright. 'He's been supporting Leeds now for 48 years,' explains Susan. 'But even that was not enough for Ralph. As soon as it became possible to commit to Leeds he became a Leeds United steward in August 1995. His wife is not a football fan in the slightest, so is a true football widow in every sense of the word. Ralph and Linda got married a week before the FA Cup semi-final against Wolverhampton Wanderers at Maine Road in 1973. They came home a day early from their honeymoon just so Ralph could go to the match. It was also Linda's birthday, which was put on hold! He remembers one match he went to in the early '70s when the first team wore orange. All the fans went silent, realising it was the Leeds players that were in orange colours. Leeds lost and it was the first and last time Leeds ever played in orange.'

Susan's all-time Leeds XI, subs, manager and assistant, looks like this:

Nigel Martyn, Paul Reaney, Terry Cooper, Norman Hunter, Jack Charlton, Billy Bremner, Johnny Giles, Eddie Gray, Peter Lorimer, Allan Clarke, John Charles. Subs: Tony Dorigo, Lucas Radebe, Tony Yeboah. Manager: Don Revie. Assistant manager: Gus Poyet.

Chapter 22

HOME SWEET HOME

On the pitch – More Leeds-born Whites:

Name	Joined	Left	Apps	Goals
Richard Naylor	2009	CP	24	1
Mike O'Grady	1965	1969	120/1	16
John Overfield	1955	1959	163	20
Paul Shepherd	1996	1996	1	0
Alan Smith	1998	2004	291/37	56
Peter Swan	1985	1989	50/8	13
Nigel Thompson	1983	1986	9/2	0
Arthur Tillotson	1920	1920	2	0
Noel Whelan	1993	1995	36/22	8

Horsforth – Leeds

So then, after hot-footing it all over the globe, it is time to get back to the one place that will remain in the hearts of everyone who has either been featured in this book or simply read it – up the M1 we go then and back to Leeds. And the one place which I personally am enormously grateful to – Horsforth. On 9 August 1930, Alice (great maiden name – 'England') and Henry Huddart (or Harry as he was known), who was an Elland Road season ticket holder, had a little girl named Nancy Huddart, born at Four Gables Nursing Home, on the Kirkstall Road. Living at 60 Victoria Drive, Nancy began her education at Featherbank School, before she moved with her parents to Barrow-in-Furness in 1938. In 1956 she married Ron Starmore and seven years later I came along! The Horsforth and Leeds roots were clearly cemented into my brain, given that I can honestly say I have no idea how young I was when I realised that I was a Leeds United supporter. It just seemed to be there all along. I do not remember anyone trying to persuade me to support this team or that. It was only ever going to be Leeds. So back to where my roots lie: it is time to track down someone else from this neck of the woods who shares the same passion for the Mighty Whites.

Lee Farrer is one such person. He has attended well in excess of 1,200 matches and he caught the Leeds United bug instantly when attending Elland Road for the very first time – but it was not for a match. On that glorious Saturday afternoon on 6 May 1972, in front of 100,000 supporters and the Queen, Allan Clarke's diving header secured our only FA Cup success to date. Consequently, the Cup and the victorious team were paraded around Elland Road.

'There wasn't a game but the club opened the ground up,' recalls Lee. 'I was six years old and I was hooked [that word again] immediately. All the routes around the ground were lined up and the team sang the Cup Final song in the centre circle, dressed in purple '70s suits! As I recall the ground was pretty full, certainly 30-odd thousand or so.

'The first Leeds away game I went to was Nottingham Forest in the League Cup semi-final in 1978. It was called off the first time we went because of fog, so we had to go back the following week. We'd been looking forward to it for weeks but when we were approaching Nottingham the fog was so thick it wasn't surprising to hear on the radio that the game was off. It was incredibly disappointing. We went back the following week but we got knocked out, of course. It was great excitement going away to watch Leeds, though, and we were in with a chance for a while until Forest, who were top dogs at the time, rattled in a few goals and that was that [Forest won 4–2 after beating Leeds in the first leg at Elland Road 3–1, so a miserable 7–3 aggregate defeat]. No Wembley trip that year!

'I've had a season ticket at Elland Road since 1977. I'm not quite up to Gary Edwards's standard but then who is? I don't know how he's managed it. I've only missed one home League game since 1981 and one away League game since 1989. So I don't know how he's been able to go to every game for 40 years. You've just got to make sure you can go to the next one, that's all you can do.'

And a highlight for Lee? 'I think when we got promoted at Bournemouth in 1990. We'd been in the old Second Division for such a long time. It seemed like a long time, although you kind of got used to it. That's got to be right up there as a massive high for the club. The tension was enormous. If we'd have lost that game there was a chance that we might not have gone up, so it was pure relief when we won and we were back in the top flight. It was a scorching hot weekend. We got down there on the Saturday morning about 5am and it was already full of Leeds everywhere. There's been plenty of highs but that really stands out for me does that. The week before that match when we beat

Leicester City [2–1 – Sterland and Strachan for Leeds – McAllister for Leicester] at home, that was probably the loudest I've ever heard Elland Road. Obviously when we won the League two years later and beat our arch rivals to the title, that was a bit special as well.

'One of the European trips we went on was the three days in Moscow with no match, when the game against Spartak Moscow in 1999 got frozen off. Everyone was ringing to find out what was going on and when I got home I was saddled with a £450 phone bill. We didn't realise it was £3.50 a minute to receive a call. We can laugh about it now but it wasn't funny at the time. We started hearing rumours that the game could be off and then on the morning of the match we found out that it was, due to a frozen pitch. We weren't going home until the following afternoon though, so it was like three days in sub-zero temperatures for no reason. We'd been the month before for the Lokomotive game so we didn't want to do any sight-seeing. The bars kept us warm though!'

Does Lee have a favourite goal and a favourite player? 'I cheer every goal with the same passion to be honest. It doesn't matter how they go in. Obviously the Yeboah goals stand out, and Clarke's winner at Wembley, of course. Chapman's winner at Bournemouth was special as well for what it meant. They're all certainly up there in the top bracket. As for my favourite player, for me it's got to be Bremner from the old team, and I would say possibly Strachan and Sheridan from more recent times.'

Lisa Woods also comes from Horsforth and can boast that, along with Mark Hunter, John Merrick and Uldis Tamsons, they have taken Leeds to the very top in England, Scotland and Wales. Back in 2000 the four of them, armed with a Leeds United flag, climbed the three highest peaks in all three countries in the incredible time of just 23 hours and 32 minutes, raising money for the Childrens Aid Direct charity. Ben Nevis was conquered in Scotland, which was followed by Scafell Pike in England and then Snowdon in Wales.

Seacroft

Dermot Broadhurst was brought up in the north-east of the city of Leeds in Seacroft and attended his first-ever game on 2 November 1963, which was a 1–1 draw at home to Charlton Athletic (Jack Charlton scoring for Leeds). It was the season in which Leeds prevailed as the old Second Division champions, breaking records in the process. Leeds got the record amount of points in that

Division (63) to gain promotion and they also achieved a record number of away wins (12) and fewest defeats (three). Dermot recalls happy days: 'There was Alan Peacock, Jim Storrie, Don Weston and my dad's favourite player John Charles, who all played at that time. I started watching Leeds regularly as I got older, from about the age of 14. I used to go in the old Scratching Shed and the best match for excitement when I was about 14 was Leeds against Glasgow Rangers in the old Fairs Cup. Everybody was crushed to pieces because it was an invasion from Glasgow [attendance: 50,498]. I'd never seen Elland Road so full, it was jam-packed and it was so exciting. And Leeds won 2–0 [through a Johnny Giles penalty and a Peter Lorimer goal]. Leeds went on to win the Fairs Cup that year [1968].'

As a young teenager Dermot and his mates had an interesting way of getting to matches whenever Leeds were playing in the capital. He says, 'If Leeds were playing in London we used to get the 2.16am mail train from Leeds that would get in at Kings Cross at 6am. There were never any inspectors on that train so we never paid. The first time we did that it was for a game against Tottenham and there were about 50 of us on this night train. I don't know how we all got away with not getting a ticket but we did.'

Dermot and his fellow Leeds pals, including John Manuel from Armley, couldn't quite get away with not paying when they went to Paris for the ill-fated 1975 European Cup Final, and as if being cheated out of the trophy was not bad enough, they were also stranded in Paris for longer than they would have liked. Dermot recalls the situation and talks fondly about another Leeds supporter he has since lost touch with, but will remember forever. 'I went to Paris for the European Cup Final and I remember not being able to get back for three days because the ferries were on strike, so we were stuck in Boulogne. There was a dwarf who used to come to matches with us as well, Dave Russell. He was our mascot and his brother Ronnie Russell from Beeston was always at games as well. We used to sit Dave on top of the old barriers and everyone around England knew Dave. He used to wear a leather jacket and a scarf that was longer than him! I don't know why, but in the early '70s people used to pinch opposing supporters' scarves and collect them. We were all from different areas in Leeds and just became good mates. It was my life when I was young and we went to every match home and away. It was all bred into me from my whole family who are all Leeds fans. I don't go and watch them now but every Saturday I look for their results. In the early '70s I would say Man City, Leeds and West Ham were probably the best supporters.'

Dermot's all-time Leeds XI looks like this:

David Harvey, Paul Reaney, Tony Dorigo, Billy Bremner, Jonathan Woodgate, Norman Hunter, Albert Johanneson, Allan Clarke, Peter Lorimer, Alan Smith, James Milner. Subs: Bobby Collins, Jim Storrie, Paul Madeley. Manager: Don Revie. Assistant manager: Dermot Broadhurst!

He contemplated putting Jermaine Beckford on the subs' bench but then opted for Madeley, saying, 'He's an ideal sub. He was a born sub.'

Beeston

Just round the corner from our sacred ground, Beeston-based Billy Hobson has been supporting Leeds for almost half a century. 'I've followed Leeds since 1961,' he says. 'And I can recollect the whole of the old ground. My first game was I think against Swansea Town [finished 2–2 with Jack Charlton scoring both Leeds' goals]. Among the first team were Alan Humphreys, Alf Jones, Bobby Cameron, Freddie Goodwin and Gerry Francis. Albert Johanneson was the first coloured player to play in an FA Cup Final, but Gerry Francis was the first coloured player to play for Leeds. There was also Billy Bremner, John McCole and Colin Grainger in the side that day. It used to cost one and three half. Two and six for an adult. I used to climb over the wall at the back of the Kop or get in Lowfields. There was only one way out and if you were slim like me you could get *in* that way.'

Moortown/Roundhay

Alan Johns, who was born and bred in the Moortown/Roundhay area of Leeds but now lives on the south coast, also picks his all-time XI, which is another interesting line up and one that, given his brief explanations for why he chose certain players, is difficult to argue against. 'Eddie Gray is my all-time favourite player,' says Alan. 'He had poise, precision and is an all-round nice guy.' Johns puts Eddie on the subs' bench however, with a line up that looks like this:

'Gary Sprake (those who saw him regularly can't deny he was world class 99 per cent of the time), Trevor Cherry (calm, skilful), Big Jack (Charlton), Woody (Jonathan Woodgate), Terry Cooper (see Cherry), Billy and Johnny (Bremner and Giles – linked by telepathy), Strach and Speedo (Gordon Strachan and Gary Speed), Clarkey and Chappy (Allan Clarke and Lee Chapman – we've had more skilful but their records speak for themselves goal-wise). Subs: Madeley (the ultimate super-sub), Eddie Gray and Gary Mac. Manager: The Don. Assistant manager: David O'Leary (you can't deny it was a wonderful team and great memories).'

Alan adds, 'Big Jack was a great guy at Leeds. I came across him a few times, through local youth football where he used to coach me at Matthew Murray on a Sunday afternoon after I was still caked in mud from a morning game. He and Willie Bell taught me loads that I still remember. Jack took me back home sometimes as he lived up our way. He presented a couple of trophies in Cup Finals that I was fortunate to appear in, the best memory of which was at ER getting changed under the "Keep Fighting" sign. Eight years later in Sheffield he remembered me and always used to have a quick word and he invited me to Hillsborough for treatment on an injury. He, St John and Maurice Setters used to drink in the pub near the ground and where I was working.'

Alan Johns's first match he recalls was way back on 25 February 1961 against Sunderland, so he was privileged to have seen the birth of the Revie side that would sweep any opponent away with breathtaking authority – eventually. It did not quite begin that way though, as Johns explains. 'We lost that game 4–2 and were 3–0 down at half-time, I think to a hat-trick from a player called Goodchild, who they had signed from Brighton that week. My brother and I stood on the wall at the halfway line in the Lowfields. I was 10 years old. We had been going home and away with Leeds Rugby League, so were used to rugby as they played it at primary school. I cannot remember being particularly excited at watching Leeds United as we were watching a poor side then. It certainly wasn't glory-hunting as we finished close to the bottom of the League that season [five points clear of relegation]. Don Revie was playing that season and everything changed the following year. The first game of the 1961–62 season we played a friendly against Leicester City, losing FA Cup finalists to double-winning Spurs the previous season. We wore the all-white kit for the first time at home and Harry Reynolds, the chairman, announced that we had a new kit and a new manager, and that we planned to get promoted into Division One and then get into Europe. I can't say that we laughed, but it all seemed pie in the sky at the time. History showed that it all happened!'

For the record the 1961–62 season was actually worse than the previous one, with Leeds finishing just three points off the drop and fourth from bottom of the old Second Division table. The following season though, 1962–63, saw a massive improvement and Leeds finished fifth. One season further on Leeds gained that promised promotion to Division One by storming up as Second Division champions having suffered just three defeats all season. In the next 10 seasons in the top flight Leeds would finish no lower than fourth and were a joy to watch, not just in England but, as Harry Reynolds had predicted, in Europe as well.

An extremely proud Leeds-born man, Alan Johns says, 'You don't have to ask if anyone's from Leeds because they'll already have told you!' Having attended countless games home and away for almost half a century it is no wonder Alan has a few stories to tell. There is the toothless Grimsby Town goalkeeper, some ever-so-slightly-dishonest Everton fans, a cheeky chappy knife borrower (!), a spooky tale involving Newcastle United and a 'free' away day that almost did not happen.

We'll start with the latter, or rather Alan Johns will, 'We had drawn home and away against Sunderland in the FA Cup [1966–67 – both 1–1 – Jack Charlton and Johnny Giles with the Leeds goals] and a chap from work said he'd get my brother and me tickets for the second replay at Hull City's Boothferry Park ground. He said he'd pick us up outside Addlestone's on York Road. I thought he must mean Addleman's, the department store, and we waited there until it looked as though we'd been stood up. We crossed the road and thumbed a lift with some plasterers in their white van. They parked near the ground and said to wait at the van if we needed a lift back. We got to the ground just after kick-off and there was no one on the turnstile so we jumped over, picked up a programme in the ground and moved into the crowd. By coincidence, we ended up next to the guy who should have picked us up. He said he had waited and then gone without us. When I queried his claim he said "Outside Addlestone's". I said "You mean Addleman's?" The place he was referring to, further down York Road, had been bombed during the war and was now something completely different. We didn't pay him for the tickets, had seen the game for nothing (which we won 2–1 with goals from Rod Belfitt and a Giles penalty – Sunderland had two sent off, Mulhall and Kerr), obtained a free programme and got a lift home, with fish and chips courtesy of the guys in the van. All in all it was a great, totally free, away trip!'

And what's this about a toothless Grimsby 'keeper? 'In the 1960s I was in my favourite spot on the wall in the middle of the old Scratching Shed when Grimsby's goalkeeper Charlie Wright had his front teeth missing, so I asked him during the warm-up what had happened to them? He replied that a big centre-forward in Scotland had knocked them out. I was peeling an orange and threw some peel at him and said "Here, have a suck on this" and he laughed. At the end of the half he came back to the goal to pick up his cap and drink and shouted

"See you Beatle-bonce" (a reference to my teenage haircut). The following year he came out, looked at me and said "no oranges this year Beatle-bonce?" Nice guy, long memory!

'Also back in the 1960s we were queuing at the little station near Burnley's Turf Moor ground. Someone in the queue went into a little corner shop and came out with a loaf of bread, butter and some cheese. On being told that he didn't have a knife he went back into the shop, through to the living area at the back and came out with a knife. The cheek of it! I also remember Everton fans walking out of the newsagents opposite Elland Road with crates of pop that used to be stacked just inside the entrance. Everton fans again, this time outside Goodison Park, stole boxes of programmes from between the seller's legs and ran off with them to sell elsewhere.'

Alan Johns does not profess to having a sixth sense or being able to look into the future, but on one occasion, again back in Revie's Super-Leeds building days, thoughts of becoming a clairvoyant must have been on his mind, if only very briefly.

This spooky story begins with a kick-about on Stonegate Road, Moortown, with a bunch of mates. Johns: 'I bent down to tie my bootlace and as I looked up to follow the game I had a vision of a Newcastle player on the ground saying to me "I've broken my leg". At the home game later that evening, an Easter Monday game, I was again on the wall behind the goal as Johnny Giles challenged for a cross into the box and a Newcastle player, full-back George Dalton, cleared it. My eyes followed the ball out of the area and then became aware of the player on the ground, holding his leg but not obviously in any pain, mouthing towards the 'keeper who was just in front of me. The 'keeper obviously couldn't hear above the crowd and shouted "What?" and I said to whoever was next to me "He's saying that he's broken his leg". It was exactly as I'd seen it a few hours earlier.'

Alan recalls some great times following Leeds everywhere and remembers one fellow White Phil Dobreen, who, as Alan says, 'was from the same Moortown/Roundhay area and was a big bugger with dark curly hair. He used to take his guitar home and away and he would start the singing every time.'

And what exactly does Alan think of the current United regime? 'We're off the critical list at last and should regain full health with the right care and attention. I think if we gain financial stability we will be back in the Premier League and then we can go as far as a serious investor wants to take us.'

Alan signs off by explaining a frustrating but wonderful trip to St Mary's Stadium, Southampton, in 2005. 'My sons and I were on the second row at the far end to all seven goals, but we had a great view of the amazing, galvanising power of the fans that day. At half-time my brother texted me from Leeds asking "3–0, what's going on?" I replied "we're not that bad". Friends of my boys were going past us taking the mick, but as we were among Saints fans we couldn't react. As the fans started their "We're gonna win 4–3" song, the home fans just laughed. Dennis Wise [playing for Southampton at the time] may have been the catalyst. We were still three down when he was substituted to a standing ovation. Then the rest is history and I had to bite on my hat (with the LUFC logo hidden) to stop laughing and shouting as the goals went in. At 3–3 my eldest said "Let's go" because he didn't think we could hide the fact that we were Leeds any longer as the people round us were getting really lairy. At the final whistle we hid our joy until we reached the car and then let out a massive roar of "YES!" This was followed by a joyous drive home, making and taking calls.'

Dave Whittaker is from Roundhay and he has followed Leeds since the late 1960s, getting into trouble with his parents at the age of 14 when he decided to go to Elland Road on his own for the visit of Manchester United. His defiance and use of all his paper round money for the week and the risk of receiving punishment from his parents was to be fully rewarded as Leeds spanked the enemy 5–1 in one of the greatest matches seen at Elland Road. 'It was one of the best days of my life,' reflects Dave. 'And, probably, the best 15 pence admission I have ever spent!

'As a 14-year-old schoolboy, broke and football mad, there was no way on this planet I was going to miss this game. Who cared if it was likely to cost me my paper round. Who cared if my mother would beat the crap out of me for going to a football match without parental supervision. As far as I was concerned this was worth every single punishment anybody could throw at me! This was one of my first games at Elland Road, and what a game it was. Clad in my green parka with its red lining, the traditional white scarf with the yellow and blue bands and there I was, on the Lowfields Road, witnessing the likes of George Best, Bobby Charlton, Denis Law, Alex Stepney etc, getting their arses well and truly kicked by the likes of Sprake, Reaney, Cooper, Bremner, Charlton, Hunter, Lorimer, Clarke, Jones, Giles and Eddie Gray. Talk about taking the mick. On that memorable day, Mick Jones scored a hat-trick with Allan Clarke and Peter Lorimer scoring the other two. I can't remember who scored the consolation goal for them but it didn't really matter. The chant from the Geldard End was "What's it like, to be outclassed, Man United?" That same season Super Leeds beat Southampton 7–0, Nottingham Forest 6–1 and Newcastle United 5–1, but still only managed to finish second in the League. Apart from the glorious result,

I remember shouting at George Best (though I doubt very much if he heard me) "Don't forget your handbag", only to hear, from directly behind me, "Big 'ard Leeds fan", from a crombie-clad Man Utd skinhead, and at the end of the game I remember being carried in the crush out of the ground, with my feet being unable to touch the terracing. Ah, those were the days.'

On another occasion in 1976 Whittaker recalls an unbelievable incident at Goodison Park, Everton, which if you were to say it was fairly scary it would be a bit of an understatement. Football violence was rife in those days, but he lived to tell the tale. 'Just over a week earlier Leeds had drawn at home 1–1 against West Ham. The atmosphere in the back of the Geldard End was the same as usual for a home game against any London club. All the anti-cockney songs were being sung, who to I don't know. We couldn't see any West Ham fans in the ground. In those days not many away fans travelled, this was 1976 and there was no Leeds Service Crew. When Leeds fans travelled away, they did so in their own small groups. There was no main gang, you just went away and hoped for the best. I remember the chant, "If you're going to Everton clap your hands." There wasn't a great response, but enough joined in to make you feel there would be some strength in numbers for the following Saturday's game in Liverpool. I was 18 years old and my life had two values, Leeds United Football Club and beer, that was it.

'In those days Everton was known to be a bad ground for visiting fans, and so none of my mates from Roundhay and Chapel Allerton would go. That pissed me off but I still had some college mates who were up for it. Mick P from Headingley, who worked as a doorman in some of the city's most notorious pubs for years, came along, so too did a guy from Bramhope and another couple who I did not know. So there were five of us on the football special which left Leeds City Station at about 10.30 that cold, grey, Saturday morning.

'The train journey over the Pennines was quite uneventful, and the entire number travelling could have filled just three carriages. There weren't many of us travelling, maybe between 70 and 120, not a great number. Anyway, our group of five crammed round a seated table and played three-card brag for part of the journey. Mick P and I cheated and worked together; needless to say I won a few pounds and we shared the takings later. There was one of West Yorkshire's finest police officers watching the game. I saw him smile as he clearly witnessed Mick and I giving each other the nod as we looked at other players' cards. He said nothing.

'We disembarked at Lime Street Station about lunchtime. The double-decker buses were awaiting our arrival, and the entire number from Leeds only managed to fill two of them, which wasn't too promising. I can't remember much about the bus journey to Everton's ground, Goodison Park, but I definitely remember what happened when we climbed off. Once outside the stadium, there was quite a large group of Everton fans hanging around and they weren't there to share toffee! What did surprise me was the reaction of the Leeds fans. Without a moment's grace they charged at the home fans. I think this was as much a shock to the home fans as it was to me, but the Everton fans fled as the Leeds fans ran at them. I don't remember any contact being made as the mounted police soon charged at us wielding those Merseyside metal-tipped batons. They were very liberal with them.

'The mounted police surrounded the Leeds fans, and as they unleashed their weapons, they screamed at us. As they crushed us together next to some turnstiles into the ground I saw one fan drop to the floor with blood coming from a police baton head wound, then came the police with dogs. It became a matter of gaining entry to the ground or being beaten and trodden on. This is where the complete madness of the day really started. We were forced through the turnstiles of the Everton home end. I think they called it the Gwladys End, it was about 1.30pm. Once inside there was total confusion. Nobody knew where we were but that was soon to change. We climbed the concrete staircase to the terracing and then, once there, at the bottom left-hand corner of the terracing, we looked up. There was a sea of blue and white only yards away from us. The entire home end was half full and every single eye among them seemed to focus on this group in the corner of their patch. Like a swarm of bees the entire mass of blue and white seemed to move, a sea of like-minded fans just charged down the terracing at us. Luckily there were no barriers to stop fans climbing from one part of the ground to another or onto the pitch. I didn't take much notice of the others around me, I just climbed over a barrier into the adjoining part of the ground as fast as I could. Everybody else seemed to do the same, and within a minute or two, all the Leeds fans had regrouped and congregated on the terracing in the corner of the opposite side of the stadium. After that little shock, I didn't believe the day could become any worse. I was in for a rude awakening! Leeds won 3–1 [Billy Bremner, Joe Jordan and Carl Harris on target] – that was the only good part of the day. At half-time I went to the food shack beneath the terracing. I was wearing the fashion statement of the time, Oxford Bags, and one of those green and yellow jumpers with three stars spread across the front. I stood out like a lighthouse. Apparently a girl serving the food commented how she liked my jumper and how the fashion hadn't reached Liverpool. She also stated how brave we were, in the way that we were the first away fans to actually show ourselves at Goodison that season. I wasn't sure what to make of that, and I'd lost my mates. I was alone in a group of Leeds fans, none of whom I knew. Throughout the game we sang various songs, one I remember was "Hey rock 'n' roll, Clough is on the dole", a reference to the much-disliked former manager Brian Clough. I had a silk scarf with me, it had "Super Leeds" printed across it, and a couple of times I held it out, baiting the home fans in the adjoining part of the ground. It worked. The atmosphere was hostile to say the least, and as the second-half minutes ticked away I was becoming very worried about whether we were going to make it back to Lime Street in one piece. The odds felt very much against it. With about 10 minutes of the game remaining, the home fans were really pissed off. They had been beaten 3–1 and the hooligan element wanted revenge. I was stood at the back of the Leeds fans. I could see down the stand and noticed how the gates had been opened. Then I saw a face I recognised. It was Eddie C from Harehills with two of his mates. This guy's reputation was legendary. At one time he was the leader of one of the biggest skinhead gangs in Leeds, the Harehills Skins. He and his two mates were leaving, and as they didn't know me, and I knew of him, I thought it might be a good idea to tag along behind them. We had not been outside the ground for a minute when the trouble started. There were home fans everywhere waiting for us. The first thing I saw was a Leeds fan being chased right past me. There were four or five chasing him. I don't know what happened to him. I think he found protection from the police, but what really struck me was the next event. Five or six home fans confronted Eddie C and his two mates. I was only a few feet behind them and they were baying at Eddie, his mates and myself to get us to fight. I couldn't believe what happened next. Eddie unfastened his sheepskin jacket, pulled out a gun and pointed it in the face of the Everton fan who was doing all the mouth actions. In disbelief I froze where I was. These home fans didn't expect that, I didn't expect it, nobody expected it! These guys turned white. The expression on their faces has never left me. This was madness. A guy with a gun at a football match.

'Seconds later the chaos started for me. About 10 home fans were running at me, directly at me. The jumper had given me away. Well, I just bolted back towards the ground. There was a queue of buses next to some railings and a park. I just ran as fast as I could towards them. I was fast in those days. I have never been a fighter, I've never been violent, but on this occasion I had no choice. I ran past some of the buses. I didn't know how many were chasing me. I bolted between two of the stationary buses and decided to make a stand. I didn't know how many were still chasing me but, much to my surprise, and his, there was only one. He was on his own, the others had lost interest. I turned and confronted him. He didn't expect it. He didn't think he was alone but it was just the two of us between two parked buses. I was buzzing by this time. My adrenaline was up there with the lions. I was ready for him. Thing is, he wasn't ready for me. I looked at him and screamed at him to fight me. He wore glasses, had a scruffy denim jacket on, scraggly long black hair and, to his horror, he was alone. I didn't hesitate in punching him. The punch was beautiful, straight in his mouth. I knocked him straight to the ground and saw the blood instantly. It was over in a couple of seconds but it felt like an eternity. He jumped back up and like the arsehole he was, fled the scene. I laughed, the bus driver smiled approvingly at me and put his thumbs up. He agreed that I had dealt a good one. I walked away from the ground in a direction that wasn't going towards the city centre, jumped on the first bus that came along and made my way back into Liverpool city centre and Lime Street Station. I met the rest of the fans back there; they all had their own tales to tell. I saw Eddie C and he was looking at me, wondering how I had managed to get back. I met up with Mick and the others. It had been an interesting day. On the way back I was sat on a table on the train, sharing stories, when as we left Liverpool a brick hit the window I was leaning against. Luckily it didn't shatter. It was a farewell gift from the lovely Everton fans. The story of Eddie C and the gun became legendary at Elland Road. Everybody heard about it over the years. Everybody seemed to have been there and witnessed it. Sorry lads, I know what happened because I was there and, believe me, it wasn't pleasant viewing! I have had a couple of incidents at games over the years, as most lads have, and, if I'm totally honest, I felt proud of myself. As for the Everton fan, UNLUCKY!! I hope I broke a tooth or two.'

Chapter 23

THE EDWARDS VIEW PART III

In Part Three of 'The Edwards View' I ask Gary just exactly how many consecutive games he has attended?

'I have always been reluctant to actually add up all the consecutive games I've seen since the Derby game in 1968, because it's sod's law that I'd miss the next one!'

Don't worry Gary, no need to work it out, so no threat to the superstitious notion. This book has done it for you and a comprehensive table of stats can be found at the end of the book. It is an incredible record to hold and one that must be almost impossible to beat by any other football supporter in the world. Next I could not possibly avoid asking Gary to describe in his own words his all-time Leeds United side, with substitutes, a manager, an assistant manager and a coach. Of course, we all have our own ideas of what the ideal all-time Leeds United side would look like. But it's fair to say that Gary Edwards's views have to be noted. His answers were not difficult for him, apart from the goalkeeper – we'll start there:

Goalkeeper: Gary Sprake / David Harvey

The goalkeeper is a tricky one. Gary Sprake was part of Don Revie's early set-up and remained so for over 10 years. He was my boyhood hero as I went on to become the school team goalkeeper right through my school years. Remaining true to Sprake, I even let one through my legs on my school debut. Sprake received much criticism for some costly blunders, all of which were televised, but he contributed to some of Leeds's early successes with countless world-class saves. He was a superb 'keeper. I turned against Sprake when he sold a story to the *Sunday People* and *Daily Mirror*, wrongly claiming that bribes played a big part in Revie's Leeds. Revie and Leeds sued the newspapers and received £200,000 compensation (a record amount at the time). Throughout Sprake's playing career, David Harvey was his understudy. Harvey got his chance in the FA Cup Final replay in 1970 after Gary Sprake's famous blunder in the Final at Wembley against Chelsea; a blunder that almost certainly cost Leeds their first FA Cup triumph. Apart from a handful of appearances by Sprake, Harvey remained the number-one 'keeper under and beyond Revie. Shortly before his death in 1989 Don Revie admitted that he should have used David Harvey long before he actually did – I have to agree with him. Another 'keeper worthy of note is Nigel Martyn.

Right-back: Paul Reaney

'Speedy Reaney' was by far the best right-back anywhere in Great Britain if not Europe. His goal-line clearances were legendary. George Best said that Reaney was his most difficult opponent ever.

Left-back: Terry Cooper

Cooper scored the only goal at Wembley in 1968 to give Leeds the League Cup, their first-ever trophy. Similar to Reaney, he was an expert in the overlap role. He was highly praised by Pelé during the Mexico World Cup in 1970.

Right-half: Billy Bremner

His very name says it all.

Centre-half: Jack Charlton

The 'Giraffe' was the best and most famous centre-half of his day. He was the backbone of England's World Cup victory in 1966. I can still close my eyes today and see him charging up and down the field in the famous all-white strip of Leeds United. He had the opposition defence crapping themselves for every corner-kick.

Left-half: Norman Hunter

Norman 'bites yer legs' was outstanding. His presence alone was almost enough to deter the opposition from entering Leeds's half. His no-nonsense tough tackling was a major factor in Leeds's rise to the top in the 1960s. Groundstaff up and down the country used to hate it when Norman was in town. They would have to spend half an hour after each game sweeping limbs and other body parts from the stand roofs!

Outside-right: Peter Lorimer

'Hot Shot' was reputed to have the hardest shot in football and not many 'keepers would disagree. Play was regularly held up while the 'keeper had new hands sewn on. He is the only Leeds player to score over 200 goals and he scored 176 in one season while still at school.

Inside-left: Allan Clarke

A big favourite of mine, Clarke was phenomenal. Nicknamed 'Sniffer' because of his uncanny knack of always being in the right place at the right time, he scored some priceless goals for Leeds and is still a big fan of the club today. I saw every game that Allan Clarke ever played for Leeds and saw every goal.

Centre-forward: Mick Jones

The unsung hero. Jones was Revie's first £100,000 signing and he was worth every penny. His partnership up front with Clarkey was feared across Europe.

Inside-right: Johnny Giles

Stolen from across the Pennines for a mere £35,000, he formed the famous midfield duo with Bremner and tore the rest of Europe to pieces. His ball skill was superb and his 'football brain' was the envy of every opposition manager. It was overwhelming public opinion that he should follow Revie as manager, but the buffoons in the boardroom had other ideas.

Outside-left: Eddie Gray

His ball control was admired the world over. Despite cruel injuries throughout his career he was one of the most exciting left-wingers in football. He was also an amazing coach and nurtured a brilliant crop of youngsters from Leeds's youth set-up and watched them execute their skills throughout Europe.

Substitutes:
Anywhere! Paul Madeley

Football should be a 12-man sport, because Madeley was far too good to be left out of Don Revie's team. Fortunately, because Madeley was, without doubt, the best utility player anywhere in Europe, he was almost always included in the team. 'Mr Versatile' and 'Rolls Royce' were just a couple of descriptions he picked up along the way.

Forward: Mark Viduka

Viduka, in my opinion, was one of the best target men in Europe. He didn't get nearly enough recognition for the effort he put in. The way he brought supporting players in to the game was second to none. And he has been known to knock a few in himself.

Forward: Tony Yeboah

One of the best strikers I have ever seen at Leeds United. His scorcher against Liverpool in 1995 won BBC's *Match of the Day* Goal of the Season. His power was awesome and he would shoot, literally, from anywhere. Leeds dispensed of his services far too early for my liking.

Midfield: David Batty

Bats was almost a parody of Billy Bremner. I say 'almost' because unfortunately a large part of his career was away from Elland Road. When at Leeds in his early days he displayed a fearless attitude in the tackle, despite invariably being the smallest player on the pitch. When he returned to Leeds some years later he had obviously matured into a fine player, demonstrating superb holding skills and player support, as well as maintaining his natural tackling ability.

Defender: Lucas Radebe

In this day and age of disloyalty amongst players, Lucas is a breath of fresh air. Leeds gave him his chance in English football and even after a call from over the hill from Alex Ferguson he chose to stay with Leeds. 'I'm very flattered,' he said at the time. 'But Leeds have been good to me, I'm happy to stay here'. On a personal note, I've met Radebe on a number of occasions and he is a top bloke!

The Management
Manager: Don Revie OBE

If 'The Don' had achieved anywhere else what he achieved at Leeds, he would have been recognised for what he was – quite simply the greatest English club manager ever. It is no secret that Leeds were, and still are, hated throughout the land and that Revie's great success was all but ignored by the press. It must have really hurt when he was awarded Manager of the Year, 1969, 1970 & 1972 and received the OBE in 1970, but even then the authorities were loathe to accept Revie's unequalled record.

Assistant manager: Eddie Gray MBE

Eddie's insight and knowledge of the Leeds youth teams, and his ability to nurture them into established first-team members, leaves me in no doubt that he would be the perfect right-hand man to Don Revie.

Coach: Syd Owen

Don Revie appointed the then Luton Town manager as his coach, and what a coach he turned out to be. Ably assisted by trainer Les Cocker, Owen worked closely with Revie's young stars of the early 60s and watched them grow into a united force that took the rest of the League by storm.

Chapter 24

CARDIFF REVISITED –
UNFORTUNATELY!

The 2005–06 season ultimately ended in heartache. A feeling we have all felt far too often over the years. Near the beginning of this book some of the South Wales Whites were featured. And the idea was to have this chapter towards the end of the book, revisiting Cardiff, where we were to emerge victorious after a brilliant Millennium Stadium Play-off Final day out. It never happened, and we went down miserably 3–0 to Watford. Needless to say, this was a tough chapter to write.

A couple of weeks prior to the Final, for the second leg of the semi-final against Preston at Deepdale it was impossible to get tickets, and so, as already mentioned, a few of us jumped on a train and headed along the south coast to a place called Woolston in Southampton. We met up with the Hampshire Whites for what turned out to be a superb night. There were around 50 of us, all wearing our colours and all emotionally drained even before kick-off with nerves jangling. Everyone in that pub and many other thousands of Leeds fans across the globe had trouble sleeping the night before. The prize of going back to the Premiership via the Play-offs was possibly just 180 minutes of football away. And the massive financial implications were all too apparent. The heartache of the last few years was tantalisingly close to being put to bed and laid to rest in the history books. We were on the brink of going back to where our great club belongs.

Kick-off was fast approaching and before you knew it, following the 1–1 draw at Elland Road on the previous Friday, and with no away goals counting double, we had got to half-time in the second leg and it was still effectively 0–0. As if our nerves were not bad enough, suddenly the lights went out at Deepdale. Someone hadn't remembered to put 50p in the meter, obviously! All the nerves building up to this match could have to be relived if they could not find enough 50 pence pieces. A quarter of an hour had passed and it was looking increasingly likely that the match would be abandoned and rescheduled for another night of anxiety. However, the moment came. One light on one floodlight began to shine. This was met by a huge cheer inside Woolston's the Bridge pub. Another light. Another cheer. Minutes later and we were back on. There was a delay of around 20 minutes, but at least we knew we were not going to have to rearrange for another night. Then there was better to come. Much, much better. Some of the Preston players and indeed their manager Billy Davies had come out in the press prior to the game and said that the two-legged semi-final was pretty much over and that they'd done their job by getting a draw at Elland Road. What more motivation did Kevin Blackwell's outfit need? Not a jot more. With just over 10 minutes gone after the restart from the Deepdale floodlight farce, Rob Hulse buried a header beyond the Preston 'keeper to put us one up. It was time to bounce. Five minutes later we were bouncing again when Frazer Richardson watched his shot sneak in for 2–0. We were on our way, although there was still just under half an hour to go. Stephen Crainey then got himself sent off with a second yellow card, meaning he would miss the Cardiff showdown should we get there. Even though we were two goals to the good, going down to 10 men was not going to help matters. Then substitute Richard Cresswell also saw red following his second yellow and he too would be absent from the Millennium Stadium. Despite us being down to nine players by the end of the contest, however, we held on and we were indeed off to Cardiff. It was a great feeling. A great, great feeling. It was time to bounce again! I'd never been to Cardiff before and always said that I would never go unless Leeds were there. Leeds *were* there, so *now* I was going. Wow. I was bouncing more than Tigger and Zebedee put together! It was hugs all round before we headed back to Bournemouth for the best night's sleep for some time. For a night when I was not actually at the game, it was probably the best night I have ever had watching Leeds on the box. The desperately disappointing moments in football are part and parcel of the game (certainly in our case anyway), but they just make nights like that all the more enjoyable. For that particular evening my grateful thanks go out to the Hampshire Whites.

A day short of two weeks passed by and it was time to get a little stressed once more. Every day during that fortnight I was waking up with thoughts of Cardiff. Waking up with thoughts of the Premiership. Waking up with a burning hunger and desire for Leeds to end their two-year exile from the big time. Being a Leeds member but living on the south coast meant I had to apply for my ticket for Cardiff by post. The queues round Elland Road for people getting them in person were astronomical. The first person started queuing at 4am on the Wednesday morning. The ticket office opened at 10am. It finally shut after they'd served the last fan in the queue at 3.30am on the Thursday morning! The fact that supporters had their tickets in their hands and I was sweating on the post simply made for more restless nights. You couldn't ring because initially the phone lines were so hot, it actually shut down the whole network in Leeds! The club therefore stuck an automatic message on the phones. They were not taking email orders for tickets either, or even via the old-fashioned fax machine. You simply had to wait for the postman. No need to worry though in the end. Sure enough, a few days later they came through the letter box. Phew!

Now it was time to get ready for the big day. It is a simple journey from Bournemouth. The 8.18am train, arriving in Southampton at 9.09am, meant a 46-minute wait for the direct train to Cardiff. Simple! Or so it should have been. When my brother Baz, son Ben and I arrived at Southampton Central, there were a couple of Leeds fans on the platform and a couple of Watford. Slowly but surely a few more Watford appeared and loads and loads more Leeds. By the time the train was due there was an announcement. 'The 9.55am service to Cardiff Central is delayed by approximately…' There was a worrying pause for everyone on the platform…'five minutes', continued the announcement. Relief! Followed by 'because of overcrowding'. We then heard that there were only three carriages. Now let's think. The train is already full. The platform at Southampton was packed. There must have been around 200 Leeds and around 10 Watford. And there were just three carriages. And it was the only train from Southampton to Cardiff that day. Nobody was going to miss that train, however, and so getting on it was like bundling into Harrods on the first day of the January sales. Amazingly Ben and I got a seat each and about half an hour later Baz somehow managed to get one as well. The one thing that worried me slightly was how on earth I was going to manage to visit the toilet en route, which was more than likely given the four cans of John Smiths Smooth in my possession. For the last half hour of the two and a half hour journey I could have burst and was surprised I didn't. We pulled up at Cardiff Central and you can guess where the first port of call was.

Then the realisation struck. We were right outside the Millennium Stadium. I had seen it on telly loads of times but never stood right outside. Not only that but Leeds fans were everywhere. Simply brilliant! There were a few people I had hoped to meet up with once we got to Cardiff, but given the chaos everywhere and the sheer numbers of Leeds supporters, the best idea was to just dive into the nearest pub you could get in. 'Edwards' it was then. It was heaving but had no queue like some of the others. As soon as we walked in, the songs were at full pelt. *And We've Had our Ups and Downs, When I was just a Little Boy, We all love Leeds,* and so on. With this kind of phenomenal support, surely Leeds were going up? Surely they could not do anything other than win. We had drawn at their place 0–0 and beaten them at Elland Road 2–1, so nothing to fear then?

Sadly, Leeds don't seem to *do* Cup Finals. It ended up being 1996 all over again, only this meant so much more. Ten years previously we were simply awful, going down 3–0 against Aston Villa in the Coca-Cola Cup Final. Alright, that was for a place in the UEFA Cup, but it still was not as big as a place back in the Premiership. A decade on, the performance was not quite so bad but the score, and more importantly the outcome, was exactly the same. A 3–0 loss to a Watford side that were favourites for relegation at the start of the season. How on earth did that happen? The 3–0 scoreline definitely flattered Watford, but they did deserve the win. They were better than us on the day. You always think of the 'what ifs', though. What if Eddie Lewis's free-kick just before the break had crept in under the bar for 1–1? What if Shaun Derry's header in the second half had not been frantically cleared off the line? What if the assistant referee had got the decision on a throw-in right? The throw that was clearly ours but given to Watford. The throw that led to the freakiest of second goals for Aidy Boothroyd's team. What if we had *really* turned up!? As it turned out we were not even able to celebrate a goal, which would have taken the closed Millennium Stadium roof right off. Is it that we do not *do* Cup Finals or that we simply do not *do* Cardiff? I am not quite sure. It certainly is not the happiest of hunting grounds for us. Maybe it is nothing to do with Cardiff at all. Maybe it is pinstriped shirts. Remember 1982? Pinstriped home shirt = relegation. Remember 2004? Pinstriped away shirt = relegation. This was now 2006 – pinstriped home shirt = no promotion. Coincidence? Probably. Worth taking the risk again? No. Ditch the pinstriped shirt idea for good. By the way, our goalkeeper in the Watford match was Neil Sullivan, who was making his 100th appearance of an eventual 110 for Leeds. He was hardly celebrating his century of Leeds outings, but he was celebrating promotion two years later. Unfortunately, he was wearing a Doncaster 'keepers' top *against* Leeds!

One day short of six weeks after the Millennium misery, the pain of watching your team lose in an important match flooded back when England crashed out of another World Cup, again on sodding penalties – against Portugal. What a year 2006 promised to be. And what a year it turned out to be. Leeds going up, England bringing football home – that was the dream. The reality was a tad different. On a happier note, before we move on, here is *my* all-time Leeds line up, with five subs and a manager.

David Harvey

This was a close-run thing between Harvey and Nigel Martyn for me. Both excellent 'keepers, both played for their country (Scotland and England respectively, despite Harvey having been born in Leeds!) and both huge favourites with the fans. We've been privileged over the years to have some outstanding 'keepers at Elland Road. Gary Sprake got some stick in his day, but he could not possibly have survived longer than five minutes under Revie if he had been a real duffer. Paul Robinson became England's regular number one, nurtured at Elland Road. And other more than competent 'keepers we have had are David Stewart, John Lukic (apart from against Rangers in 1992), Mervyn Day and the one that got away, David Seaman.

Paul Reaney

'Speedy Reaney' was, as his nickname suggested, super quick. He possessed an excellent touch and I'll never forget that during Leeds's mickey-taking of Southampton in 1972, when we won 7–0, the passing after we had scored our seventh involved some lovely touches from the England right-back. Danny Mills and Mel Sterland were both good performers for Leeds in the right-back position and deserve a mention as well.

Terry Cooper

Terry Cooper was an awesome left-back. By far and away the best in his position throughout the land at that time. Ian Harte and Tony Dorigo both played an excellent part in this position for Leeds, but it's TC that gets my vote.

Billy Bremner

Although David Batty was a superb number four for us, there can be no doubt whatsoever about who the real number four in a Leeds United shirt was. Every time I go to Elland Road I always make a point of having another look at the statue of dear old Billy, which was created by Frances Siegelman and unveiled prior to a game against Derby County on 7 August 1999. He was a phenomenal player who never played with less than 100 per cent effort for Leeds. He simply did not know how to. The goals against Man Utd in so many Cup games typified his sheer guts, determination and will to win, not matched by anyone before or since. It is tragic that he passed away at the age of just 54, ironically the same number of caps he was awarded for Scotland, and on a personal note very frustrating, given that I had booked tickets for a sportsman's dinner which was to be hosted by Billy himself three months after the great man left us. I would have been so proud to have met the man. RIP Billy, you will never be forgotten.

Lucas Radebe
The ever-smiling South African, who was once shot in the leg, clearly lives for every day. His infectious grin is as big a part of the man as was his immense influence on the pitch. When he first arrived from South African outfit the Kaizer Chiefs even Howard Wilkinson, who bought him for peanuts, could not have known what a massive part he would play for Leeds United. His testimonial played in front of 38,000 fans at Elland Road proved just how enormously popular he was and will always be with the Leeds faithful. He also inspired the brilliant band 'The Kaiser Chiefs' to name themselves as such. They are not just a brilliant band, but they always have LUFC written on one of their giant speakers at venues. Good lads!

Norman Hunter
Another part of Revie's dream team, Hunter was a rock in the heart of the Leeds defence, picking up the tag 'bites yer legs' for a reason. And if he had not become a footballer, then maybe a successful career in boxing would have materialised given his points victory over Franny Lee at Derby County in 1975!

Gordon Strachan
Ah, the wee ginger-haired Scot. Funny that we have only ever won the major English prize on three occasions, all with a fiery ginger-haired Scot captaining the side from midfield. Strachan was awesome for Leeds. It took a while for many fans, me included, to accept him given his previous club, but he soon put in brilliant display after brilliant display, changing our minds completely.

Allan Clarke
'Sniffer' simply has to be in the all-time side. After all, who else has scored a winning goal for Leeds in an FA Cup Final? It was not just his classic diving header from the edge of the box against Arsenal in 1972 that swung it for me, though. He just seemed to know exactly where the back of the net was. And like all good strikers, he always seemed to be in the right place at the right time. A defender's nightmare. A joy to watch for us.

Peter Lorimer

Normally wearing the number-seven shirt, I have given 'Lash' the number-nine shirt for my all-time side in order to fit Strachan in. In two spells at Elland Road, 'Hot Shot' Lorimer found the back of the opposition's net no fewer than 238 times in 703 appearances, making him the all-time top goalscorer for Leeds. And with reputedly the hardest shot in football, goalkeepers would quake in their boots at the thought of facing him.

Johnny Giles

A real craftsman in the heart of the midfield. He and Billy Bremner bossed the show week in, week out and nobody knew how to handle them.

Eddie Gray

The wizard on the wing. Eddie Gray is my all-time favourite player, purely for the fact that I just used to love watching him drop a shoulder and destroy full-backs every week. Not only was he an awesome player for Leeds and a massive part of Revie's maestros, but he has also worked tirelessly for the Leeds cause ever since he hung up his boots and as a true hero to all Leeds fans around the world. He was the scorer of what I believe to be the greatest goal in Leeds's history when he made six Burnley players look like they were auditioning for the Keystone Cops before belting the ball home with the grace of a footballing genius. He also scored a second in this match, which was on 4 April 1970 in front of an awestruck Elland Road, when he chipped the Burnley goalkeeper from fully 30 yards.

Substitutes

Nigel Martyn

As mentioned under the 'keeper I chose for the first XI, David Harvey, Martyn was a superb 'keeper for Leeds. His consistency should have earned him more caps for England than the 23 caps he did get. He was a cool customer who never lost his rag like so many shot-stoppers do, and a 'keeper any defender would be glad to have behind them. One of the most popular 'keepers ever to play at Elland Road.

Tony Yeboah

Tony Yeboah sneaks onto the subs' bench simply because he was so exciting to watch. His two goals against Liverpool and then Wimbledon at the start of the 1995–96 season were amazing strikes. The goal against Liverpool won the BBC's

Goal of the Season award, but the goal against the Wombles, where he got a hat-trick, was in my opinion slightly better. He scored 10 goals in the opening nine games that season and was a huge favourite with the fans.

Duncan McKenzie

What can you say about the super skills of the outrageous Duncan McKenzie? He was simply a showman. Not content with performing some breathtaking skills on the pitch to embarrass opponents, he had his party tricks as well. He once threw a golf ball the full length of Elland Road and, on one occasion, frightened the life out of his insurance company by leaping over a Mini inside the ground. He is now a very funny after-dinner speaker and his impersonation of Brian Clough, if ever you get the opportunity to enjoy it, will have you in stitches.

Tony Currie

Ah yes, Tony Currie. He did not quite make it into the first XI but he had to be on the bench for me. He was a player with an enormous amount of talent, scoring the first Leeds goal I ever saw at Elland Road, against Coventry City in 1979. It was a moment I will never ever forget and one which cemented my love for the club. Thanks Tony. I will forever be indebted to you for that.

Trevor Cherry

Trevor was a real fighter who did not know how to give up – and he had no shortage of skill either. He picked up a League champions' medal in 1974 and captained the side from when Billy Bremner left in 1976 until his own departure in 1982. I will never forget watching Leeds against Manchester City in an FA Cup fifth-round tie on 26 February 1977, when, with just four minutes left on the clock, Cherry burst through the City 18-yard box and with sheer guts and determination slid the ball under big Joe Corrigan to put us into the quarter-finals. City were a very good side at the time and it was a Cup tie and a half. I only saw it on TV, but I will never forget John Motson's commentary. 'And Cherry's coming in. [Raised voice] He's still there. [Higher pitched voice] And Cherry has scored. With four minutes to go, at last the breakthrough comes.' It sends a tingle down my spine thinking about it. Cherry played 27 times for England.

Manager: Don Revie

Awesome is sometimes a word used too frivolously, but the Don was exactly that. His tactical nouse, his motivational attributes and his eye for players that were to become international superstars were just fantastic. He would and should, if it weren't for many a dodgy refereeing decision, have won far more silverware for Leeds than he did. But what a record and what football to behold in his time as manager of the club. He was not just the greatest manager Leeds United FC have had, but also one of the all-time greatest managers of any club.

Gordon McQueen was a terrific centre-half, but when I was 15 years old, I stood outside the players' entrance after a game at Elland Road, with my autograph book and pen to hand, and McQueen came out with his best buddy Joe Jordan. I had already got Jordan's autograph, so was just homing in on McQueen for his. They had stopped to chat and McQueen had his back to me. Looking up at this giant of a centre-half I said 'Excuse me.' No reply. 'Excuse me,' once again no reply. I then bravely tapped him on the shoulder before I went for it. 'Can I have your autograph please?' McQueen stopped talking to Jordan before looking round at me to give me a look that suggested I was something that a mountain of flies had just come off. He then turned his head back and began talking to Jordan again. I walked away disappointed, but also really upset by his dismissive attitude. How long does it take to sign an autograph? Whenever I see him on Sky Sports now it always reminds me of that day. He did, of course, go over to the dark side, so in hindsight I am glad he kept his pen in his pocket.

Chapter 25

STATS AND SHORT STORIES

2006–09 Referee Stats

The following tables (in chronological order) show the outcomes of matches, goals scored and goals conceded, League points won from however many available (eg 3/6 = three points from a possible six) and Cup matches won, drawn and lost under the officialdom of whichever referee over three seasons starting from 2006–07:

2006–07	League					Cup					
Referee (33 in total)	W	D	L	F	A	W	D	L	F	A	Lg Pts
Graham Laws	1	1	0	2	1	0	0	0	0	0	4/6
Kevin Friend	0	1	1	3	4	0	0	0	0	0	1/6
Rob Styles	0	0	3	2	6	0	0	0	0	0	0/9
Nigel Miller	0	1	1	1	2	0	0	1	1	3	1/6
Andy D'Urso	0	0	1	1	3	1	0	0	1	0	0/3
Steve Bennett	1	0	0	1	0	0	0	0	0	0	3/3
Lee Mason	0	0	1	0	1	0	0	0	0	0	0/3
Andre Marriner	1	0	2	3	8	0	0	0	0	0	3/9
Iain Williamson	0	0	1	0	1	0	0	0	0	0	0/3
Darren Drysdale	0	0	0	0	0	1	0	0	3	1	0/0
Steve Tanner	2	0	1	4	3	0	0	0	0	0	6/9
Trevor Kettle	0	0	1	0	4	0	0	0	0	0	0/3
Colin Webster	0	0	1	1	2	0	0	0	0	0	0/3
Grant Hegley	0	0	1	1	5	0	0	0	0	0	0/3
Michael Dean	0	0	0	0	0	0	0	1	1	3	0/0
Chris Foy	1	0	0	2	0	0	0	0	0	0	3/3
Phil Crossley	0	0	2	2	5	0	0	0	0	0	0/6
Michael Jones	1	1	1	4	2	0	0	0	0	0	4/9
Scott Mathieson	1	0	1	2	4	0	0	0	0	0	3/6
Dean Whitestone	1	0	0	2	1	0	0	0	0	0	3/3
Phil Dowd	0	0	1	1	2	0	0	0	0	0	0/3
Kevin Wright	0	1	0	2	2	0	0	0	0	0	1/3

	W	D	L	F	A	W	D	L	F	A	Lg Pts
Keith Stroud	0	0	1	0	1	0	0	0	0	0	0/3
Mark Clattenburg	0	1	1	0	1	0	0	0	0	0	1/6
Graham Salisbury	0	0	1	0	2	0	0	0	0	0	0/3
Mike Pike	1	0	0	2	1	0	0	0	0	0	3/3
Neil Swarbrick	0	0	1	2	3	0	0	0	0	0	0/3
Phil Joslin	1	0	0	2	1	0	0	0	0	0	3/3
Clive Oliver	1	0	0	2	1	0	0	0	0	0	3/3
Tony Bates	0	1	1	0	1	0	0	0	0	0	1/6
Lee Probert	0	0	1	2	3	0	0	0	0	0	0/3
Peter Walton	1	0	0	1	0	0	0	0	0	0	3/3
Alan Wiley	0	0	1	1	2	0	0	0	0	0	0/3

2007–08			League					Cup			
Referee (35 in total)	W	D	L	F	A	W	D	L	F	A	Lg Pts
Lee Mason	3	1	0	7	3	0	0	0	0	0	10/12
Andy Penn	0	0	0	0	0	1	0	0	1	0	0/0
Neil Swarbrick	1	0	0	4	1	0	0	0	0	0	3/3
Keith Hill	1	0	0	2	1	0	0	0	0	0	3/3
Andy D'Urso	1	0	0	2	0	0	0	2	0	4	3/3
Clive W Oliver	1	0	1	2	2	0	0	0	0	0	3/6
Pat Miller	1	0	0	2	0	0	0	0	0	0	3/3
Keith Stroud	3	1	0	7	1	0	0	0	0	0	10/12
Graham Laws	1	0	0	2	0	0	0	1	0	1	3/3
Danny McDermid	0	1	0	1	1	0	0	0	0	0	1/3
Phil Joslin	1	0	0	1	0	0	0	0	0	0	3/3
Anthony Taylor	1	0	0	1	0	0	0	0	0	0	3/3
Michael Jones	1	0	0	4	0	1	0	0	1	0	3/3
Nigel Miller	0	1	0	1	1	0	0	0	0	0	1/3
Paul Taylor	1	0	1	1	1	0	0	0	0	0	3/6
Mark Halsey	1	1	0	5	3	0	0	0	0	0	4/6
Phil Dowd	1	0	1	3	4	0	0	0	0	0	3/6
Steve Bennett	1	0	0	3	1	0	0	0	0	0	3/3
Tony Bates	0	0	0	0	0	0	1	1	1	2	0/0
Kevin Friend	1	0	0	1	0	0	0	1	1	2	3/3
Lee Probert	1	0	2	3	4	0	0	0	0	0	3/9
Eddie Ilderton	1	0	0	3	0	0	0	0	0	0	3/3
Colin Webster	1	0	0	1	0	0	0	0	0	0	3/3
Andre Marriner	1	0	1	3	3	0	0	0	0	0	3/6

	W	D	L	F	A	W	D	L	F	A	Lg Pts
Mark Clattenburg	0	0	1	1	3	0	0	0	0	0	0/3
Graham Salisbury	1	0	0	3	0	0	0	0	0	0	3/3
Steve Tanner	0	1	1	1	2	0	0	0	0	0	1/6
Mike Dean	0	1	0	1	1	0	0	0	0	0	1/3
Scott Mathieson	1	0	0	2	0	0	0	0	0	0	3/3
Mike Pike	0	1	0	1	1	0	0	0	0	0	1/3
Chris Foy	1	0	0	1	0	0	0	0	0	0	3/3
Rob Shoebridge	1	0	0	2	0	0	0	0	0	0	3/3
Clive Penton	0	1	0	3	3	0	0	0	0	0	1/3
David Foster	0	1	0	0	0	0	0	0	0	0	1/3
Alan Wiley	0	0	0	0	0	1	0	0	2	0	0/0

2008–09

Referee (36 in total)	League					Cup					
	W	D	L	F	A	W	D	L	F	A	Lg Pts
Iain Williamson	2	0	0	6	4	0	0	0	0	0	6/6
Graham Salisbury	1	0	0	4	1	1	0	0	5	2	3/3
Mike Russell	0	0	1	0	2	0	0	0	0	0	0/3
Dean Whitestone	0	1	0	1	1	0	0	0	0	0	1/3
Kevin Friend	0	0	1	0	2	1	0	0	4	0	0/3
Kevin Wright	0	1	1	2	3	0	0	0	0	0	1/6
Anthony Taylor	1	0	0	3	1	1	0	0	2	1	3/3
Trevor Kettle	1	0	0	5	2	0	0	0	0	0	3/3
Darren Deadman	1	0	0	3	1	0	0	0	0	0	3/3
Peter Walton	2	0	0	4	0	0	0	0	0	0	6/6
Andrew Penn	0	0	0	0	0	1	0	0	3	2	–
Graham Laws	1	0	0	1	0	0	0	1	1	2	3/3
Lee Probert	0	0	1	0	2	0	0	0	0	0	0/3
Scott Mathieson	1	0	0	3	2	0	0	1	2	4	3/3
Carl Boyeson	1	0	0	3	1	0	0	0	0	0	3/3
Andre Marriner	0	1	1	3	5	0	0	0	0	0	1/6
Colin Webster	1	0	0	2	1	0	0	0	0	0	3/3
Grant Hegley	1	0	0	3	0	0	0	0	0	0	3/3
Pat Miller	1	0	1	2	2	0	0	0	0	0	3/6
Fred Graham	1	0	0	1	0	0	0	0	0	0	3/3
Michael Oliver	0	0	0	0	0	0	1	0	1	1	–
Mark Halsey	0	1	1	2	3	0	0	0	0	0	1/6
Phil Crossley	0	0	0	0	0	1	0	0	5	2	–
Chris Foy	0	0	1	1	2	0	0	0	0	0	0/3

	W	D	L	F	A	W	D	L	F	A	Lg Pts
Neil Swarbrick	1	0	0	2	0	0	0	1	0	1	3/3
Rob Shoebridge	0	0	1	1	2	0	0	0	0	0	0/3
Nigel Miller	0	0	1	1	2	0	0	0	0	0	0/3
Tony Bates	0	0	1	1	3	0	0	0	0	0	0/3
Richard Beeby	1	0	0	3	1	0	0	0	0	0	3/3
David Foster	1	0	0	2	0	0	0	0	0	0	3/3
Alan Wiley	1	0	0	2	0	0	0	0	0	0	3/3
Paul Taylor	0	0	1	0	1	0	0	0	0	0	0/3
G. Horwood	0	0	1	0	2	0	0	0	0	0	0/3
R. Booth	0	1	0	1	1	0	0	0	0	0	1/3
A. Haines	1	0	0	4	0	0	0	0	0	0	3/3
Keith Stroud	1	0	0	1	0	0	0	0	0	0	3/3

2006–07, 2007–08 & 2008–09 in total

Referee (56 in total)	League					Cup					
	W	D	L	F	A	W	D	L	F	A	Lg Pts
Graham Laws	3	1	0	5	1	0	0	2	1	3	10/12
Kevin Friend	1	1	2	5	6	1	0	1	5	2	4/12
Rob Styles	0	0	3	2	6	0	0	0	0	0	0/9
Nigel Miller	0	2	2	3	5	0	0	1	1	3	2/12
Andy D'Urso	1	0	1	3	3	1	0	2	1	4	3/6
Steve Bennett	2	0	0	4	1	0	0	0	0	0	6/6
Lee Mason	3	1	1	7	4	0	0	0	0	0	10/15
Andre Marriner	2	1	4	9	16	0	0	0	0	0	7/21
Iain Williamson	2	0	1	6	5	0	0	0	0	0	6/9
Darren Drysdale	0	0	0	0	0	1	0	0	3	1	0/0
Steve Tanner	2	1	2	5	5	0	0	0	0	0	7/15
Trevor Kettle	1	0	1	5	6	0	0	0	0	0	3/6
Colin Webster	2	0	1	4	3	0	0	0	0	0	6/9
Grant Hegley	1	0	1	4	5	0	0	0	0	0	3/6
Mike Dean	0	1	0	1	1	0	0	1	1	3	1/3
Chris Foy	2	0	1	4	2	0	0	0	0	0	6/9
Phil Crossley	0	0	2	2	5	1	0	0	5	2	0/6
Michael Jones	2	1	1	8	2	1	0	0	1	0	7/12
Scott Mathieson	3	0	1	7	6	0	0	1	2	4	9/12
Dean Whitestone	1	1	0	3	2	0	0	0	0	0	4/6
Phil Dowd	1	0	2	4	6	0	0	0	0	0	3/9
Kevin Wright	0	2	1	4	5	0	0	0	0	0	2/9

Keith Stroud	4	1	1	8	2	0	0	0	0	0	13/18
Mark Clattenburg	0	1	2	1	4	0	0	0	0	0	1/9
Graham Salisbury	2	0	1	7	3	1	0	0	5	2	6/9
Mike Pike	1	1	0	3	2	0	0	0	0	0	4/6
Neil Swarbrick	2	0	1	8	4	0	0	1	0	1	6/9
Phil Joslin	2	0	0	3	1	0	0	0	0	0	6/6
Clive W. Oliver	2	0	1	4	3	0	0	0	0	0	6/9
Tony Bates	0	1	1	0	1	0	1	1	1	2	1/6
Lee Probert	1	0	4	5	9	0	0	0	0	0	3/15
Peter Walton	3	0	0	5	0	0	0	0	0	0	9/9
Alan Wiley	1	0	1	3	2	1	0	0	2	0	3/6
Andy Penn	0	0	0	0	0	2	0	0	4	2	0/0
Keith Hill	1	0	0	2	1	0	0	0	0	0	3/3
Pat Miller	2	0	1	4	2	0	0	0	0	0	6/9
Danny McDermid	0	1	0	1	1	0	0	0	0	0	1/3
Anthony Taylor	2	0	0	4	1	1	0	0	2	1	6/6
Paul Taylor	1	0	2	1	2	0	0	0	0	0	3/9
Mark Halsey	1	2	1	7	6	0	0	0	0	0	5/12
Eddie Ilderton	1	0	0	3	0	0	0	0	0	0	3/3
Rob Shoebridge	1	0	1	3	2	0	0	0	0	0	3/6
Clive Penton	0	1	0	3	3	0	0	0	0	0	1/3
David Foster	0	1	0	0	0	0	0	0	0	0	1/3
Mike Russell	0	0	1	0	2	0	0	0	0	0	0/3
Darren Deadman	1	0	0	3	1	0	0	0	0	0	3/3
Carl Boyeson	1	0	0	3	1	0	0	0	0	0	3/3
Fred Graham	1	0	0	1	0	0	0	0	0	0	3/3
Michael Oliver	0	0	0	0	0	0	1	0	1	1	–
Neil Swarbrick	1	0	0	2	0	0	0	1	0	1	0/3
Tony Bates	0	0	1	1	3	0	0	0	0	0	0/3
Richard Beeby	1	0	0	3	1	0	0	0	0	0	3/3
David Foster	1	0	0	2	0	0	0	0	0	0	3/3
G. Horwood	0	0	1	0	2	0	0	0	0	0	0/3
R. Booth	0	1	0	1	1	0	0	0	0	0	1/3
A. Haines	1	0	0	4	0	0	0	0	0	0	3/3

More Worldwide Whites and Your Top Players

On the pitch – More International Whites from the four corners of the globe:

Name	Joined	Left	Apps	Goals	Born
George Affleck	1909	1919	191	1	Scotland
James Allan	1925	1927	74	0	Scotland
John Ashurst	1986	1988	108/1	1	Scotland
Mansour Assoumani	2009	2009	1	0	France
Hugh Baird	1957	1958	46	22	Scotland
John Bell	1960	1967	260	18	Scotland
Hugh Beren	1909	1910	3	0	Scotland
Noel Blake	1988	1990	59/1	4	Jamaica
Adam Bowman	1908	1909	16	7	Scotland
Raúl Bravo	2003	2003	6	0	Spain
Billy Bremner	1959	1976	772/1	115	Scotland
John Brock	1920	1920	6	0	Scotland
Vince Brockie	1987	1987	2	0	Scotland
John Buckley	1986	1987	7/5	1	Scotland
James Bullions	1947	1949	37	0	Scotland
James Burnett	1908	1910	24	3	Scotland
Kenneth Burns	1981	1983	64/2	4	Scotland
Steve Caldwell	2004	2004	13	1	Scotland
Zoumana Camara	2003	2004	15	1	France
Robert Cameron	1959	1961	63	11	Scotland
Alex Campbell	1911	1911	1	0	Scotland
Eric Cantona	1991	1992	25/10	14	France
Sebastien Carole	2006	2008	30/22	3	France
Cyril Chapuis	2003	2004	1/2	0	France
Kenneth Chisholm	1947	1948	40	17	Scotland
Andy Clark	1906	1907	24	0	Scotland
Bobby Collins	1962	1966	167	25	Scotland
Stephen Crainey	2004	2007	61	0	Scotland
Alec Creighton	1910	1912	69	0	Scotland
Gui Da Costa	2007	2007	1/6	0	Portugal
Olivier Dacourt	2000	2003	78/4	3	France
Mark De Vries	2007	2007	3/5	1	Suriname
Russell Doig	1986	1987	5/5	0	Scotland
Didier Domi	2003	2004	9/5	0	France
John Donnelly	1982	1984	40/4	4	Scotland

Name	Joined	Left	Apps	Goals	Born
David Dougal	1908	1910	25	2	Scotland
Thomas Drain	1905	1907	10	3	Scotland
James Dunn	1947	1958	443	1	Scotland
John Ferguson	1912	1912	17	0	Scotland
John Finlay	1951	1951	1	0	Scotland
Peter Flynn	1953	1953	1	0	Scotland
Dougie Freedman	2007	2007	12/2	6	Scotland
James Frew	1920	1923	99	0	Scotland
Scott Gardner	2007	2009	2	0	Luxembourg
Mark Gavin	1982	1984	24/11	4	Scotland
Jimmy Gemmell	1907	1910	73	14	Scotland
Andy Gibson	1912	1912	5	0	Scotland
Archibald Gibson	1954	1959	170	5	Scotland
Arthur Graham	1977	1982	259/1	47	Scotland
Eddie Gray	1965	1983	561/18	69	Scotland
Frank Gray	1972	1984	396/9	35	Scotland
William Gribben	1928	1928	3	0	Scotland
Leandre Griffit	2005	2005	0/1	0	France
Edward Hamilton	1909	1909	3	0	Scotland
John Hamilton	1908	1909	25	0	Scotland
John Harkins	1910	1912	66	0	Scotland
Joseph Harris	1922	1925	134	14	Scotland
Danny Hay	1999	2001	3/3	0	New Zealand
John Henderson	1954	1955	15	4	Scotland
Thomas Henderson	1962	1963	34	2	Scotland
John Hendrie	1989	1989	26/5	5	Scotland
Martin Hiden	1998	2000	31/1	0	Austria
David Hopkin	1997	2000	83/10	6	Scotland
Tom Hynds	1907	1908	38	0	Scotland
John Jackson	1913	1915	58	12	Scotland
Tom Jennings	1924	1930	174	117	Scotland
Joe Jordan	1971	1977	183/38	48	Scotland
Tresor Kandol	2006	2007	47/19	12	The Congo
Robert Kane	1935	1946	61	0	Scotland
John Kemp	1958	1958	1	0	Scotland
Jimmy Kennedy	1906	1909	60	1	Scotland
James Kirkpatrick	1925	1926	10	0	Scotland
Radostin Kishishev	2006	2008	15/2	0	Bulgaria
Pierre Laurent	1997	1998	2/2	0	France

Name	Joined	Left	Apps	Goals	Born
George Law	1912	1915	110	2	Scotland
Gary Liddell	1972	1974	4/2	1	Scotland
Derek Lilley	1996	1998	4/22	1	Scotland
Valentine Lawrence	1914	1914	6	0	Scotland
Peter Lorimer	1962	1985	677/28	238	Scotland
James Lumsden	1966	1969	3/1	0	Scotland
Gary McAllister	1990	1995	294/1	45	Scotland
Andrew McCall	1952	1954	64	8	Scotland
George McCluskey	1983	1985	67/19	17	Scotland
John McCole	1959	1961	85	53	Scotland
Robert McDonald	1986	1987	24	1	Scotland
William McDonald	1908	1909	14	0	Scotland
John McDougall	1934	1936	59	1	Scotland
John McGee	1920	1920	1	0	Scotland
Billy McGhie	1976	1976	2	1	Scotland
William McGinley	1972	1972	0/2	0	Scotland
John McGoldrick	1983	1983	12	0	Scotland
John McGovern	1974	1974	4	0	Scotland
John McGregor	1985	1985	5	0	Scotland
John McGugan	1960	1960	1	0	Scotland
Neil McNab	1982	1982	6	0	Scotland
Samuel McNeish	1950	1950	1	0	Scotland
David McNiven	1975	1977	16/7	6	Scotland
Gordon McQueen	1972	1977	171/1	19	Scotland
Rui Marques	2005	CP	89/5	4	Angola
Dominic Matteo	2000	2003	147	4	Scotland
George Meek	1952	1959	200	19	Scotland
James Melrose	1987	1987	3/3	0	Scotland
William Menzies	1923	1931	258	2	Scotland
Lubomir Michalik	2007	CP	49/4	1	Slovakia
David Murray	1905	1909	85	7	Scotland
Thomas Murray	1960	1960	7	2	Scotland
William Nimmo	1957	1957	1	0	Scotland
George O'Brien	1956	1958	43	6	Scotland
John O'Hare	1974	1974	7	1	Scotland
Salomon Olembe	2003	2004	10/4	0	Senegal
Derek Parlane	1979	1982	48/5	10	Scotland
David Rennie	1985	1988	113/6	7	Scotland
Bruno Riberio	1997	1999	43/9	6	Portugal

Name	Joined	Left	Apps	Goals	Born
David Robertson	1997	2000	29/2	0	Scotland
Jimmy Robertson	1912	1913	34	8	Scotland
David Robinson	1926	1927	5	0	Scotland
Tom Rodger	1908	1909	25	4	Scotland
Robert Ross	1951	1951	5	0	Scotland
David Russell	1924	1924	9	0	Scotland
Armando Sa	2007	2007	6/6	0	Mozambique
Lamine Sakho	2003	2004	10/9	1	Senegal
John Shaw	1971	1973	2	0	Scotland
Enoch Showunmi	2008	CP	6/8	5	Nigeria
Ronald Sinclair	1985	1988	9	0	Scotland
John Smith	1960	1962	72	3	Scotland
Robert Snodgrass	2008	CP	34/17	11	Scotland
James Speirs	1913	1915	78	32	Scotland
David Stewart	1973	1978	74	0	Scotland
Jim Storrie	1962	1966	153/3	67	Scotland
Gordon Strachan	1988	1994	234/10	45	Scotland
George Stuart	1920	1920	3	0	Scotland
Peter Sweeney	2007	2007	6/3	0	Scotland
Paul Telfer	2008	2009	18	0	Scotland
John Thom	1924	1924	7	3	Scotland
John Thomson	1936	1938	41	11	Scotland
James Toner	1954	1954	7	1	Scotland
Thomas Townsley	1925	1930	167	2	Scotland
Neil Turner	1913	1914	4	2	Scotland
Andy Watson	1983	1984	42/1	7	Scotland
John Watson	1908	1910	49	0	Scotland
Percy Whipp	1922	1926	154	47	Scotland
John White	1926	1929	108	38	Scotland
David Whyte	1976	1976	1/1	0	Scotland
Clyde Wijnhard	1998	1999	14/11	4	Suriname
George Wilson	1928	1928	3	0	Scotland
Martin Woods	2002	2003	0/1	0	Scotland
Ronald Wright	1960	1960	2	0	Scotland
Tommy Wright	1982	1986	80/12	28	Scotland
Anthony Yeboah	1995	1997	61/5	32	Ghana
Thomas Younger	1961	1962	42	0	Scotland

Throughout this book a handful of Leeds supporters have named their all-time Leeds United XI, some have included substitutes, a manager and an assistant manager, and one (Gary Edwards) includes a coach. The following list shows the number of votes each player received for either a first-team place or a place on the bench. Not surprisingly, topping the list in the first team is one Billy Bremner. Clarkey sits in second place, and again unsurprisingly leading the way on the subs' bench is the cultured 'Rolls-Royce' utility player that was Paul Madeley. There are some interesting assistant managers, but no prizes whatsoever for guessing who comes out on top as your favourite boss. For the first team then, this is how the votes panned out:

22: Billy Bremner. **20:** Allan Clarke. **19:** Nigel Martyn. **18:** Peter Lorimer, Eddie Gray. **16:** Norman Hunter, Johnny Giles. **15:** Paul Reaney. **13:** Gordon Strachan. **12:** Terry Cooper. **11:** Lucas Radebe. **10:** David Batty,: Jack Charlton. **8:** Tony Dorigo, Gary Kelly, Tony Yeboah, John Charles. **7:** David Harvey. **6:** Jonathan Woodgate. **5:** Lee Chapman, Paul Madeley, Gary McAllister, Rio Ferdinand. **4:** Harry Kewell, Mel Sterland, Mick Jones. **3:** Ian Harte, Gary Speed, Alan Smith, Tony Currie. **2:** Paul Robinson, Dom Matteo, Mark Viduka, Lee Bowyer, Jimmy Floyd Hasslebaink, Gary Sprake. Frank Gray. **1:** Mick Bates, Simon Walton, Matthew Kilgallon, Gordon McQueen, Liam Miller, Shaun Derry, Chris Fairclough, David Wetherall, Eric Cantona, Olivier Dacourt, Ray Hankin, David Healy, Vinnie Jones, Rod Wallace, Albert Johanneson, James Milner, Trevor Cherry, Arthur Graham.

On the substitutes' bench: 10: Paul Madeley. **9:** Tony Yeboah. **5:** Gordon Strachan, Gary McAllister. **4:** Mark Viduka. **3:** Tony Currie, Eddie Gray, David Harvey, David Batty. **2:** Gary Speed, Jonathan Woodgate, John Sheridan, Lee Bowyer, Bobby Collins, Duncan McKenzie, Robbie Keane, Jimmy Floyd Hasslebaink, Lee Chapman, Lucas Radebe. **1:** John Charles, Joe Jordan, Mick Jones, Carl Shutt, Mick Bates, Frazer Richardson, Neil Sullivan, Gary Sprake, Ian Harte, Rod Wallace, John Lukic, Alan Smith, Rio Ferdinand, Jack Charlton, Vinnie Jones, Allan Clarke, Jim Storrie, Nigel Martyn, Trevor Cherry, Tony Dorigo, Carl Harris, Scott Sellars, Gary McAllister.

Manager: 12: Don Revie. **1:** Howard Wilkinson.
Assistant manager: 3: David O'Leary, Eddie Gray. **2:** Gus Poyet. **1:** Brian Clough, Sgt Wilko, Dermot Broadhurst!
Coach: 1: Syd Owen.

And just for the record, here are a few other short tales from Leeds supporters scattered across Europe:

There's the story of Sandra and Lizio Velle from Malta, who proudly named their son 'Elland'.

There's Stanislava Kaneva from Bulgaria, who would love to hear from any Leeds fans anywhere. To help her keep in touch with her heroes, you can write to her at this address: ul.Hristo Botev 10, ap.15 Box 15, BG-Sevlievo–5401, Bulgaria. The Teesside Whites boast a list of foreign recruits among their ranks, in Daan Schilperoord from Holland and Fredi Kurth and Heinz Alder from Switzerland.

If ever you are over in Benidorm on Spain's Costa Blanca, you could do far worse than to visit 'The Leeds Arms'. Decked out in blue, yellow and white, the whole pub is a shrine to Leeds United. There are Leeds beer mats, pictures, posters and pennants, and a wall that displays countless names of players that have played for the Mighty Whites over the years, as well as the lyrics to *Marching on Together*.

Finally, there is the tale of Ricky Smithers and John Wood, who on a trip to a Stoke City v Leeds encounter on 23 February 1988 (lost 2–1) were cursing their car, which broke down around an hour away from the old Victoria Ground. Deciding to abandon the vehicle, they put their thumbs out and attempted to hitch the rest of the way. From thinking they might miss the match, they suddenly ended up travelling in luxury as the Stoke City chairman at the time, Mr P. Coates, picked them up in his top-of-the-range brand new Rolls-Royce!

With kind permission from leedsunited.com the following quotes were first published on the official Leeds United website.

Han Seung Jong – South Korea

'I agree that Japanese are good Leeds fans but South Koreans are also wonderful Leeds fans! As you know, we can't see many Leeds games, especially this year, but I have an account with LUTV, and we usually listen to the radio, and watch the highlights and reserve games live. I became a Leeds fan when we were high-flying in Europe seven or eight years ago. I was big fan of Kewell. But while we go through hardships, I felt I'm not a Kewell or Viduka or Smith fan, or anyone, I'm just Leeds fan. When we lost to Watford in the Play-off Final we watched it by computer in a pub together. It's not a good memory but we can't forget that time. After the game we sang *Marching on together*. It's not easy to bear to see our downhill road. However, Leeds United has many many fans around the world (specially in South Korea) I believe it will make Leeds as top club of the Europe. We are making plans for visiting Elland Road as soon as possible. Leeds has really, really big fan base not only in Britain – and I'm really proud of that.' Han runs a Leeds United fan website in Korea and has over 600 members.

Carlo Zerola – Juazeiro, Brazil

On Seville utility player and Brazilian international Dani Alves (a 13 times capped player who almost joined Chelsea in summer 2007):

'I own a pizzeria. It's the same town as Daniel is from and his brother eats here three times a week. Every time Dani comes back he eats here too. When he comes next time he's promised to have his photo taken wearing a Leeds home shirt. I'm from Leeds but I've been living here 20 years, coming back to watch Leeds twice a year. I listen every Saturday on the internet. Forever Whites fan Carlo.'

Himalayan Allan – Kathmandu

'I started supporting Leeds when I was eight or nine years old. I lived in Beeston then and used to go in the boys' pen at the Geldard Road end. Jimmy Milburn, Jimmy Dunn, George Meek, Albert Nightingale, Harold Brook and of course the late great John Charles are players that spring to mind from those days. I went to Cross Flatts school and was in the same under-11s team as Paul Madeley. I went regularly to Elland Road through the Revie years but then I started working overseas. Even now I work in Oman but I actually reside in Kathmandu with my Nepali wife and two young daughters. We watch games regularly on TV and my wife has been to Elland Road and had photos taken on both sides of the ground.'

In the 2007–08 season leedsunited.com ran a Greatest Fans in the World competition whereby entries would automatically be entered into the computer and one lucky winner, along with a guest, would be flown from wherever in the world to the final League match of the season against Gillingham. Almost 8,000 supporters entered from over 170 countries worldwide and the lucky winner was Leisa Simpson, who couldn't have come much further than from her home in Coffs Harbour, Australia. Along with her husband Steve they enjoyed a fabulous experience and in their own words of enormous gratitude this, courtesy of *leedsunited.com*, is what hubby Steve said:

'Leisa and I have been given an insight into Leeds United that most fans only ever dream of, we both feel very privileged and honoured to have been given this opportunity. Hence I would like to share some of our experiences with you, the fans. We had seven wonderful days in Leeds visiting Thorp Arch, watching the first-team squad prepare for the final game against Gillingham, meeting the staff, coaching staff, the players and ultimately having lunch with the squad. We had a stadium tour, lunch and dinner with Mr and Mrs Bates, had the privilege of visiting the players in the dressing room before the game, we watched the game with the chairman and his wife and experienced Elland Road at its best with a full house present. To top all of this off we attended the annual awards dinner. Really it does not get any better than that, in fact the Elland Road faithful put on such a wonderful show that the fans had my wife in tears as the emotion was just too great. What became apparent to my wife and I was that Leeds United represents more than just a football club, it is the people within the club and the fans that support Leeds United that make it so special. Everyone we spoke to holds a pride and passion for the club that we have never witnessed before. A big thank you to Mr and Mrs Bates, you need to be congratulated and supported by all Leeds fans, they truly have Leeds United Football Club at heart and I am sure that with Mr Bates' vast experience and knowledge of running a big football club that we will be back in the Premier League in the not too distant future. Also you know that they say behind every good man there is a good woman, well having met Mrs Bates I can tell you that there is no one better, she is truly a very special lady and we are very fortunate to have her support at Leeds United. We both feel very honoured to have spent time with Mr and Mrs Bates over lunch and dinner and it is a memory that will always be close to our hearts. We would like to thank everyone within the club and the city of Leeds who made us feel so welcome with true Yorkshire hospitality. A special mention must be made to Mr and Mrs Bates, Hayley Kelly (marketing manager), Peter STIX Lockwood (you truly represent what Leeds United stands for), Gary McAllister, the coaching staff and players, Nicky and the staff at Bewleys Hotel, James Broughton at Leeds Bradford airport and KLM Airlines. And, finally, we must say that we have left a piece of our hearts in Leeds and that we will be back because we want to be a part of the family that is Leeds United. To all the Leeds United fans you are definitely without a shadow of a doubt the greatest fans in the world, so lets give all our support to everyone associated with this great club and keep on Marching on Together.'

The following is a list of Leeds United Regional Members' Clubs and contact details, should anyone reading this publication wish to become a member:

Barnsley Kevin Airstone — barnsleywhites@hotmail.co.uk
Beckwithshaw David Naylor — davidnaylor2000@btinternet.com
Blackpool Mark Jordan — blackpool_whites@msn.com
Carlisle Paul Armstrong — Lorna Tinker 0113 367 6242
Cheshire Whites Kev Lindley — snoweagle@btopenworld.com
Chiltern Hector McFarlane — www.chilternwhites.co.uk
Cleethorpes Whites Andy Hartley — www.cleethorpeswhites.co.uk
Conwy County Whites Ann Hughes — simon.ann1@yahoo.co.uk
Coventry/Warwickshire Jonathan Hardie — www.covwarkswhites.co.uk
Desborough & Rothwell Luke Hill — lukehill@live.com
Essex Paul Downer — essexwhiteslumc@aol.com
Grimsby Whites Brett Taylor — www.grimsbywhites.com
Hampshire Andy Crawford — chairman@hampshirewhites.com
Hereford Whites Dean Cholmondeley — dean@herefordwhites.co.uk
Hope Inn (Leeds) Gary Barrass — garypaulbarrass@yahoo.co.uk
Ilkley Richard Fox — www.ilkleywhites.com
Keighley Stephen Pickles — picklesfamily@blueyonder.co.uk
Kent Whites Steve Humphrey — stumps4leeds@aol.com
Lincs Whites Richard Maynard — richard.maynard1@ntlworld.com
LUDO (Leeds United Disabled Organisation) Nicky Chapman — www.ludo1992.net
Norton & Malton Andrew Butterworth — andymandybutts@aol.co.uk
Nottingham Mark Brinley — www.nottinghamwhites.co.uk
Preston Sean Rafferty — sean1966@btinternet.com
Scarborough Dave Exley — dave.exley@scarborough.gov.uk
Shropshire Whites Gary Sleat — gvsleat@gmail.com
Snaith Keith Colby — keithcolby1@btinternet.com
South West (Bristol) Dave Jones — Lorna Tinker 0113 367 6242
Stockport Whites Jon McGonigle — stockportwhites@yahoo.co.uk
Wensleydale Laura Mason — Loopylaura35@yahoo.co.uk
Whitby Graeme Smith — graemesmith1919@yahoo.co.uk
Woodman (Outwood) Lee Gilbertson — leegilby@blueyonder.co.uk
Cookstown (NI) Thomas Patterson — thomaspatterson@hotmail.co.uk
County Laois Colm O'Hara — allbooks@eircom.net
Dubai Paul Mather — pem@emirates.net.ae

Isle of Man Steve Cain

stevecain@manx.net

Kilkenny Padraig Lawlor

gourmetstore@hotmail.com

Malta (Real Leeds Malta) Hilary Attard

hilary01@maltanet.net

NW N. Ireland (Londonderry) Ian Culbert

Lorna Tinker 0113 367 6242

Park Inn (Belfast) Calvagh O'Donnell

calvagh_parkinnlumc@yahoo.co.uk

Thanks for the journey so far Leeds. No doubt there are plenty more ups and downs to come. There will be changes in personnel at Elland Road over the next weeks, months and seasons. Players will be bought and sold, managers and coaching staff will come and go, and board members will occupy the hierarchy of positions and try their utmost (in some cases maybe a little misguided) to make Leeds the best club in the land, but one thing will never change – the fans.

AS PROMISED...
THE EDWARDS STAT ATTACK

Gary Edwards's consecutive match stats up to and including the end of the 2008–09 season, which include all Cup competitions but do not include the countless friendlies, testimonials or games prior to the consecutive marathon of 90 or more minutes, is as follows:

Season	Attended	W	D	L	For	Against	Gl Diff	Success %
1967/68	26	14	6	6	35	23	+12	65
1968/69	55	33	15	7	84	42	+42	74
1969/70	63	34	19	10	127	60	+67	69
1970/71	59	36	15	8	105	45	+60	74
1971/72	56	32	12	12	92	40	+52	68
1972/73	64	33	18	13	106	56	+50	66
1973/74	54	28	19	7	82	43	+39	69
1974/75	65	27	20	18	89	69	+20	60
1975/76	46	23	9	14	69	50	+19	60
1976/77	48	19	12	17	59	58	+1	52
1977/78	49	22	10	17	81	64	+17	55
1978/79	53	23	18	12	92	64	+28	60
1979/80	49	15	15	19	55	66	-11	46
1980/81	46	17	11	18	41	53	-12	49
1981/82	46	11	12	23	42	67	-25	37
1982/83	49	15	23	11	61	53	+8	54
1983/84	49	17	15	17	65	69	-4	50
1984/85	46	21	12	13	71	52	+19	59
1985/86	48	16	10	22	59	76	-17	44
1986/87	55	25	11	19	70	54	+16	55
1987/88	51	21	14	16	71	60	+11	55
1988/89	53	21	16	16	66	57	+9	55
1989/90	53	26	14	13	81	57	+24	62
1990/91	56	27	12	17	85	56	+29	59
1991/92	49	25	17	7	85	43	+42	68

Season	Attended	W	D	L	For	Against	Gl Diff	Success %
1992/93	55	17	18	20	80	83	-3	47
1993/94	47	19	17	11	74	49	+25	59
1994/95	50	24	15	11	79	54	+25	67
1995/96	56	22	10	24	66	80	-14	48
1996/97	46	15	15	16	40	48	-8	49
1997/98	46	23	8	15	75	52	+23	59
1998/99	49	22	16	11	74	43	+31	61
1999/00	55	31	8	16	88	58	+30	64
2000/01	59	29	13	17	94	70	+24	60
2001/02	49	22	14	13	73	51	+22	59
2002/03	50	20	8	22	74	67	+7	48
2003/04	41	9	9	23	45	88	-43	33
2004/05	50	16	18	16	52	57	-5	50
2005/06	51	23	16	12	65	45	+20	61
2006/07	50	15	7	28	52	79	-27	37
2007/08	55	30	11	14	78	47	+31	65
2008/09	57	31	8	18	101	66	+35	60
Total	2154	949	566	639	3083	2414	+669	57

Gary's 1,000th competitive match he attended consecutively was in the old Second Division on 24 January 1987, which turned out to be a goalless draw at home to Blackburn Rovers. The crowd was 14,452.

Gary's 2,000th match was unfortunately the 3–0 defeat at home to Sunderland in the Championship on Wednesday 13 September 2006. The crowd that day was 23,037.

The 500th victory he saw during this incredible journey came on 10 March 1999 in a 2–0 win over Tottenham Hotspur at Elland Road. Goals from Alan Smith and Harry Kewell secured three Premiership points in front of a crowd of 34,521.

The 500th draw Gary saw was a 1–1 stalemate at home to Chelsea on 6 December 2003 in front of 36,305 supporters. Jermaine Pennant scored the goal for Leeds.

Alan Smith scored Leeds's only goal in Gary's 500th defeat, which was a 3–1 reverse at Newcastle United on 12 January 2002.

Here is a small table of significant goals Gary has seen in this quite remarkable 41-year period of not missing a single competitive match:

Significance	Date	Opponent	Venue	Comp	Score	Gate	Goalscorer
Goals For							
1st goal	7 Feb 1968	Derby Co.	H	Lge Cup	3–2	29,367	Rod Belfitt
500th goal	23 Dec 1972	Man Utd	A	Div 1	1–1	46,382	Allan Clarke
1,000th goal	26 Feb 1979	West Brom	H	FAC 4	3–3	34,000	Arthur Graham
1,500th goal	17 Oct 1987	Plymouth	A	Div 2	3–6	9,358	Bob Taylor
2,000th goal	9 Feb 1994	Oxford Utd	H	FAC 4r	2–3	22,167	David White
2,500th goal	31 Jan 2001	Coventry C.	H	Prem	1–0	36,555	Robbie Keane
3,000th goal	6 Sep 2008	Crewe Alex.	H	Lge 1	5–2	20,075	Alan Sheehan
Goals Against							
1st goal	7 Feb 1968	Derby Co.	H	Lge Cup	3–2	29,367	Kevin Hector
500th goal	8 Oct 1977	Bristol C.	A	Div 1	2–3 (1st)	26,215	Tom Ritchie
1,000th goal	16 Oct 1985	Sheff Utd	H	FMC	1–1	2,274	Colin Morris
1,500th goal	28 Feb 1994	Oldham Ath.	A	Div 1	1–1	11,136	Darren Beckford
2,000th goal	11 Jan 2003	Man City	A	Div 1	1–2 (2nd)	34,884	Niclas Jensen

Incidentally, the third goal that Bristol City grabbed in the 2–3 defeat above was scored by one Norman Hunter. In total, whether it has been a goal for Leeds United or the opposition, Gary Edwards has witnessed no fewer than 5,497 competitive goals while watching the Mighty Whites.

BIBLIOGRAPHY

Leeds Leeds Leeds magazine, published by Ignition Publications, The Reading Room, High Street, Doveridge, Derbyshire, DE6 5NA. Editor: Neil Jeffries.

Website: www.leedsunited.com

The Essential History of Leeds United, by Andrew Mourant, published by Headline Book Publishing, a division of Hodder Headline, 338 Euston Road, London, NW1 3BH.

Leeds United – A Complete Record 1919–1989, by Martin Jarred and Malcolm Macdonald, published by Breedon Books Publishing Company Limited, Breedon House, 3 The Parker Centre, Derby, DE21 4SZ.

The Who's Who of Leeds United, by Martin Jarred and Malcolm Macdonald, published by Breedon Books Publishing Company Limited, Breedon House, 3 The Parker Centre, Derby, DE21 4SZ.

BV - #0072 - 280426 - C0 - 210/136/15 - PB - 9781780911717 - Gloss Lamination